Thriving in the Wake of Trauma

Thriving in the Wake of Trauma
A Multicultural Guide

Thema Bryant-Davis

Contributions in Psychology, Number 49
Paul Pedersen, Series Editor

Westport, Connecticut
London

Library of Congress Cataloging-in-Publication Data

Bryant-Davis, Thema.
    Thriving in the wake of trauma : a multicultural guide / Thema Bryant-Davis
    p. cm. — (Contributions in psychology, ISSN 0736-2714 ; no. 49)
    Includes bibliographical references and index.
    ISBN 0-275-98507-5 (alk. paper)
    1. Post-traumatic stress disorder—Cross-cultural studies. 2. Post-traumatic
stress disorder—Patients—Cross-cultural studies. 3. Psychiatry, Transcultural.
I. Title. II. Series.
    RC552.P67B794 2005
    616.85'21–dc22   2005006043

British Library Cataloguing in Publication Data is available.

Library of Congress Catalog Card Number: 2005006043
ISBN: 0-275-98507-5
ISSN: 0736-2714

First published in 2005

Praeger Publishers, 88 Post Road West, Westport, CT 06881
An imprint of Greenwood Publishing Group, Inc.
www.praeger.com

Printed in the United States of America

The paper used in this book complies with the
Permanent Paper Standard issued by the National
Information Standards Organization (Z39.48-1984).

10 9 8 7 6 5 4 3 2 1

To Survivors

Those in silence and those who scream
Those who were believed and those who were ignored
Those who are surviving, those who are thriving
And those who are just making it a day at a time;
Those walking, those soaring, those crawling, and those lying quite still on
*   the path to wholeness.*
May this work help you remember the power of your wings.

Contents

Series Foreword

Thema Bryant-Davis gives us a look at trauma from the inside out in her excellent and victim-sensitive book *Thriving in the Wake of Trauma*. From the acknowledgments at the very beginning of the book, where she acknowledges the help she has received from specific victims of specific trauma, and throughout the book she brings the facts of trauma up close and personal to the reader. Many if not most readers will find themselves or people they know among the victims addressed in this book. The reader can expect to become personally engaged both in the trauma and in the recovery process, which is the book's central theme.

She describes culture as "the answer" to the question of identity for all of us and particularly for those who have experienced trauma. The cultural context is described broadly to include disability, gender, migration status, race, religion, sexual orientation, and socioeconomic status. Cultural identity is defined orthogonally where each of us belongs to many different cultures at the same time, even though some may be more salient with regard to the experience of trauma at a given point in time. Culture is necessarily complex, and a simplistic understanding of culture is rejected, no matter how convenient that simplified version might seem. The cases of trauma might include physical, sexual, verbal, and/or emotional examples of assault to the victim. Trauma is also necessarily complex, and she rejects simplistic answers to the healing process of recovery from trauma.

Understanding the meaning of trauma in its cultural context is essential to recovery and the healing process she advocates. Trauma disempowers survivors, leaving them with a feeling of helplessness unless the survivor can be helped to recover. It is no surprise that so few books have avoided simplistic solutions regarding both trauma and culture. Thema's book is a very personal and sometimes emotionally difficult journey for the reader, and especially for survivors. She not only identifies with the individual survivor but also with the many others surrounding the cultural context in which the survivor lives in an example of inclusive cultural empathy.

The chapters describe specific examples, guidelines for healing, and "themes of recovery" such as safety, self-care, trust, shame, memories, mourning, anger, body image, sexuality, coping, and thriving. The afterword of this book is significantly a poem, where Thema expresses some of her own feelings as well as the feelings of survivors she has known in a personalized, specific, and moving testimony. The book is a unique experience.

This book fits well with the other books in the Contributions in Psychology series in describing how psychology serves society. The many books in this series define the cutting edge of psychology as it is applied to social issues. Each book has focused on a specific issue of importance, providing building blocks to those who deliver psychological services in our society. It is with great pride that we welcome this most recent contribution to the series.

Paul Pedersen, Series Adviser
Dept. of Psychology, University of Hawaii

Preface

I WRITE THIS

I write this for every Haitian child who has crossed oceans of terror in search of peace and safety.

I write this for the Rwandan rape survivor who sat in my office in America and asked, "Am I safe here? Are there rapists here?"

I write this for the Arab client who before 9/11 was upset that he was constantly mistaken as Latino and was therefore discriminated against.

I wonder if he now hesitates to tell people his accurate ethnicity.

I write this for the mentally retarded, mute adolescent who was raped in her residential treatment center by a nurse.

I write this for the Asian incest survivor who told me she had two wishes: that her father had never touched her breasts and that she had been born white.

I write this for the Native American survivor of domestic violence who had patients taunt her in her day care treatment program; they made a circle around her imitating Indian chants.

I write this for the Liberian woman who in the aftermath of war, violence, and torture looked me in the eye and said with conviction, "Praise Jesus. We're still here."

I write this for every person who has been chased, beaten, and harassed because of his or her sexual orientation or gender identity.

I write this for the biracial rape survivor whose white mother was afraid the rape of her daughter would be taken less seriously than the rape of a white girl.

I write this for the young woman from Botswana who, in a class discussion on race and racism, looked around at her all white peers and said, "I still feel strong."

I write this for the young white gay man who was raped and told me, "Dr. Bryant-Davis, I don't want to be a 'survivor.' I want my life back. I just want to be me again."

I write this for the Asian international student who tried to kill herself; she didn't want to tell her parents back home that her professor was sexually harassing her. I write this for the bisexual Native American assault survivor whose mother forbade her from acknowledging her partner at graduation.

I write this for the African-American man whose hands still shake from his experience of being bused to all-white schools for desegregation.

I write this for the Christian Latina rape survivor who prayed to God to forgive her for not being a virgin—still believing the rape of her body was her fault.

I write this for the Haitian and Dominican employees who were forced to sit through a sexual harassment prevention workshop although they spoke no English and no translator was provided.

I write this for the Jewish bisexual young woman who used to practice magic but stopped after she was raped because she couldn't make sense of the fact that her rapist had "greater magic" than she did.

I write this for the African-American rape survivor who told me she knows if she were white, the man who raped her would have been convicted.

I write this for every person who has sat through a sermon about the need for women to stay with abusive husbands or for survivors to forgive and get over it. I write this for every person who has spent years in mosques and temples and churches, years in prayer and meditation, years speaking with spiritual leaders, and still the violation they experienced makes them feel dirty, evil, unworthy, guilty.

I write this for my grandfather, uncle, and brother-in-law—all of whom served in the U.S. Army—treading water in the trauma of war and racism.

I write this for my mother—a womanist theologian who dares to preach about mental health in sanctuaries of silence.

I write this for me—a therapist, professor, and researcher; a survivor of rape, racism, and sexual harassment.

I write this for every person who has ever advocated for the invisible, fought against oppression, resisted the laziness of stereotypes, and spoke truth to power. I write this for each person who at this moment is living at midnight, hoping that joy will come in the morning.

I write this for you—survivors, therapists, ministers, researchers, doctors, nurses, police officers, judges, advocates, and students.

Those who are in helping professions or are students of helping professions, those who have sought knowledge on the cultural context of trauma recovery and have found little information readily accessible.

And those who are in recovery, who have read books or been in therapy sessions where you had to leave your sexual orientation at the door, your race at the door, your experiences with classism at the door, your wheelchair at the door, your religion at the door.

I say to you, in this place of healing, all of you are welcome.

I write this for you.

Acknowledgments

Thanks to Susan Roth, Judith Herman, Mary Harvey, Corann Okorodudu, and Jessica Henderson Daniel for their professional support.

Thanks to my wonderful family, especially my husband Kwesi Davis, my father John Bryant, my mother Cecelia Bryant, as well as Jamal Bryant, Gizelle Graves Bryant, Jimiyu Davis, Aisha Davis, Brenda Morgan Davis, and Purnell Davis Jr.

Special thanks to my editors at Praeger Press Debora Carvalko and Paul Pedersen and Kim Hoag of Bytheway Publishing Services.

A very warm thank you to Shanisha Gordon, my undergraduate research assistant, for her research skills.

My greatest gratitude for the survivors I have worked with as a counselor, researcher, educator, and advocate. I appreciate your trust, honesty, and courage. May you continue to press, grow, soar, and thrive.

Finally, thanks to my sisters in spirit: Amini Williams, Vanessa Nyborg, Edith Arrington, Joy Jones, Annette Santiago-Espina, Roslyn Brookins, Deborah Blanks, Chrystal Green, Amada Sandoval, Allison Stratford, and Vera Alexander.

1

Introduction

While there has been a history of distorted research that has stressed the emotional pathologies and behavioral deficits of marginalized communities, less research has illustrated their strength, resources, and resilience. There is a need to give ear to the hardships endured by many and the ways in which they have coped with their experiences. The stories these survivors tell highlight the remarkable recovery of many and simultaneously give attention to the pitfalls that impede the progress of others.

What Is Culture?

Culture is at the root of sociology and psychology. It represents the answer to the question of identity. It gives children their ideas about life, relationships, spirituality, and sexuality. It is the possession of elders of a particular community; the gift they pass down to future generations. It is stated directly and whispered. It is implied and recited. Culture is the pattern of learned behaviors, attitudes, rituals, languages, and beliefs for a particular group of people. Within any one person there are multiple cultural traditions that are intersecting in each moment of each day. While there are many cultural traditions, this book will focus on seven cultural categories. They are disability, gender, migration status, race, religion, sexual orientation, and socioeconomic status.

A shared cultural understanding of people who have a similar physical or mental disability exists. Without question, there is a cultural heritage among persons who are deaf just as there is a cultural experience of those who are blind. Not only do experiences of discrimination against the disabled carve out cultural identities, but also the strengths and skills of each group carve out cultural expressions.

In terms of gender, males and females are socialized into a cultural understanding of manhood and womanhood ideals. We receive direct and indirect socialization messages from family, friends, school, religious teachings, and the media. These messages teach the cultural role expectations of women and men. Whether these expectations are for men to be providers or for women to be nurturers, there are cultural prescriptions for gendered behavior and there are consequences for not following the script that has been given to us. There are also people who are transgendered, whose psychological and social experience of their gender is different from the biological sex of which they were born—persons who were born biological males but emotionally and cognitively experience themselves as female, or vice versa. In addition, there are some people who experience themselves as "gender queer," those who do not ascribe to notions of masculinity or femininity. More states and schools are adopting policies that cover not only discrimination based on sex or gender but also based on gender identity, which covers persons who are transgendered or gender queer.

Migrating to a new country also shapes the cultural beliefs, behaviors, and attitudes of a particular people whether the migration is by choice or by force. One's cultural traditions are greatly affected by multiple migration dynamics including if one migrated due to slavery, escape from war and political oppression, or for economic opportunity. Migration also manifests its impact on the individual depending on one's level of acculturation, language acquisition, financial resources, social support, degree of exposure to discrimination against immigrants, and one's desire and/or ability to return home.

Race is a social construction based on phenotypes or physical characteristics. Racial experiences can be both positive and negative. Positive experiences are based in shared experiences, rituals, language, customs, and traditions. Racism, on the other hand, is bias against a person or group of people based on their race. Racism can be covert or overt, individual or institutionalized. Specific racist incidents include but are not limited to housing discrimination, racial harassment, hate crimes, racial slurs, and employment discrimination as well as stereotypical depictions of members of a racial group. Racial equality is an important factor in the struggle for human rights in general and mental health specifically.

What Is Interpersonal Trauma?

Interpersonal trauma is a physical, sexual, verbal, or emotional violation of one person or group of people that is perpetrated by another person or group of people when that violation results in feelings of intense fear, powerlessness, hopelessness, or horror. As Herman (1997) notes, events are traumatic not because they are rare, but because they overwhelm the internal resources that usually give us a sense of control, connection, and meaning. Another trauma expert, van der Kolk (1996), defines trauma as "an inescapable stressful event that overwhelms people's existing coping mechanisms" (p. 279).

Examples of interpersonal trauma include physical assault, sexual assault, abuse, harassment, discrimination, racially motivated hate crimes, harassment based on sexual orientation, domestic violence, war, community violence, and torture. Herman (1997) describes the manner in which the investigation of particular traumas has flourished in the context of particular political movements. The antiwar movement brought to light the post-traumatic stress of veterans, and the women's movement brought to light the post-traumatic stress of domestic and sexual violence. In this post–civil rights era and this era of global human rights advocacy, we need to address and acknowledge the impact of societal traumas such as racism and homophobia.

In terms of victimization, it is important to consider familial, community, and national violence. Being a victim of violence conceptually applies to not only direct personal exposure (being the victim of the violence), it also includes exposure through witnessing and vicarious exposure (knowing someone to whom violence has happened). Risk for community violence exposure is higher among the poor, those ages fifteen through nineteen, the nonwhite, and those who live in densely populated urban areas.

While many traumas are self-explanatory, I will provide a brief description of sexual assault. Definitions of sexual assault vary by nation and by state. For the purposes of this discourse, sexual assault is any unwanted physical sexual contact, including fondling of genitals, breasts, and buttocks as well as oral, anal, and vaginal penetration. This contact may be precipitated by physical force or coercion. Sexual assault also occurs when sexual contact occurs with a person who is unable to give consent; this inability may be a result of intoxication, being asleep, or being under the influence of date rape drugs or other drugs. *Rape*, a subsection of sexual assault, is defined as unwanted penetration as a result of force or coercion. The penetration may be oral, vaginal, or anal and may involve persons of the same or different genders. Rape involves any penetration whether it is committed with a penis, finger, or object. When sexual assault is perpetrated against a child the term *child sexual abuse* is often utilized, and when the perpetrator is a family member the term *incest* is utilized. Child sexual abuse, including incest, does not have to include actual physical contact; it may also refer to exposure to pornography, exhibitionism, or exposure to sexual verbal or written material (Etaugh and Bridges, 2004). Childhood sexual abuse is the compelling of children to engage in sexual activities to which they are psychologically and developmentally unable to consent (Wyatt, Newcomb, and Riederle, 1993).

What Are the Effects of Interpersonal Trauma?

Interpersonal trauma disempowers the survivor as the perpetrator(s) has essentially violated the survivor's humanity. Interpersonal trauma leaves emotional, cognitive, physical, relational, and spiritual wounds (Bryant-Davis, 2003). It is the work of the survivor along with counselors and other support persons to work toward the healing of these wounds. Cognitively the survivor may experience difficulty concentrating, problems with memory, negative thoughts about the self, intrusive memories, flashbacks, hypervigilance, and difficulty thinking about the future.

Emotionally the survivor may feel anger, sadness, guilt, shame, fear, confusion, and even numbness or blankness (Herman, 1997). Physically, the perpetrator may have caused the survivor to have broken bones, bruises, sexually transmitted diseases, pregnancy, organ damage, brain damage, burns, loss of body parts (i.e., cutting off a person's hand), and even death. Relationally, survivors may find it difficult to trust others, to interact with people in authority, to interact with people who remind them of the perpetrator, or to tolerate intimacy emotionally or sexually. In addition, they may have difficulty setting boundaries, asserting themselves, or being alone as a result of both fear and past experience with their rights being ignored.

Trauma can also have behavioral consequences for the survivor including but not limited to eating disorders, substance abuse, and other self-destructive or high-risk behaviors. In addition to all of these effects, trauma also affects the soul, the spiritual integrity of the survivors (Bryant-Davis, 2003). They may be left questioning their prior understanding of God, faith, justice, and humanity.

Both clinical case studies and empirical data have supported the proposition that violent childhood experiences have significant emotional, cognitive, and behavioral effects on survivors. Long-term effects of childhood trauma include generalized hyperarousal and difficulty modulating arousal; alterations in neurobiological processes involved in stimulus discrimination, such as problems with attention and problems with somatization; loss of capacity to put feelings into words; conditioned fear responses to trauma-related stimuli; shattered meaning, such as loss of safety, trust, and/or hope; and social avoidance (Wyatt, Newcomb, and Riederle, 1993; van der Kolk, McFarlane, and Weisaeth, 1996). Roth and Batson (1997) summarize the effects of violent childhood experiences as organized around the following symptoms: anxiety, fear, depression, somatic complaints, aggression, sexualized behavior, learning problems, post-traumatic stress disorder, behavior problems, and self-destructive behavior.

Violence, including childhood victimization, may have negative behavioral effects that are not always understood as being related to the trauma. For example, in a sample of 2,973 black and white adolescent males, more black than white males reported experiencing physical violence, incest, and extra-familial sexual violence. As for outcome risk-taking behaviors, blacks were more likely to use illegal substances, run away, skip school, attempt suicide, force partners into sex, and commit violent crimes; however, the racial effects decreased when violence histories were taken into consideration (Hernandez, Lodico, and DiClemente, 1993). In this light, the significance of research and interventions focused on one's trauma history becomes clear if one seeks to break the cycle of violence, both that aimed at others and at the self. This also negates some of the self-blaming research that is directed at proving a lack of morality and/or impulse control among racial minority males. Within the context of post-traumatic stress and even more likely continued traumatic stress, the behavior of survivors who "act out" is better understood.

For racial minorities who have been victimized, the shattering of self-concept may be connected to the cultural conception of the self. For example, as opposed to the Cartesian notion that has influenced European thought, "I think therefore I am," Africentric thought focuses on the belief, "I am because we are" (Akbar, 1985; Robinson and Ward, 1991). In this light, being victimized by others and witnessing the victimization of others would affect the survivors' self-concept. The sense of self as part of community may in a positive way lead some to identify themselves with a community of survivors who have historically persevered through many difficulties. On the other hand, if one comes to define oneself by the way one is treated in the community, one may see the self as being more devalued and powerless in the aftermath of community violence. Although it may have a positive or a negative effect on the survivor, the sense of community influences the self-concept of the survivor.

Not only does direct victimization affect survivors, but the observation of violence can also have long-term effects as well. Pynoos and Nader (1988) as well as Jenkins 2002, for example, indicate the following effects of exposure to community violence: emotional pain; emotional and behavioral disturbances, such as post-traumatic stress; maintenance of states of chronic stress, suspicion, and paranoia; fear of and loss of faith in others; fear of invasion violence in community institutions such as schools; loss of hope; detachment, shame, guilt, acting out behavior (drug use and aggression); desire to take revenge; maintenance of personal apathy; and increased hostility. Other studies of community violence among urban youth have also revealed positive correlations between the degree of exposure and reported levels of psychological distress (Burton et al., 1994; Lynch and Cicchetti, 1998). Among adolescents who have witnessed a large number of community violence incidents, high rates of PTSD (25 to 30 percent) have been found (Saigh, 1991). Although direct victimization and witnessing victimization have been demonstrated to induce PTSD in children, direct victimization correlates more strongly with measures of distress than does exposure via witnessing (Saigh, 1991).

What Is Thriving?

There has to be a safe space to acknowledge and begin the work of healing all of these wounds. The goal however does not end with the cessation of symptoms; thriving in the wake of traumatic experiences requires the empowerment of the survivor to regain his or her voice, body, power, and sense of self. For some survivors, like those who were violated as children, this process may not just be one of regaining one's voice and power, but of actually finding one's voice and power for the first time. Thriving requires empowerment and the healing of one's self-esteem. Every survivor deserves the opportunity to thrive (Bryant-Davis, 2003). Symptom reduction and elimination is important for trauma recovery, but thriving necessitates a healing of one's sense of self, including an awareness of one's strengths and skills.

Why Is It Important to Look at Cultural Context?

"Although this is an area that has received very little attention, the cultural context of trauma is an important dimension because the meaning of trauma is culturally specific, and the social and religious rituals surrounding loss and disaster have an important healing role in both individual and community trauma" (van der Kolk, McFarlane, and Weisaeth, 1996, p. xv).

To heal the wounds of interpersonal trauma requires that the survivor and those working with the survivor truly bear witness to the traumatic experience and that the experience happened within the cultural context of the survivor's life. As a therapist, I cannot say I truly am present to the pain of a rape survivor if I do not also acknowledge that her disability, religion, race, sexual orientation, migration status, and socioeconomic status all influenced her experience of the rape as well as how she and her community have processed the rape since it occurred.

While there are some universal statements that can be made about trauma, such as it is frightening or overwhelming, there are also some culturally specific factors that affect each person's experience of a traumatic incident (Bryant-Davis, 2003). To work toward healing we have to begin to ask and answer the more complicated questions such as (1) How does a woman's faith affect her feelings about her own anger in the context of domestic violence?; (2) How does a man's sexual orientation affect his sense of safety in the context of being discriminated against in the workplace?; (3) How does an adolescent girl's race affect her body image in the context of being gang raped?; (4) How does a boy's mental disability affect his sense of shame in the context of being physically assaulted on the playground? Essentially, the work of recovery, the pathway to thriving, can never be complete when we require survivors to leave themselves at the door. If there is only room for the rape or war or domestic violence in the therapist's office, but not room for acknowledgment and exploration of the cultural context of these traumas, we as professionals do our clients a major disservice. Healing the wounds of trauma requires hearing and seeing the humanity and violation of another person, and to see and hear them requires that we make room for the powerful influence of cultural traditions, experiences, and beliefs.

What Has Been the Resistance to Looking at Cultural Context?

While there is a growing interest in the role of culture, there are currently a limited number of trauma texts that give serious consideration to the cultural context of trauma recovery. To name a few of these texts, one published by the American Psychological Association is entitled *The Ethnocultural Aspects of Posttraumatic Stress Disorder*. This book reviews the current literature and the need for further research on variations in PTSD with survivors of various ethnicities. Additionally, Judith Herman's book *Trauma and Recovery* addresses issues of gender, religion, and political terror, including the Nazi concentration camps. The afterword of her 1997 edition also names racist incidents within the discourse of traumatic experiences. Additionally, the important text, *Traumatic Stress: The Effects of Overwhelming Experience on Mind, Body, and Society*, by van der Kolk, McFarlane, and Weisaeth, includes a chapter on "Trauma in Cultural Perspective." To explore issues specific to societal traumas such as racism and homophobia, one would have to explore an array of articles in various scientific journals although they are not currently compiled into a text.

Some researchers and counselors believe that the way to equality is to claim to be color-blind or culture-blind. Some may fear or assume that if they acknowledge a person's culture they will be guilty of discrimination, when actually the opposite is true. When we ignore the cultural heritage of survivors, we are being incompetent clinicians at best and discriminatory at worst. I am reminded of a client I worked with who was in a wheelchair. She shared that her prior therapist had worked with her for a year without ever acknowledging or asking about her disability. Likewise, there are religious clients who have never talked about the centrality of their faith to their lives with their counselors because they were never told that therapy was a safe place for them to talk about the intersection of their faith and their recovery process. When counselors meet ethnic minority clients and then say they didn't notice the person's race, this is not a compliment, it is erasure. Erasure and denial of the person's heritage and their experience in the world as an ethnic being is as harmful as denial and erasure of a person's trauma history. Some people value the notion of color-blindness because they believe that acknowledging a person's culture is somehow rude or automatically discriminatory. This perception occurs because people have blended the notions of race and racism or gender and sexism. In other words, some people falsely believe that all cultural markers are negative and lead to oppression, so they have set as a goal the ability to ignore culture. This is quite problematic. When people say "I don't see you as a gay person, I see you as a human being," this implies that being gay makes one no longer human. It is important to acknowledge and respect our various cultures as well as our humanity.

Some therapists, educators, and professors also believe that the experience of trauma is universal. There is the assumption that because traumatic incidents are caused by such atrocities, those who experience them are automatically having the same experience. This assumption ignores the impact of cultural context on psychology. While there are some intrapsychic factors that we see across cultures, the manifestation of these factors as well as the cultural lens of interpretation and response to the factors can be quite varied. It is poor practice and invalid research that does not consider these factors. Marsella, Friedman, and Spain note, "While a universal neurobiological response to traumatic events most likely does exist, there is room for considerable ethnocultural variation in the expressive and phenomenological dimensions of the experience...." (p. 107).

The final reason culture is ignored is quite simply the extra work that is required when one acknowledges that these factors are important. As counselors, researchers, and educators, it is simpler to avoid it. It is easier to present a cookie-cutter approach to recovery that works with all people without any need for variation or additional thought. To acknowledge the full person means I have to address the full person, not just the dissected notion of trauma existing separate from the person. As we know, easier does not equate to competent care, valid research, or inclusive curriculum development. While it may require more work, exploring the cultural context of trauma recovery is essential to providing competent mental health care, research, and education.

What Is My Personal Investment in Writing This Book?

I am an able-bodied, African-American, Christian, female, heterosexual, middle-class doctor of psychology. I believe all of my cultural identities are significant and shape my experience, thoughts, values, and behaviors. Along with the richness of my various cultural traditions, I also find it important to acknowledge the ways I have been a target of discrimination based on some aspects of my culture such as my race and gender, and I must also acknowledge the ways that I hold privilege based on other aspects of my culture such as my able-bodied status, nationality, class, and sexual orientation.

As a trauma therapist, I have worked with trauma survivors of various cultures. While bearing witness and assisting in the recovery process, I have noticed the power of culture in people's understanding of the ways they have been violated as well as the power of culture in the ways they make meaning of themselves, their recovery, and the world around them. It is important for mental health professionals to engage and dialogue around this issue so that we don't provide incompetent care. Trauma recovery is difficult enough; as professionals we do not need to exacerbate the problem by dismissing, ignoring, and minimizing the cultures of those we serve. I feel a responsibility to the clients I have seen, to those who have been seen by others, and to those who refuse to seek service. I am compelled to write this book due to the experiences of survivors, those who were made to feel invisible by the very persons who were supposed to help them.

Along with being a trauma therapist, I am a trauma survivor. This book is for me and for every survivor on the path of recovery; those of us who have not seen our truths represented in self-help books or even in the protocols of some counselors. I write this book because I see you—you and I are not invisible— our life experiences are significant and worthy of attention.

What Is the Format of This Book?

The overarching themes of recovery from this book are based generally on the work of Judith Herman's book entitled *Trauma and Recovery* and the psycho-educational Stage One Trauma Recovery group designed at the Harvard Medical Center Victims of Violence program, directed by Judith Herman and Mary Harvey, both of whom were my clinical and research supervisors during my postdoctorate training. The themes are safety, self-care, trust, shame and self-blame, memories, mourning the losses, anger, body image, sexuality, coping strategies, and thriving. While Herman and Harvey incorporate issues of meaning making and self-esteem, thriving is a component that I have added to their model. Specifically, it looks at issues of growth, enhancement, and fulfillment. It is the step after moving from victim to survivor. It is the empowered state of going from surviving day-to-day to thriving—being your best self and using your gifts, skills, and abilities to a higher degree.

Within each theme I explore both theoretical and empirically based concepts related to the cultural context of recovery. Specifically, this book provides a guide, an overview of the ways identifying markers of culture intersect with the various components of recovery from interpersonal trauma. It is important to note at the outset that for all people there is an *intersectional* component of cultural variables. Within this text I talk about the cultural dynamics of economic status, disability, migration status, race, religion, and sexual orientation. It should be noted however that each of these factors intersects in each person. There are unique realities that are not merely additive but also multiplicative, unique to the experience of living at the intersections of multiple cultural categories. The intersection of multiple forms of oppression complicates the experience of trauma and the trauma recovery process (Holzman, 1996).

Each chapter also includes examples of clinical activities that can be done with survivors. Acknowledging the fact that many survivors may not be comfortable with traditional talk therapy, the activities provided in this text make use of alternative therapeutic strategies, namely journaling, art, music, movement, nature, social support, spirituality, and activism.

This guide is useful for counselors and helping professionals of varying clinical approaches. Whether the counselor is using psychodynamic, cognitive-behavioral, eye-movement desensitization and reprocessing, exposure therapy, support, or psycho-educational counseling, it is important to keep these themes and factors in mind when working with survivors.

For survivors who may be reading this guide, it is important to remember that culture is a framework for our lives, yet our lived experiences also make us unique. This means that some of the factors discussed will fit your experience, thoughts, and values and some of the factors discussed may not match your experience. You are the expert on your life, so it is important to take in the parts that feed and nurture your recovery and discard those parts that don't seem to match your experience. It is important to recognize that reading books is helpful, but it is not a substitute for therapy. Therapy is a place where you not only can take in information about trauma recovery, but also a place where you can be heard and supported. If you are a survivor, I encourage you to consider counseling if you have not already tried it.

Whether the reader is a helping professional and/or a survivor, it is most helpful for you to read the book in order. However if you are working with a client or are a client who is currently dealing with a particular theme, you may want to read that section immediately. That is fine, but I do encourage you to read the entire text in your own time.

It is also important to note that reading about trauma can be distressing for the reader. We are affected by traumatic stories, whether we live them, hear about them, or read them. It is important to pace yourself and take care of yourself. The case studies and survivor quotes within the text are based on over ten years of trauma counseling and trauma research. My work started with being a volunteer crisis counselor and community educator with local rape crisis centers and has continued in various settings, including hospitals, community agencies, clinics, and universities. After reading about traumatic material you may find that you have any number of responses including but not limited to anger, anxiety, sadness, intrusive thoughts about what you read, tension in your body, or questions about your faith or the way you make sense of the world. This is a normal reaction to hearing about the various traumas that occur in our world. You can take care of yourself by reading at your own pace, talking with others about the thoughts and feelings that come up for you, engaging in activities you enjoy, and becoming involved in activism, such as raising awareness in your community about trauma recovery and prevention. Most important, know that as the reader you are not alone. There is a community of people who care about these issues, and being aware of these issues is one step in the healing of society.

Why Have I Integrated Poetic Language into the Text?

By penning these words, Omalade (1994, p. 110) has inspired and freed me to integrate poetry and the voices of survivors throughout this text:

> The Black woman ... [scholar] must wrestle herself free of the demons of discipline which deny her. Eventually she must break the fetters of the academy and its shadows on Black women's thoughts. She must retrace the steps of our people, allowing the capacity of her dreams and her struggle to guide her through the raw material and data of our history. She must embrace the men and women ... who push their voices into her body and mind ... The Black woman scholar faces the index cards of facts and reference as she sits down to write, and the voices of the academy come to haunt: "Your language is too subjective. Quote from authorized sources. Demonstrate how this is significant to the entire society not just Blacks. Your work is too rhetorical, too lyrical." She sits immobilized, caught between these voices and the voices of her mothers and fathers ... [until she] uses the language of the people of everyday life without apology ... and reinforces the dignity of [Black] people as brilliant insightful commentators on [their own] human experience.

... and so I write for scholars, researchers, counselors, students, and survivors. I write with an integration of the art, science, and spirit of psychology; this is the way I honor the stories, rhythms, and songs of survival. These words are motivated by the strained voices of the previously silenced, those who are moving from victim to survivor, from survivor to thriver.

2

Safety

"So, after (I got shot) I was real apprehensive about going out at night—you know, like with any of my boys or anything like that—because it was like, you know, I didn't know what to expect. So that's how I kind of dealt with it, being more careful. Um, it kinda sobered me up a lot as far as, you know, "You need to stop being a little juvenile delinquent and, you know, get your shit together." I think that's how it affected me the most—is that it kinda made me realize that, you know, life's a little bit too short to, to uh, sit around and . . . You're not invincible. I don't care, you know, if you think you are as a teenager, you're not. You know. You need to stop screwing around in school and, uh, take life a little more seriously and watch your back, you know."

—a survivor of community violence

"Nobody is going to speak up for you but you. Ain't nobody else going to do it for you. And I learned this. I learned it the hard way. I took it and took it until I had to stand up and face facts. And if I didn't speak up then I was going to still be that way for a long time. And I knew that's not what I wanted. So I had to speak up and let somebody know what was going on. At least if I didn't get no help and nobody didn't do anything; at least I could say I did tell somebody. You know what I'm saying? I spoke up, I didn't keep it, you know what I'm saying, hidden the whole time, I told somebody. And telling somebody, it paid off. Each time they moved me, it may have not been the best place but at least, the last home they placed me in, it was the best. I'm not saying social services is the best place for nobody's child to go because it's not. Because I've been through some foster homes that just, you know, these foster parents, they have beat me and stuff. And I learned ain't nobody going to speak up for you but you, so I spoke up."

—a survivor of child abuse

What Is Safety?

Safety is a sense of protection, well-being, and security. It is the feeling people experience when they are not in danger. During times of safety, one is not worried about harm to the body, heart, mind, or spirit. If people are safe, they feel comfortable expressing themselves, their dreams, thoughts, and feelings. Feeling safe means there is an absence of anxiety and tension. Times when a person feels safe are times of feeling a sense of relaxation and ease.

How Often Do People Feel Safe?

Everyone has had different experiences with safety. Some may have felt safe for all of their childhood, and some may never remember a time when they or she felt safe.

How Does Trauma Affect Safety?

When someone is traumatized, their sense of safety is taken away. Traumatic events create anxiety and distress because they endanger the survivor emotionally and/or physically. During the traumatic experience and/or after the event, it is common to feel tense and afraid. The trauma the survivor experienced may make the survivor feel that certain people, places, or situations are not safe. The survivor may even feel that the world in general is not safe. Traumatic experiences violate our sense of safety. After the experience, the survivor may feel unsafe around the person who violated the survivor or around people who remind the survivor of that person. The survivor may feel unsafe in the place where it occurred or in places that remind the survivor of that place. The survivor may feel uncomfortable in situations that are similar to the situation in which the trauma occurred. This unsafe feeling may be occasional or constant. It may have lasted for a month after the experience, or it may be years later and the survivor continues to feel unsafe.

What Are Signs That a Person Doesn't Feel Safe?

- Does the person often look over their shoulder in fear?
- Does the person often hold their breath?
- Does the person have panic attacks?

- Does the person have tension in their body, such as in their back or neck?
- Does the person stay away from people, or is the person afraid of being alone?
- Does the person feel that they have to constantly watch what they say and do?
- Does the person often experience an upset stomach?
- Does the person have trouble sleeping?
- Does the person constantly feel that something bad is going to happen to them?

How Might One's Economic Situation Affect One's Sense of Safety?

A survivor who experienced a traumatic experience and has limited finances may feel even more vulnerable. This person may not have the resources to do the things that would make them feel safe, such as moving or leaving a job where the violation occurred. The survivor may also have few or no family or friends who have enough money or resources to share with the survivor. In addition, a survivor who lives in a lower-income area may have been vulnerable to multiple traumatic experiences over the course of their life. While child maltreatment crosses economic lines, some of the factors in low-income families that are associated with increased risk for maltreatment are parental unemployment, overcrowding, frequent moves, and poor parental social networks; lack of material and social resources make it more difficult for impoverished families to maintain safe environments for their children (Jones & McCurdy, 1992; Sidebotham, Heron and Golding, 2002).

In addition, the survivor may not have had the money for therapy, medical treatments, or legal action. There may be resources in the survivor's area for people who have limited finances, but the survivor may not have been told about these resources. In addition, the survivor may have felt looked down on by those who were supposed to provide help. Some counselors discriminate against those who cannot pay, and this can increase feelings of vulnerability and anxiety. If this has happened, the survivor may feel less safe than survivors who have more money and resources available to them. The survivor should know however, that reclaiming their sense of safety is possible.

How Might One's Gender Affect One's Sense of Safety?

If the survivor is a female, she may have had several prior experiences that have affected her sense of safety. Violence against women is one of the biggest human rights violations in the world. In North America, 40 to 51 percent of women have experienced some form of violence in their lifetime, including child abuse, physical violence, rape, and domestic violence (Robinson, 2003). Women are particularly vulnerable when the perpetrator is a family member, as the general public is often hesitant to get involved in matters that are considered "private" or familial. Along these lines, in a national study conducted in Great Britain, 12 percent of women had experienced sexual abuse before the age of sixteen, and 14 percent of them were abused by family members (Naker, 1985).

Intimate partner violence includes psychological, physical, and sexual abuse, and all three of these types of abuse have negative consequences for the woman's emotional and physical safety. Women who are survivors of physical intimate partner violence are also at risk for health consequences that impede their physical well-being and safety; these possible consequences include but are not limited to physical disability, chronic pain, migraines, sexually transmitted infections, chronic pelvic pain, stomach ulcers, and frequent indigestion (Coker and colleagues, 2000). Addressing the safety concerns of survivors should therefore include recommendations of physical health assessments and treatment as well as mental health assessment and treatment. Experiencing, witnessing, or hearing about sexual harassment, stalking, pornography, sexual objectification, prostitution, sexual assault, and discrimination all may have affected the survivor's sense of safety. As a woman or girl, the survivor may in general have felt unsafe in the world even before the traumatic experience. The trauma may have then increased the sense of danger that was already present. The establishment of safety is an important component of recovery for female survivors (Herman, 1997).

If the survivor is a male, he may feel unsafe but be unable to talk about his feelings. In one survey with male and female survivors of sexual abuse, the boys reported much lower levels of disruption associated with abuse (Moisan, Sanders-Phillips, and Moisan, 1997). Men are often taught to ignore their feelings and not share them with others. This may have put the survivor in a difficult situation. The survivor may feel unsafe but worried that expressing those feelings will result in more vulnerability. In terms of sexual abuse and safety, while girls are more likely to be sexually abused by family members and strangers, boys are more likely to be abused by nonfamilial but known males such as neighbors, family friends, or authority figures (Moisan, Sanders-Phillips, and Moisan, 1997).

Other cultural factors also interact with gender. For example, adolescent males in rural areas are more likely than urban adolescent boys to report having been victimized by intimate partner violence, particularly to have reported being slapped, hit, or kicked by an intimate partner (Spencer and Bryant, 2000).

For men and women, traumas such as intimate partner violence can negatively affect the sense of safety by precipitating depression, PTSD (symptoms include hyperarousal, avoidance, and reliving the experience), substance abuse, and additional abusive relationships later in life (Coker and colleagues, 2000). Whether the survivor is male or female, restoring the survivor's sense of safety is an important step in recovery.

How Might One's Mental or Physical Disability Affect One's Safety?

A survivor who has a mental or physical disability may have had multiple experiences of feeling unsafe due to being stigmatized in school, their home, their neighborhood, and society in general. The stigma surrounding disabilities may increase vulnerability to violation, as perpetrators know that the tendency to blame or disbelieve victims has particular potency when the victim has a disability. There are myths surrounding the disabled; for example, the perception that the disabled are not sexually abused because of either the assumption that no one would seek to harm them because of their disability or the perception that a perpetrator would not find them "attractive" because of their disability (Balogh and colleagues, 2001). Additionally, the abuse often is minimized by nondisabled persons who falsely assume that, as a result of the survivor's disability, they won't be affected by the abuse (Balogh and colleagues, 2001). Abused children with intellectual disabilities are often abused by family members and care staff; disabled boys and girls are neglected and sexually, emotionally, and physically abused, with a higher rate of disabled boys being abused compared to nondisabled boys (Balogh and colleagues, 2001; Firth and colleagues, 2001; Kvam, 2000; Sobsey, Randall, Parrila, 1997). While intellectually and physically disabled survivors may have difficulty communicating the occurrences and details of abusive behaviors, the disability may also make it additionally difficult if not impossible to escape abusive perpetrators.

Although disabled survivors may have difficulty with verbal communication, they may communicate that they are not sure by loss of appetite, sleeping problems, crying, nightmares, rage, introverted behavior, and/or apathy; unfortunately these signals are often falsely attributed to bullying, failure, fear of the hospital, or being on the wrong medication (Balogh and colleagues, 2001). Even though there are significant challenges, it is possible to detect abuse of the disabled and it is necessary for us to work to create safe environments for those who are intellectually and physically disabled.

How Might One's Migration Status Affect One's Safety?

Survivors who recently left their home country may feel that their sense of safety is additionally threatened. They may have left their home country because of a traumatic experience, such as war. Or, they may have felt safer in their new country, but then had a traumatic experience there that makes them question if there is any safe place. In addition, they may be unfamiliar with the language, resources, agencies, and legal rights available in their new country. This exacerbates feelings of vulnerability after a traumatic event. Some survivors may be illegal residents in their new country and therefore unable to gain access to certain services and protection. In a study of South Asian immigrant women, a higher prevalence of intimate partner violence was found (approximately 40 percent) with the following factors being associated with greater risk: lower social support, no family in the United States, and lower acculturation; additionally many of the women had no awareness of intimate partner violence services (Raj and Silverman, 2003). Regardless of their legal status or knowledge of their new country, survivors 'safety is important.

How Might One's Race/Ethnicity Affect One's Safety?

A racial or ethnic minority survivor of a traumatic experience may have had multiple experiences that threatened their sense of safety. Experiences of racism, discrimination, bias, and hate crimes are traumatic in and of themselves. In addition, the survivor may have felt that professionals have not valued the survivor's safety in the same way that a majority group member's safety would be valued. As a result, seeking help from police, therapists, or medical personnel, may not have felt like real options for the survivor.

The specific dynamics around the safety violations of survivors should be explored in terms of cultural context and patterns of trauma. For example, although Wyatt (1985) found similar rates of childhood sexual abuse in a non-clinical sample of black and white women, she found that black women were more likely to be abused during preadolescence while white women were more likely to have been abused in early childhood. While African-American girls are more likely to endure abuse that includes penetration than Hispanic girls, Hispanic girls who have been sexually abused usually have a greater number of episodes of sexual abuse, wait longer to disclose abuse, then to be abused by their father or stepfather, and have confusion regarding family values and rules (Shaw and colleagues, 2001). The age at which one is violated can certainly impact one's sense of safety, particularly if the feeling of safety is now linked to development and physical maturity. An additional example of differential dynamics regarding safety is a study of child rape among South African women, which found that among these women who had been raped before the age of fifteen, the most common perpetrator was a schoolteacher (Jewkes, Mbananga and Bradshaw, 2002; Madu and Peltzer, 2001). A survivor's safety concerns may vary not only due to the age she was at the time of the assault, but also based on her relationship to the perpetrator.

Safety is also affected by the treatment of children and women of one's ethnicity. This is largely manifested in the prevalence of trafficking of women and children. Those who are economically disadvantaged from developing countries are vulnerable to economic, physical, and sexual violations of their human rights (Bertone, 2000). One report on sexual exploitation of children in Sri Lanka found that out of the 145 schoolchildren, studied, the participants reported both knowing other children who had had sex with adults (some for money), and some of the children (6 percent) reported that they had sex with an adult in exchange for money; few of the children reported learning about sex at school or at home (Miles, 2000). This shows how ethnicity, economics, and age can intersect to increase vulnerability to violations and establishment of safety. These factors also interact in the histories of young abortion-seeking women in China who report an incident of sexual coercion; coercion is associated within the population of Chinese women who have a poor education as well as intimate partner violence, sex for money, sex after abusing alcohol, younger age at first intercourse, and a larger age difference between themselves and their partner (Yimin, et al., 2002).

A number of violent acts toward children are socially sanctioned and deemed "acceptable" in many countries (Berrien and colleagues, 1994; Schlagenhauf, 2003; Segal, 1995). Certainly in communities where not only physical punishment on a milder end of the spectrum but also physical abuse on the other end of the spectrum are socially accepted, people will grow up with an altered sense of physical safety in the world. In terms of physical safety, youth and young adults who reported incidents of sexual coercion in Lima, Peru, also had higher rates of sexually transmitted diseases and less knowledge about sex in general (Caceres, Marin, and Hudes, 2000).

If many members of the survivor's family or community have experienced traumatic events, they may also minimize the survivor's experience and tell the survivor that it is not a big deal. When traumatic events are prevalent, people may advise the survivor to just get over it. This makes it difficult to feel safe talking about the trauma that the survivor experienced. For example, researchers have found higher rates of intimate partner violence against African-American and Mexican women as compared to white women (Rickert and colleagues, 2002). Femicide is the leading cause of premature death of African-American women, with the following factors contributing to lack of safety for them: poverty, problem drinking and illicit drug use of the victim and perpetrator, unemployment of the perpetrator, and past intimate partner violence (Campbell and colleagues, 2002). In a study of over one thousand American Indians, 9 percent of men and 5 percent of women had experienced physical violence; those reporting these incidents had higher levels of physical and mental health concerns, and very few of them had ever been assessed for physical violence or safety (Harwell, Moore, & Spence, 2002). With a high community prevalence of safety violations, women of these communities may begin to minimize abusive behavior as a way of coping with its prevalence.

Members of ethnic minorities are also combating the negative stigma majority group members often believe about them. Regardless of the stereotypes others hold about the survivor's race or ethnicity, the survivor's safety is important. Racism is a reality, and counselors must work with an awareness of that reality to honor the survivor's life integrity, value, and right to be protected and treated with respect. Members of ethnic minorities may present themselves as being quite strong as a way of coping. Counselors should build on this strength but not miss the possibility that the client is indeed feeling unsafe regardless of presentation.

How Might One's Religion Affect One's Sense of Safety?

If the survivor is a religious person, he or she may feel guilty about having feelings of vulnerability. This person may believe that if they have enough faith, they should never feel unsafe. The truth is that all people have times when they feel unsafe, and those feelings are not a reflection of the survivor's religious faith. There are dangers in the world that affect us all. People in the survivor's religious community may advise that person to pray and believe that they are safe. These are valuable strategies, but there may continue to be times when the survivor feels unsafe because of the trauma they experienced. In addition, the survivor may have had the experience of sharing the their faith with those who were supposed to help (such as counselors), but instead they put down the survivor's beliefs. This may have left the survivor feeling unsafe talking to certain professionals. It should be noted that the survivor's safety as well as faith are important, and a point should be made to connect with helping professionals who will respect the survivor's religious beliefs.

How Might One's Sexual Orientation Affect One's Sense of Safety?

A survivor who is gay, lesbian, bisexual, or transgender may often feel unsafe because of homophobia and past experiences of interpersonal trauma. One study of 521 youths at a gay, lesbian, and bisexual youth rally found the following regarding safety: bisexual adolescent males were most likely to report any type of abuse, bisexual females were more likely to report experiencing sexual abuse, lesbians were more likely to report feeling scared about their safety compared to heterosexual females, bisexual were more likely to be threatened with outing than both gay males and lesbians (Freedner and colleagues, 2002).

Before the traumatic experience, the survivor may have experienced, seen, and/ or heard about hate crimes and harassment incidents. Survivor who have been traumatized by a homophobic incident or a different traumatic event may now feel unsafe in their own environment. It may be their neighborhood, school, job, or a social setting. Survivors may also feel unsafe talking to professionals about their safety concerns because of fear of possible homophobic responses. For example, a survivor may have spoken with someone about his safety concerns and been dismissed or ridiculed because of the counselor's homophobia. We live in a homophobic society, but know that survivors have the right to safety and protection.

Why Is Safety Important to One's Recovery?

It is important for the survivor to regain a sense of safety so that anxiety and tension can be reduced and so she can reconnect with the self. It is essential for this person to be able to take action to increase safety and see the warning signs that distinguish a possibly unsafe situation or person from a safe one. It is not always possible to predict safe people and places, but it is essential to maximize the survivor's emotional and physical safety.

It is vital for the survivor to determine possible ways that she or those around her may endanger her well-being. Safety is a first step in recovery. If the survivor is currently in a dangerous situation that continues to traumatize her, it will be very difficult to move from victim to survivor to thriver. The first step is to honestly assess her safety, and if she is not safe, determine the steps she can take to increase her safety. This person's traumatic experience may have negatively affected her self-esteem, and as a result she may not believe that she is worthy of protection and safety. The survivor is worthy.

What Are Things Survivors Do That Threaten Their Safety?

- Excessive drinking and drug use
- Unprotected sex; sex with strangers
- Suicidal attempts
- Cutting and burning
- Not seeking medical treatment or getting routine checkups
- Consistent pattern of selecting dating partners and friends that endanger the survivor

Whether others continue to endanger the survivor or the survivor is a danger to himself, it is important that he seeks help, by speaking with a professional and/or engaging in self-help activities, such as reading this book. Seeking help is a sign that the survivor values his safety and wants to work toward recovery. I encourage counselors to work with survivors on the activities that follow to address their sense of safety. Before the survivor does the activities, consider the following steps that could assist him in establishing safety in emergency situations before addressing the more reflective aspects of safety.

1. If the survivor is feeling suicidal, a clinical assessment should be done at a nearby hospital to determine if inpatient care is needed.

2. If the survivor is feeling unsafe because of someone else, you can help this person to consider reporting it to the police, obtaining a restraining order, pressing criminal charges, filing a harassment or discrimination complaint, going to a shelter, and/or avoiding contact with the perpetrator.

The following activities use a variety of formats including affirmation, writing, music, movement, nature, art, activism, and spirituality. Use of the arts, in and out of traditional therapy, has the power to help survivors give voice to their experiences. The arts may be used to explore themes related to sexual assault and release negative effects and beliefs precipitated by sexual assault. For example, Bryant (1999) found that African-American adult survivors of childhood sexual abuse reported using the arts to gain power over experiences of sexual violence. The arts may include visual art, drama, dancing, story telling, music, and poetry. In working with child survivors, all of these artistic approaches may be incorporated in play therapy (Webb, 1999).

The use of the arts has been found to give the survivors the opportunity to resist the stereotypical depictions of rape by having them create their own imagery and representation that is more authentic and related to their own experience (Backos and Pagon, 1999). The arts are also a powerful tool because, instead of silencing women and girls, it provides a tool for affective expression, including affect that is usually restricted such as anger and shame (Backos and Pagon, 1999). Visual artistic expression has been found to be healing for women survivors of sexual childhood violence by giving them an opportunity to experience personal growth and increased self worth (Spencer, 1997).

Lev-Wiessel (1998) found that drawing is an effective tool for survivors to break the silence and secrecy that was imposed by the perpetrator of their abuse. Poetry has also been discussed as a tool for the exploration and transformation of self-perception and self-understanding (Fox, 1997). Payne (1994) has explored the use of dance and movement for gaining a sense of self, strengthening body image, and developing personal strength and trust. Writing has been used as a way to name violence as a weapon of warfare against humanity; the act of writing is utilized to reclaim the power needed to change society and resist oppression (Adisa, 1997).

Activism as a coping strategy is the use of helping others who are violated or oppressed in order to decrease the likelihood of others being violated, to gain a sense of empowerment, to counter feelings of self-doubt, and/or to make sense of the trauma by finding ways of taking the negative experience and using it for the good of others who are facing similar situations (Bryant, 1999). Whether they educate their communities about rape, volunteer at rape crisis or battered women shelters, or lobby to improve rape laws, many women find the act of helping others an integral part of their recovery (Benedict, 1994).

Activism may also speak to the specific realities of a sociocultural context and in this way provide special meaning in survivors' lives. For example, some antirape education campaigns in African-American communities have taken on a black feminist framework while incorporating highly publicized issues such as the mass community support of convicted rapist Mike Tyson and accused perpetrators Michael Jackson, R. Kelly, and Kobe Bryant. Significantly, African-American women who are involved in activism report a higher rate of rape myth rejection than nonactivists (White, Strube, and Fisher, 1998). Likewise, involvement in political activism has been found to build empowerment, collective identity, and sense of belonging for Latina women (Abrahams, 1996). Activism may include engaging in a number of activities, including but not limited to working with community watch programs, rape crisis centers, and children's rights groups. Whether through formal or informal involvement, finding ways to have voice and power through action can be a key component to thriving for survivors.

Garbarino (1996) argues that interventions should not just focus on physiological and psychological issues, as is often the case; instead there should be a focus on the metaphysical and spiritual challenges that arise from violation. Among survivors who were violated as children, Ryan (1998) notes that a significant number of them in some way alter their spiritual beliefs or practices as a result of the violation and then utilize their religious and spiritual beliefs and practices to cope and make meaning of their lives after the violation. While extreme religiosity has been found to have negative effects, strong religious beliefs have been found to have positive effects on coping and serve as an important tool for some families in responding to crisis (Joseph, 1998; Walsh, 1998). Within the African-American community, Blaine and Crocker (1995) found that religious belief salience and psychological well-being were moderately correlated. Along with individual belief systems, membership in a spiritual or religious group may serve the purpose of increasing one's support networks, thus making one's faith organization a community resource (Anderson-Scott, 1998). Along these lines, Bryant (1999) found that many African-American adult survivors of childhood violence report using spirituality as a tool of growth, meaning-making, and empowerment in the aftermath of violation.

The instructions below are instructions for the survivor. Of course, they are all optional. The survivor may choose to do some activities and for whatever reason choose not to do other activities. The survivor is the expert on his or her own comfort level and needs. (If the survivor is not literate and the activity requires writing, the survivor can share their responses verbally with the health care professional.)

Journaling/Poetry

Read and try to remember this affirmation.
Affirmation: I deserve to live in safety.

Activities:

1. Write a short story describing a specific time when you felt safe.
2. Write a poem about a person that makes you feel safe. If you are uncomfortable writing a poem, simply write a description of the person.
3. Write a list of the five times in your life when you felt the least safe. You do not need to describe them in detail, just list them using a short phrase or sentence.
4. Write a description of the things that would need to change within you and within the world to make you feel safer.

Movement

Read and try to remember this affirmation.
Affirmation: I can breathe deeply. I am safe.

Activity:

Imagine yourself during the most recent traumatic experience. Position your body in a way that represents how you felt. It may be frozen and rigid or you may have felt unable to pull yourself together. Use your entire body to make your position—the position of being unsafe. Now slowly breathe in and out seven times. Now slowly move your body until you are in a position that represents safety. Once you are in a pose or position of safety, breathe deeply seven times.

Arts and Crafts

Read and try to remember this affirmation.
Affirmation: My safety is important.

Activities:

Think about the feelings you have when you aren't safe and draw a picture to represent those feelings. The drawing may be abstract or specific symbols, people, or places. You can use pencils, crayons, or markers. Now think about the feelings you have when you are safe and draw a picture to represent those feelings. If you can never remember feeling safe, draw a picture of what you imagine it would be like to be safe.

Music

Read and try to remember this affirmation.
Affirmation: I value my life.

Activity:

Think of a song that makes you feel safe. What about it makes you feel safe? Is it the lyrics, the rhythm, the person who taught it to you, the time of your life when you first heard it? Play the song now and either sit quietly and listen to it or sing along with the recording. Allow the feeling of safety to surround the survivor.

Drama/Theater

Read and try to remember this affirmation.
Affirmation: I choose to live in safety.

Activity:

Imagine a historical figure that you respect. It may be a politician, an artist, a deceased member of your family, or anyone you choose. Then pretend that you are that person. What would that person say to you considering what you are going through right now? You may want to write out the words that they would say and then read them aloud, or you may want to just start talking and see what words come out. Think about their body language. Would they stand or sit? Would they smile or be serious? Would they whisper to you or speak loudly? Would they advise you or simply tell

you about their life and how they survived? After you have done the
exercise, write a reflection of what it was like to take on the personality of
the person you respect.

Spirituality

Read and try to remember this affirmation.
Affirmation: My body, heart, mind, and spirit are worthy of protection.

Activity:

Look through a book of spiritual wisdom, whether it is the Bible, Koran,
Torah, a book of poetry or proverbs, or a book written by a spiritual leader
of your faith. Find a passage that speaks about safety and protection. Read
it and sit in silence to meditate on the words that you have read. Think
about how the passage relates to you specifically and allow yourself to find
wisdom, peace, and assurance from the reading.

Social Support

Read and try to remember this affirmation.
Affirmation: I will seek friends who are safe.

Activities:

1. Think of a few people with whom you spend time. Consider each
   person and how they respond when you share your feelings. Are
   they supportive, judgmental, manipulative, dismissive, competitive,
   or affirming? Choose the person who is the most supportive and tell
   them about your safety concerns. If there is no one that you can trust,
   consider talking to a counselor or calling a hotline to talk about your
   feelings.

2. Think about how your sense of safety has been affected by the
   trauma and by your economic status, gender, migration status, race/
   ethnicity, religion, and/or sexual orientation. Consider sharing this
   with someone you can trust. It is important for you to talk about
   your feelings and enlist the support of others in making your
   environment safe. If there is no one whom you can trust, consider
   talking to a counselor or calling a hotline to talk about your
   feelings.

Nature

> *Read and try to remember this affirmation.*
> *Affirmation: I see myself living in safety.*

Activities:

Think about the size of a seed and all the forces working against it, such as wind and storm. Next consider how it is protected in the earth and the way it grows and flourishes. Now consider your life and list the different factors that have worked against your growth.

Now list the people or factors that have in some way protected you. It may be things that you did or people, such as a teacher, friend, or family member who intervened on your behalf.

Activism

> *Read and try to remember this affirmation.*
> *Affirmation: I release anxiety and walk in safety.*

Activity:

After you have established safety for yourself and maintained it for some predetermined period of time, seek out an agency that helps people who are in danger and see if there is a way you can volunteer a few hours with them. It may be a shelter, rape crisis center, counseling center, legal aid office, or victims' rights organization. You may help them organize files, clean, serve meals, or better understand the experience of those who have gone through a traumatic event.

Survivor Case Summary Joseph is a biracial gay survivor of sexual assault. He is Japanese and African-American and in his mid-thirties. He is from a middle-income family and is the middle of three children. Joseph's parents are Christian but he considers himself a generally spiritual person who does not subscribe to any one particular religion. He has no physical or mental disabilities and is a college graduate.

Joseph presented for counseling after his self-destructive behavior resulted in a number of negative legal consequences. During the assessment process it was discovered that Joseph was sexually assaulted in a night club a week before his destructive behaviors intensified.

While Joseph had already begun using alcohol, drugs, and casual sex to cope with anxiety related to both his racial identity and his sexual orientation, these high-risk behaviors intensified after the sexual assault.

Joseph's safety was in jeopardy for a number of reasons. He was drinking heavily, and this was having negative consequences on his social relationships as well as his physical health. He was also engaging in unprotected casual sex on a regular basis. In addition, Joseph was abusing marijuana and cocaine occasionally. The priority for Joseph was to establish safety in terms of his negative coping and avoidant strategies as well as his self-punishing behaviors.

In addressing safety we had to explore the experiences of trauma, including sexual assault, homophobia, and racism. This exploration also addressed issues of shame and self-blame as well as denial and minimization. Joseph blamed himself for the assault because he went to the nightclub and drank a lot of alcohol. He also initially used minimization and denial to cope with the assault, as well as his experiences with homophobia and racism. By naming the self-destructive pattern of Joseph's behaviors and challenging the cognitive distortions that were fueling them, Joseph was able to move toward safe and healthy behaviors. These changes included talking about the traumatic memories, mourning the losses, learning adaptive coping strategies, and making thriving, including developing positive self-esteem, a realistic goal. Along with individual counseling to address the traumatic experience, Joseph also sought treatment for his drug and alcohol abuse.

The coping strategies that Joseph found helpful were developing a healthy social network, counseling, and music, particularly singing. Counseling also focused on developing resistance strategies to enable Joseph to resist internalizing negative societal stereotypes about male survivors of sexual assault, as well as stereotypes about gay men and men of color. By actively working to embrace positive notions of his identity, Joseph was able toward the end of the therapeutic process to begin engaging in activism to educate others about sexual violence. He found this quite rewarding and plans to continue his activism in the future.

3

Self-Care

"You need a positive outlet. Your first outlet of course should be to talk to somebody. And it has to be somebody you trust, because if you give this information to somebody that doesn't deserve it, it can cause more harm. And that was one of my biggest fears. You know what I'm saying. Misconceptions . . . people spreading rumors that you're gay, so my personal outlet was always music, you know. Writing a song is a positive outlet. Something that takes that negative energy. Something that you can take what has happened and do something that you enjoy that can take your mind off it but at the same time gives you that outlet. Because right now I can be heard and I can go make a piece of music about that pain and turn that pain into something so great and so much more powerful than the pain, that I'll get away from it. That's always been my high. Music for me is just, honestly, you can't take it from me now. I can close my eyes and I can hear my music. (laughs)"

—a survivor of sexual abuse

"Doing, singing and stuff for two years. And ain't no turning back now, you know. If I—like I told these friends of mine, I said, if I know, you know, the journey I'm on now, I'd been turned my life over, you know. But I had to learn the hard way. Because of the violence I grew up around, you know. But I'm overcome it, you know. I feel down, sometimes I just get the Bible and read it, you know. Cause, I'm at home mostly by myself. Or I'm looking at TV. Or I find something to do, you know. Like, you know, working in the yard, you know, planting flowers and stuff. Far as that, I'm looking in the Bible. It helps me a lot, and I got medications that I took. I take Prozac. I take one of them every day. Yeah. And I got to go back and see my doctor next month too. The twenty-first. See if he can give me some more medicine. I tried to come off of it by myself but my nerves just, you know, like I said, much as I been through, and then messing with that cocaine, it just made things worse, you know, sometimes, you know, like things ain't going to be like I want it to be, you know, and the Bible tells you that, you know: "The sun ain't going to shine on you all of the time." You going to have some bad days, too. But I think it's just to test my faith, you know. You know, to be a Christian, you have to be [bold] and you have to take some stuff that normal people won't take, you know. Cause it's easy to get off the right road. But I heard once you get off that road it's hard to get back on that road again. You know. So I'm just trying, you know, day—taking it day to day, you know. I'm not rushing [after it]. You know, we got a nice little group. We sing. We fixing to do a program September the twelfth—so, we're not getting nothing out of it, you know, we're just doing it for the Lord, you know, helping them out. . . . It helps me a lot, you know, cause my mind be on songs, you know, and I be thinking about Jesus when I'm singing. You know, how He died for me, you know, and all us, you know. He gave us His only son. That's the greatest gift [of love], you know. We owe Him. But we can't pay Him what he gave it to us, you know. We just got to do our best, you know, till our day come. So that's all I'm waiting on, you know, till my day comes. I just want to be ready."

—survivor of child abuse

What Is Self-Care?

Self-care is the active decision to engage in activities that nurture and sustain the survivor. Self-care is important for every human being (Herman, 1997). Self-care activities include but are not limited to eating, sleeping, exercise, and maintaining good hygiene. When the survivor engages in self-care, she is saying to herself and to others that she values her life and health. Self-care is the opposite of self-harm. Instead of deciding to actively harm the self or passively neglect the self, the survivor chooses to care for the self. This includes the survivor's body, heart, mind, and spirit.

How Does Trauma Affect Self-Care?

When the survivor experienced the traumatic event(s), the person who violated or disrespected the survivor was sending the survivor the message that he is insignificant. That person or group of people may have made the survivor feel invisible, dirty, or inhuman, less valuable than others. Some survivors may respond to this by taking extra time and effort for self-care. The more common response however is to believe that one is insignificant and therefore neglect one's needs. In addition, the survivor may use lack of self-care as a protective measure; hoping that by neglecting the self, others will ignore them and therefore not harm them further. Roth and Batson (1997) summarize the effects of trauma on self-care by noting that post-trauma symptoms include increased self-destructive behaviors, suicidal preoccupation, and excessive risk-taking. All of these factors create barriers to caring for the self.

How Does Trauma Affect Eating?

The survivor may develop an eating disorder after the traumatic event(s). Some people begin denying themselves food. The survivor may do this as a form of regaining control. Trauma takes away control, and survivors often try to find ways to regain control over their lives. One such way is through controlling their diet. Some survivors of sexual traumas stop eating in the hope that having a thin body will make them less sexually attractive to potential perpetrators. The same mind-set is at work for those who begin to overeat. Not only may eating be a form of soothing and coping, it may also be motivated by the hope of becoming less desirable to potential perpetrators. Avoiding food or eating excessively may also be a way that the survivor is unconsciously or consciously attempting suicide. If the traumatic event has created feelings that are unbearable, self-care becomes difficult and self-harm, including suicide, becomes more and more attractive.

How Does Trauma Affect Sleep?

The memory of the survivor's traumatic experience may make sleep very difficult. The survivor may find it impossible to fall asleep or may wake up often during the night. Some survivors often worry about their current safety and so remain awake, keeping watch to protect themselves. On the other hand, the survivor may experience depression as a result of the traumatic event. This depression may in part cause the survivor to sleep constantly for most of the day. Depression makes it hard to face the day and so many people cope by sleeping.

How Does Trauma Affect Exercise?

The survivor may want to exercise constantly as a way of gaining control over her body. If she experienced physical or sexual trauma, she may engage in excessive exercise in the hope of becoming strong enough to ward off future attacks. Some survivors also engage in excessive exercise because of never feeling strong enough, good enough, beautiful enough; as a result physical strain may be used as a way for the survivor to punish herself. On the other hand, some survivors avoid exercise because it is difficult to acknowledge the physical body. If the survivor experienced a sexual assault, she may go through life trying to avoid thinking about or feeling her body. For this reason, exercise becomes very difficult. In addition, if the survivor is consciously or unconsciously attempting to gain weight to reduce the potential or future violation, she may also avoid exercising. It is important to find moderation. While exercise is important, excessive exercise can be damaging physically and emotionally.

How Does Trauma Affect Hygiene?

Some survivors become depressed and avoid bathing and/or cleaning their living space. If the survivor was sexually traumatized, he may be uncomfortable touching his body, so he avoids bathing. The survivor may also avoid bathing because he is hoping to reduce the likelihood of future violations. Some survivors do not clean themselves, their clothes, or their living environment because they feel unworthy of cleanness. The survivor may believe that he is dirty and only deserves to live in filth. It is important to the recovery process for this person to reject the notion that he is dirty or unworthy. Even if the survivor doesn't believe it, he should begin attempting to take better care of his hygiene, body, and space. As the survivor begins to change his behavior, he will begin to restructure the cognitions related to self-worth and value.

There may be some survivors who clean obsessively. They may wake up early to dust and scrub and stay up late recleaning that which he spent the day cleaning. In essence, he may feel that no matter how much he cleans, he is still somehow dirty, tarnished, or stained. While it is good to take care of one's self and one's space, know that obsessive cleaning is an indicator of a need for emotional, mental, and spiritual cleansing. Survivors will need to explore and eventually accept the cleanness of their inner woman or inner man. When the survivor can do that, he can begin to release the outer obsession with the assurance that he is good enough and clean enough at the core.

How Does Mental and Physical Disability Affect Self-Care?

For persons with disabilities who require assistance with self-care, the aftermath of trauma can be particularly challenging. Needing assistance getting to help resources, having materials in a format that one can utilize, communicating with professionals, and engaging in activities that are enjoyable are some of the challenges survivors face. Survivors with disabilities may experience an increase in feelings of vulnerability, dependence, and anxiety. They should be assured that their support system, health professionals, and/or court officials are present and willing to assist. Feelings of being a burden as well as of distrust, shame, and self-blame can cause survivors to withdraw, internalize their symptoms, and silence their needs. All of these behaviors are barriers to recovery. It is important for connections to be made with people who value the survivor and are sensitive to his post-trauma symptoms. If the survivor has moderate to severe mental retardation, it may be challenging for him to communicate or have clarity about his needs in the aftermath of trauma. It is important for members of his support circle as well as health care professionals to provide support and psycho-education at a level he can understand concerning the particular trauma he experienced as well as to normalize the aftermath of trauma. Additionally, use of the arts can be a great form of emotional self-care, communication, and affective expression for those who are verbally or mentally challenge.

How Might One's Economic Status Affect One's Self-Care?

In various countries including the United States, South Africa, Egypt, and Bangladesh, impoverished persons are more vulnerable to violation and face more barriers to accessing resources such as shelters, counseling, judicial services, and medical services (Koenig and colleagues, 2003; Kim and Motsi, 2002; Youssef, Attia, and Kamel, 1998). Impoverished women and children are particularly vulnerable to trafficking, and once they have been trafficked, their limited resources and support make escape to safety for self-preservation and care difficult (Schlagenhauf, 2003).

If the survivor's finances are limited, she may not be able to join a fancy gym or go to a fancy spa or expensive salons. There are still inexpensive ways that the survivor can engage in self-care, however. She can exercise in her apartment or in the park. She can eat inexpensive but healthy meals. Due to the survivor's current economic situation, it may be difficult for her to get a good amount of sleep. She may have to work a few jobs or live in a noisy environment that makes sleep difficult. Understanding her own financial circumstances, she should try to maximize her opportunities for rest and self-care. With the stress and strain that this survivor is facing, rest is especially important and valuable.

If, on the other hand, the traumatic event and the survivor's economic stress have resulted in feelings of depression that make it difficult to stay awake, the survivor should consider getting counseling. Many counseling services provide reduced rates or free guidance and support. The survivor is worthy of care.

How Might One's Gender Affect Self-Care?

Many women and a growing number of men suffer from eating disorders. The survivor may have had an eating disorder prior to her traumatic event, and the trauma may have magnified the disorder. There are many pressures on women to attain unrealistic physical dimensions. These are promoted in the media, peer groups, and within families. Related to these pressures is the prevalence of excessive exercise that often results in physical harm and emotional frustration and isolation. On the other hand, many females are not socialized to engage in athletics and exercise, and as a result there is a growing prevalence of obesity. The lack of socialization for exercise combined with the effects of trauma may serve as barriers for many females when it comes to self-care, particularly healthy eating and healthy exercise.

While physical activity is largely encouraged for boys and men, food preparation is not. Many men grew up being socialized with the belief that cooking is a part of the female identity. Men who grew up with this belief may never have learned how to cook healthy meals for themselves. It is important for male survivors to take responsibility for all aspects of their self-care including eating healthy meals. In addition to food and exercise, men have to strive for self-care by resisting self-harming behaviors. King, Coxell, and Mezey (2002) found that men who report childhood sexual abuse are more likely to report later psychological disturbances. In addition, men who report having "consensual" sex before the age of sixteen are more likely to report acts of self-harm. It is important for male survivors to resist alcohol and drug abuse, cutting, burning, and suicide attempts.

How Might One's Migration Status Affect Self-Care?

Much of the research on trauma survivors assumes a homogeneity of experience, but cultural background is a salient factor that affects survivors, their families, and communities (Tyagi, 2001). Research on the recovery process for survivors, including disclosure patterns and barriers to disclosure, needs to take into account environmental issues and factors associated with migration history and acculturation status.

Some survivors who are new migrants or illegal residents find themselves working in very bad conditions with long hours, low wages, and in unclean environments. Immigrants as well as low-income women are more vulnerable to job strain, particularly sexual harassment. This discrimination can negatively affect the survivor's self-image and create feelings of powerlessness and hope-lessness. Discrimination and poor living conditions can create depression, but the survivor should remember that he is valuable and deserves care and com-passion. Even when others do not make the survivor a priority, it is important for the person to value his health, body, mind, heart, and spirit. Self-care is key.

How Might One's Race/Ethnicity Affect Self-Care?

Internalized racism creates additional barriers to self-care. The survivor may have internalized some of the discriminatory messages that are promoted about her people in society. These include being dirty, insignificant, unintel-ligent, or unattractive. When the survivor believes these myths, she does not care for herself in the same way that she would if she believed that she is clean, significant, intelligent, and attractive. The trauma of racism in addition to any other traumas that the survivor experienced can result in neglect of one's health and well-being. Some survivors have been treated with such hostility and neglect, they begin to neglect and dismiss their own needs.

It should also be noted that members of racial and ethnic minority groups are more likely to live with financial strain. If the survivor is living on a small income, there are additional challenges to committing to self-care. The survivor should however remember that the racism and/or classism that she may reg-ularly have to face make it especially vital for her to be rested and cared for.

Hooks (1995) reminds us that mental health care for racial minority survi-vors must "link psychological recovery with progressive political awareness of the way in which institutionalized systems of domination assault, damage, and maim" (p. 138). Self-care must take into account the cultural context as well as the societal forms of oppression working against the survivor. Empowerment is key to self-care, and true self-care requires the acknowledgment of barriers to resource access and well as concrete strategies for those barriers to be dismantled.

How Might One's Religion Affect Self-Care?

deVries (1996) notes the lack of information that is available on the impact of religion on trauma and the trauma recovery process. He adds that it is important for mental health professionals to explore the trauma recovery process beyond the in-dividual alone, but inclusive of the sociocultural environment, including religion.

Self-sacrifice is an important principle in many religious teachings. Fol-lowers of various religions are instructed to be long-suffering, patient, and generous. They are also taught the importance of serving others and putting the needs of others before one's own needs. These teachings can lead to clients (1) feeling selfish by going to counseling where the entire session is focused on their needs; and (2) denying and minimizing the negative effects of the violation in order to make their family, friends, and even the perpetrator more comfortable.

To address the concept of attending counseling as being selfish or self-absorbed, it is important for clients to understand the value of self-care, particularly within a context of trauma recovery from a violation that attacks one's sense of self-worth. In addition, it is a religious obligation for people to take care of the gifts God has given them. Clients have to begin to see themselves as a gift, as a treasure that is worthy of protection, care, and nurturance. Additionally, to address the issue of denial of one's feelings for the comfort of others, it is important to provide psycho-education on the nature of mutuality, honesty, and reciprocity in relationship. Clients have to develop relationships that are not based on them serving others, but based on a true connection and honest sharing with another person. Building these trusting mutual relationships is a key component to recovery.

The survivor may belong to a religion that values self-sacrifice over self-care. He should be affirmed in the fact that self-care is not selfish. By investing time and energy into his rest, therapy, and exercise, the survivor will be a better person. Taking time for rest, nourishment, and even counseling is not a sign of selfishness. It is an indicator that one values one's life and well-being.

How Might One's Sexual Orientation Affect Self-Care?

Lesbian, gay, bisexual, and transgendered (LGBT) survivors may suffer from internalized homophobia. The survivor may believe some of the negative myths that are perpetuated in society. This may magnify the sense of unworthiness from the trauma and result in additional barriers to self-care. It is important to challenge these myths and spend time and energy in self-care.

Some gay men speak about the community pressure and focus on youthfulness and physical appearance. This may affect self-care, especially in diet and exercise. These pressures on self-care added to the impact of trauma may result in eating disorders and obsessive exercising.

Self-care related to escape from abusive relationships is also critical. Merrill and Wolfe (2000) found that gay and bisexual men, similar to heterosexual and lesbian women, report staying in abusive relationships because they love their partners and hope the partner will change. It is important for counselors to assess and address self-care in terms of relationships and safety for LGBT survivors and heterosexual survivors.

Why Is Self-Care Challenging for Some Torture Survivors?

Physical torture is an intrusive attack and abuse of the body. As a result, torture may result in physical scars, bruises, disfigurement, and/or general body shame. Many torture survivors have body memories that may be triggered by physical contact and physical examinations. It is important for torture survivors to receive support before, during, and after physical examinations. It is also important for the person conducting the examination to be informed that the patient is a trauma survivor, so they can be especially sensitive in informing the patient of their actions before and during the exam.

Why Is Self-Care Important for Recovery?

It is essential that the survivor reject the messages created by those who violated or disrespected him. The survivor is valuable and significant. He deserves care, not neglect. By taking care of the self, he speaks truth to his own body, mind, heart, and soul. The truth is, the survivor is worthy of care. The survivor did not deserve the treatment he received. He deserves rest, health, and life. Once the survivor has taken care of his own safety, he can now begin to care for his needs: physical, emotional, and spiritual.

How Can the Survivor Begin to Engage in Self-Care?

- Challenge the myth that the survivor does not deserve good things
- Set aside adequate time for sleep
- If the survivor can't sleep, seek help
- Eat healthy meals and healthy snacks
- Take time to clean one's body, clothing, hair, teeth, and living space
- Take time to do nondestructive, inexpensive things that the survivor enjoys, such as reading, watching a movie, talking with a friend, listening to music, going for a walk, doing arts and crafts, or going to a museum

- Schedule regular preventive visits at the doctor's and go to the hospital when one experiences a physical or emotional emergency

Below are some specific activities that can be helpful to survivors.

Journaling/Poetry

Read and try to remember this affirmation.
Affirmation: I care about my body, mind, heart, and spirit.

Activities:

1. Make a list of things that make the survivor feel good.
   A.
   B.
   C.
   D.
   E.
   F.
   G.
2. Cross out anything on the list that is not good for you.
3. Write a marriage vow to yourself promising to take time for self-care. I vow to . . .
4. Describe your sleeping and eating habits. Include how the traumatic event affected your habits and how your cultural background affects your habits.
5. Describe your hygiene and exercise habits. Include the impact of the traumatic event(s) as well as the impact of your cultural background.
6. Write a letter to yourself telling yourself that you deserve good treatment.

Movement

Read and try to remember this affirmation.
Affirmation: I will move through the universe with peace and strength.

Activity:

Imagine that your body is water. Begin to move your head and neck as though they flow easily like water. Now move your shoulders, arms, and hands as if they are waves of water. Next move your rib cage and chest in a smooth circle. Begin to move your hips in easy waterlike movements. Let your legs now move with smooth motions carrying your body around the room in waves of peace. Now sit down and let your feet move around in front of you like cascading waves of water. Finally hug yourself and say, "I care about myself. I value myself. I deserve care." Breathe in and out slowly seven times.

Visual Art

Read and try to remember this affirmation.
Affirmation: I will take care of my physical, emotional,
and spiritual health.

Activities:

1. Think about how you feel when you don't take care of yourself. Draw whatever comes to mind. It may be abstract or an actual representation of you.
2. Think about how you feel when you take care of yourself. If you can't remember ever taking care of yourself, draw what you imagine it would be like to care for yourself.

Spirituality

Read and try to remember this affirmation.
Affirmation: My spirit is free and clean.

Activity:

Take a bath or shower and while you are cleaning yourself, give thanks for each part of your body. Make this cleansing a celebration of your safety and a recognition of the gift of your birth. Even though parts of your body may have been bruised or hurt at certain points, hug yourself, embrace yourself, give thanks for your life.

Drama/Theater

Read and try to remember this affirmation.
Affirmation: I can relax now. I can take my time.

Activity:

Put an empty chair in front of you. Pretend that the part of you that doesn't take care of yourself is seated in the chair. Now you take the role of the part of you that wants to take better care of

yourself. It is your job to convince the person in the chair that
you deserve better. Decide if you will best make your case with
intensity or with humor, with compassion or reasoning. Say
aloud the need you have to be cared for. Don't stop until
you think the part of you that is in the chair is convinced. Then
breathe deeply for as long as you need and write a description
of the experience.

Music

Read and try to remember this affirmation.
Affirmation: I speak and sing words that restore me.

Activity:

Here are some lyrics. Take them and sing them to your own melody.
There is no right or wrong. This is your song. You can sing slow or fast. You
may choose high or low notes. You may tap out a beat with your foot or clap
your hands. You may choose to hum your song quietly so only you can hear
or you may present it to your friends in full concert style. It is yours.

I will care for my soul
It has been through so much
Journeyed through hills and valleys
Tossed and turned on the sea of my yesterday

But it is mine
Yes, it is mine

I will care for my mind
Seen so much

But now it's time to shine
Thought I would lose it
But I'm still here
Yes, I'm still here

I will care for my heart
It keeps beating
Never retreating
Living for today
Pushing for tomorrow

It is mine
Yes, it is mine

I will care for my body
Love myself in spite of the pain
Love myself in spite of the rain
This body is a gift
And I celebrate it
Because it is mine
Yes it is mine

Social Support

Read and try to remember this affirmation.
Affirmation: I will choose to talk to people who care about themselves
and care about me.

Activities:

1. Share your self-care goals with one other person. Pick
   someone who is supportive. Tell them one or a few of your goals.
2. Ask someone to exercise or go on a walk with you. If they
   don't want to go, you should still exercise on your own or
   consider joining an already formed walking or exercise group.

Activism

Read and try to remember this affirmation.
Affirmation: I choose self-care over self-harm.

Activity:

Consider writing an editorial letter to a local newspaper. If you have difficulty writing, ask someone to write down your words. The letter does not
need to be about your specific traumatic event, but in general cover the
effect of trauma and the importance of government funds and resources
being made available to trauma survivors. Depending on the particular
traumatic event that you experienced, your letter may focus on rights for
rape survivors, domestic violence survivors, survivors of racist or
homophobic incidents, childhood abuse survivors, physical assault survivors, or sexual harassment survivors. Many papers receive countless
letters, so if your letter is not printed, do not be discouraged. You may
consider sending it to another paper or to a community agency for them to
include in their regular mailings.

Nature

Read and try to remember this affirmation.
Affirmation: I take time to breathe and rest.

Activity:

Go outside and pick a tree that you like. If there are no trees near your home, go to a nearby park. Once you have picked your tree, sit by it for at least twenty minutes in silence. Study the similarities between you and your tree. Think about its roots, trunk, branches, and leaves. Think about your past, your growing up, your strengths, your gifts, and your beauty. Now sit for an additional ten minutes, simply breathing and relaxing.

4

Trust

"And at the time, I guess thinking back now, I didn't realize that we were a poor family. And I don't know if it's a cultural thing or not, but we didn't go to therapists and things like that. We went to church and then we went and talked to each other . . . things like, I guess, child molesting or whatever in the community, it was taken care of by the community."

—a survivor of sexual abuse

"When I go through any kind of healing process I'm doing it by myself because I—it's just the trust issue, I trust myself and don't necessarily know that somebody else is gonna understand what I'm going through, or understand the healing process of me crying or yelling or screaming or shaking or whatever—and it was like part of the progression for me to do the healing with myself. I'll either sit and think about the incident, and then I'll like say what I would've loved to have said at the time. And then I like cry, because they help move some of the energy and my dad tried to make me not cry, so either crying, or talking or screaming about it, yelling, like I'm talking to my parents, and just letting the feelings of helplessness come up and stuff and just feeling that in my body, you know."

—a survivor of domestic violence

"And I got in the bed with my parents because I knew I could always depend on them to shelter me from anything that was negative or I considered bad at the time. I had never lived in a home where there was a lot of violence. And actually I sort of like prayed we'd just get home to my mama and daddy. Cause I knew that they could take care of it, if anyone could take care of it. I relied on my parents, and I had a very strong religious background at the time. And I knew they would take care of me once I got home. And I talked to them about it the next day and we talked that night in the bed until I fell asleep. And I had other siblings that, we were able to talk about it and maybe that's what helped us through it, and by talking with other peers in the classroom about what had gone on. So by talking about it we were able to relieve some of the pent-up stress and emotion and get it out of the system. And I remember it very vividly to this day. I always had someone I could talk to and I really had a close-knit family."

—a survivor of community violence

What Is Trust?

Trust is faith in a person to act toward the survivor with compassion. It is the expectation that a person will be dependable. The survivor can have trust in a higher power, in other people, and in himself. When the survivor can trust someone, the relationship feels safe and secure. When the survivor has trust in a higher power, he has faith that he is being cared for and loved. When survivors trust themselves, they have a sense of peace and confidence in their capabilities and self-worth.

How Can Survivors Tell If They Trust Someone?

- Would the survivor feel comfortable sharing personal information with this person?
- Would the survivor make a loan to this person and believe he would be repaid?
- Does the survivor think his children would be safe in the person's care?
- Is the survivor comfortable when the other person is in his home?
- If others were putting the survivor down in his absence, does he think the person would defend him?
- Would the survivor be surprised if the person purposefully hurt him, or does the survivor expect the person to hurt him?
- Does the survivor feel confident that the person would not abuse or take advantage of him emotionally, physically, sexually, or financially?

How Can the Therapist Assess If the Survivor Has Self-Trust?

- Is the survivor able to make decisions?
- Does the survivor feel comfortable holding opinions that are different from those of others?

- Does the survivor know how he feels about something or someone before other people tell him their opinion?
- Does the survivor choose relationships and situations that are safe and edifying?
- Is the survivor comfortable spending time alone?

How Does Trauma Affect Trust?

Traumatic events destroy trust. These events teach us that people cannot be trusted (Roth and Batson, 1997). After a trauma, the survivor may feel that by opening up, relying on, trusting another person, he becomes vulnerable. He may believe that the way to prevent trauma in the future is to trust no one. One of the major consequences of interpersonal trauma is a sense of disconnection; for this reason, the repair of trust and connection is critical to recovery (Herman, 1997).

Perpetrators of traumatic events are often people we know, people we may have trusted. For this reason, traumatic events make us question our ability to determine who is trustworthy. Due to self-blame, we not only lose trust in others but also in ourselves. We may believe that if we'd had better judgment or strength, we would have been able to avoid the traumatic event. The truth is that the traumatic event was not the survivor's fault. Perpetrators of traumatic events are often charismatic and manipulative, causing us to lower our defenses.

Trust, relationships, and intimacy may also become more difficult as a result of the relational effects of trauma. Trauma can make it difficult to regulate emotions (van der Kolk and McFarlane, 1996). Survivors tend to experience intense emotions in response to stimuli even when the stimuli may appear to others as mild or innocuous. Survivors may be more sensitive or may emotionally shut down and disconnect. Trust has to build over time; as the survivor faces the traumatic memories and begins to feel safer within himself and with those in his support group, trusting relationships can be developed.

What Is the Role Of Trust and Disclosure in the Lives of Child Trauma Survivors?

Families sometimes keep secrets regarding violence and abuse, but the family can be strengthened and safety can be established by greater openness (Imber-Black, 2003). Parental reaction to disclosures of child abuse seriously affects the psychological well-being of the child; children who disclose abuse need validation and support from the adults in their life (Howard, 1993). Nondisclosure of sexual abuse is associated with long-term negative outcomes (Wyatt, 1990); it is important for children to have a safe, responsive person to whom they can disclose any experience of abuse. Feelings associated with disclosure of incest include relief, empowerment, anger, shame, and disappointment (Mize et al., 1995). Mize and colleagues (1995) found that some adult incest survivors prepare for disclosure by attending therapy, reading, meditating, sharing with friends first, attending twelve-step programs, and attending workshops. Survivors reported that family members responded to disclosure with a mixture of support, belief, blame, denial, and withdrawal; overall, however, survivors experienced a sense of reconnection after disclosing (Mize et al., 1995).

General Barriers to Disclosure of Victimization	Cultural Barriers to Disclosure of Victimization
• Feelings of powerlessness	• Lack of trust in societal institutions (police and/or legal system)
• Fear	
• Anxiety	• Belief that social stigma already attached to people of one's ethnicity, national origin, religion, or sexual orientation
• Shame; Guilt; Isolation	
• Negative perceptions of self	
• Repression of memories	• Concept of reporting as equivalent to selling out the race or betraying the race
• Perceptions of abuse as approval or affection	
• Disassociation	• Desensitization from repeated exposure to community violence
• Difficulty trusting	
• Nonsupportive response to initial disclosure	• Fear of being labeled gay in cases of male-perpetrated abuse on a male child or adult
	• Family business among ethnic minorities more important to keep private—concrete consequences of disclosure
	• Linguistic issues—Immigration issues (emotional dependence on perpetrator)
	• Clinicians and teachers miss by blaming the victim for acting out behavior, especially among ethnic minority male children
	• Economic dependence on perpetrator

Many incest survivors do not tell because of the reality-based fear that they will not be believed or protected. Roesler and Wind (1994) found that in 52 percent of cases when children disclosed sexual abuse, parents did not respond with support and the abuse continued for more than a year. Adults who disclosed incest as a child report being met with disbelief and blame (Roesler and Wind, 1994). Some of the effects of incest that may contribute to lack of disclosure are fear, feelings of helplessness and powerlessness, shame, guilt, negative self-perception, perception of abuse as affection, withdrawal, and difficulty trusting others (Wyatt, Newcomb, and Riederle, 1993).

How Does Disability Status Affect Survivor's Trust?

When choosing whom to trust, adult survivors who have disabilities have to determine whether the person with whom they come in contact has adopted myths about the disabled. These myths are usually that persons with disabilities are childlike, absolutely dependent on others, and incapable of functioning in various life roles such as spouse, parent, or professional (Etaugh and Bridges, 2004).

When working with child survivors who have disabilities, practitioners in child and adolescent psychiatric units should be aware of the prevalence of sexual abuse among the intellectually disabled and attend to the need for protection and empowerment in this population (Balogh et al., 2001). As with non-disabled children and adolescents, most disabled survivors are abused by family members. Balogh et al. (2001) note that although disclosure is difficult for the severely disabled, it is possible to establish a sexual abuse history and work on addressing those issues with the child. To address those issues, Hughes (1998) explores the ways in which the arts serve as an empowering tool for learning disabled sexual assault survivors. She (Hughes, 1998) notes that instead of a reliance on the verbal and cognitive focus on traditional therapy, use of the arts helps disabled survivors have a sense of control, power, and connection. This is necessary for the building of trust and safety.

How Might One's Economic Status Affect One's Trust?

If the survivor grew up in a family or community where resources were limited and she had to look out for herself, she may have already believed that trust is dangerous. The traumatic event may have confirmed this belief. This will make building trust in others additionally challenging. Wyatt (1997) concludes, "Of all the factors that can influence childhood sexual activity, poverty has been most strongly linked with abusive early childhood experiences. Children who grow up in poverty, often with families who are themselves disenfranchised, are at risk for a variety of social, health, emotional, and physical problems.

If the survivor is a person of wealth, she may have difficulty trusting others. This may be due to experiences of others taking advantage of her or pretending to be her friend in order to gain access to the survivor's wealth. The traumatic event may have increased this distrust.

Regardless of her income and education, it is important to find people that the survivor can trust and for her to learn to trust herself.

How Might One's Gender Affect One's Trust?

Many women are socialized not to trust themselves. Growing up, the survivor may have had her thoughts and feelings discounted and questioned. As a result, she may have always felt uncomfortable about speaking her mind or making decisions for herself. The traumatic event may have further challenged the survivor's trust of herself.

Violence against women is one of the most pervasive human rights violations around the world (Rozee, 2000). Globally, sexism and antifeminism are still very actively at work against the well-being and safety of women (Denmark, 1998). The violations women experience include but are not limited to sexual assault (stranger rape, marital rape, rape as a war crime), prostitution, incest, trafficking (the international buying and selling of women and girls), child brides, and pornography. In the general U.S. population, 15 percent of women report having been raped in their lifetime (Tjaden and Thoennes, 1998). From the National College Health Risk Behavior Survey, sexual assault prevalence rates appear even higher, with 20 percent of female college students reporting having been forced to have intercourse at some point in their lives (Brener et al., 1999). In a community sample of 104 men ranging from twenty through forty years of age, Rubenzahl & Corcoran (1998) found that 24 percent of the men admitted committing acquaintance rape based on a broad definition of the term and that 10 percent admitted committing acquaintance rape based on a strict definition of the term.

Rates of sexual assault reported on anonymous surveys are much higher than the rate of women who actually report their assaults to law enforcement agencies. Out of 360 participants, Feldhaus, Houry, and Kaminsky (2000) found that in an emergency services division of a hospital the lifetime prevalence rate of sexual assault among women was 39 percent. Only 25 percent of the women who had been sexually assaulted reported that they contacted a social service agency to obtain help after the assault.

Sexual assault occurs across lines of race, class, sexual orientation, religion, and disability. Roosa, Reinholtz, and Angelini (1999) found that rates of childhood sexual abuse were similar across racial and ethnic lines. About one-fifth of African-American, Mexican-American, Native American, and non-Hispanic whites reported experiencing rape, and about one-third of each group reported experiencing some form of sexual abuse.

Along with trust of self, family, and friends, people also face trust issues when considering counseling. Gender bias in diagnosis and treatment may also serve as a barrier in building trust with mental health professionals (Etaugh and Bridges, 2004).

Many men are socialized not to trust others. Manhood is often associated with independence and showing minimal emotional display to others. The traumatic event may have further increased the survivor's discomfort with trusting others. In addition, the relationship to the perpetrator can alter trust in specific ways. For example, Tang (2002) found in a study of Chinese young men and women in Hong Kong that while women were more likely to have been sexually victimized overall, men were more likely to have been victimized by someone they considered a friend. In a literature review on cultural factors of childhood sexual abuse, Kenny and McEachern (2000) summarize the following findings: African-American children are more likely to be sexually abused by parents' boyfriends or girl-friends as well as uncles; white children are more likely to be abused by parents and babysitters; Mexican-American children are more likely to be abused by a member of their extended family; and Asian-American children are more likely to be abused by biological fathers, especially when the child is a female. When exploring trust and relationship patterns, it is important to take into consideration the role and relationship of the person who violated the survivor.

Regardless of the survivor's gender, it is essential to have trust in the self and in others who are trustworthy. Roth and Batson (1997) remind us that while attention to post-trauma symptoms is important, it is also critical to deal with issues of self-trust or identity and trust in others in terms of social relationships.

How Might One's Migration Status Affect One's Trust?

A survivor who is a recent immigrant may not know very many people she can trust outside of her family. It is difficult to find new friends, especially if the survivor is unfamiliar with the language and traditions in her new country.

In addition, if the survivor left her home country during a time of war or political persecution, she may have already had her trust in others diminished. One study of Bosnian refugee couples found that the marital satisfaction of wives was directly related to the PTSD of husbands and the PTSD of the wives themselves (Spasojevic, Heffer, and Snyder, 2000). Trust and connection for refugees and immigrants, including marital intimacy and satisfaction, are greatly shaped by these trauma experiences.

Additionally, if the survivor is on a student or other temporary visa, or in the country illegally, it may be difficult for her to feel safe seeking professional help. She may be afraid to threaten her status in the country.

As with all survivors, in the experiences of refugee and immigrant survivors, empowerment and transformation must be contextualized. This context includes the survivor's culture, religious beliefs, and experiences as an immigrant or refugee as well as race, class, and sexual orientation (Holzman, 1994). The experience of rape within refugee camps requires prompt action both in terms of culturally relevant mental health intervention as well as the establishment of safety within the camps (Atlani & Rousseau, 2000). There also must be an awareness of the role of somatization in the presentation of immigrants and refugees. Presentations of physical complaints for which no cause is found may be an indication of the stressful experience of their migration and refugee status as well as the stressful experience of violence, including sexual violence (Castillo et al., 1995). An awareness of the physical and emotional connections of symptoms and experiences could help practitioners and survivors themselves gain a greater sense of personal understanding and power. It is especially important for survivors to find people and agencies that they can trust.

Culturally specific barriers to distrust must also be examined. While trust is affected by trauma violations against all survivors, there are cultural norms that intersect with traumatic experiences to make trust very difficult. For example, Rao and others (1992) found that Asian-Americans are the least likely to disclose sexual abuse to their mothers. Cultural traditions based on patriarchy, submissiveness, obedience, and loyalty are barriers to interracial and intraracial trust.

How Might One's Race/Ethnicity Affect One's Trust?

My voice joins our collective voices, and we shall scratch the surface of our wounds. We shall form community with our stories. We will cast spells with our disclosures.

—Charlotte Pierce-Baker (1998, p. 20)

Racism and discrimination based on ethnicity are quite prevalent. As a result, as a racial or ethnic minority, the survivor may have learned early not to trust members of racial majority groups. This is magnified when bystanders of racial injustice respond with denial and distancing (Herman, 1997). This can be very frustrating and isolating for survivors of racist incidents. The oppression of racism, sexism, and classism combine to create barriers to disclosure, whether one is contemplating trusting the police, counselors, family, or friends (Washington, 2001; Collins, 2000).

Survivors who have internalized negative messages about their racial or ethnic group may also find it difficult to trust members of the survivor's own race or ethnicity. The traumatic event may have increased the survivor's distrust of others and of himself. If those who were supposed to help the survivor deal with the trauma, such as therapists or police officers, were disrespectful or discriminatory toward him, he may find it additionally difficult to trust professionals. This is a challenge to recovery but not an insurmountable one. Trust is possible, even in a society where racism is alive.

While social support and connection has long been a cultural value associated with ethnically marginalized groups, it is noteworthy that in a sample of patients who have panic disorders and agoraphobia, African-Americans reported less satisfaction with social support and financial support than did European-Americans (Smith, Friedman, and Nevid, 1999). Coping with economic and social pressures may create strain in the time and resources that African-Americans are able to provide. The stigma in the African-American community that is still attached to mental illness may also serve to deter the provision of support that otherwise might be available. The existence and effectiveness of social support networks have to be established, and when weak there should be an attempt to build social networks of survivors to decrease their isolation and increase connection and sense of strength.

Regarding survivors of childhood violence, patterns of distrust and non-disclosure have often been reinforced by historical, legal, and societal attitudes about ethnic and racial minority groups (Root, 1996). Root (1996) writes that disempowerment based on gender and ethnicity "muffles the voices of the woman (and girl) of color and prevents her from being taken seriously" (p. 371). In terms of cultural context and disclosure, Tyagi (2001) interviewed twelve women of color who were incest survivors regarding the experience of disclosure. Factors that were found to affect disclosure of incest were value systems, community-mindedness, social attitudes, and fear of negative consequences. For children who are sexually abused, disclosure to the police usually would involve disclosure to an adult, usually the child's mother, who makes the decision regarding initiating police involvement. Racially marginalized women, however, report general and culturally specific barriers, such as distrust and negative past experiences, to reporting sexual violence to the police (Neville and Pugh, 1997). Wyatt (1990) notes that ethnic minority children, as a result of sexual abuse and racism, may experience feeling stigmatized. This stigma may make them feel that people will not respond positively to their needs. Stigma or stereotypical constructs of ethnic minority girls, such as the belief that they are bad, overly sexual, less worthy of sympathy, and more deserving of violence leads to them being blamed when others violate them (Root, 1996). With this societal blame in place, the survivor is less likely to feel comfortable disclosing incestuous abuse. Trust is also harmed by unresponsiveness to disclosures of violation. Paredes, Leifer, and Kilbane (2001) found lower levels of functioning among African-American child survivors of sexual abuse when their mothers were survivors of sexual abuse who were experiencing trauma symptomology. It is important to eradicate the cycle of violence that leaves children with less support in the aftermath of violation as their mothers are simultaneously coping with the aftermath of trauma.

Many racial and ethnic minorities are involved in religious organizations, and some may consider disclosing sexual abuse to their minister if they feel the minister is approachable. Sims (2002), however, found in a qualitative study with racial minority male and female ministers that although the participants believed the church should play an active role in dealing with child sexual abuse in their community, none of them had. If racial minority children do not hear adults addressing the issue of child abuse, they may feel that there is no safe person for them to choose for disclosure.

How Might the Survivor's Religion Affect the Survivor's Trust?

Although there is no difference in the rate of sexual abuse based on religious preference within the home (Elliot, 1994), there are unique dynamics that affect the recovery of religious survivors. The survivor's religion may teach him to always trust others as an example of his faith. He may feel guilty about his inability to trust. This may cause him to believe that he has to quickly forgive everyone and give them additional opportunities. If the perpetrator has not changed, this person will continue to harm the survivor, and he will continue to struggle between having feelings of guilt and distrust. It is important to trust that the Creator loves the survivor enough to want him to only be in relationships with those who are safe and trustworthy. The Creator does not want the survivor to place his trust in those who do not value the survivor or treat him with respect.

Trust also plays a role in domestic violence. This includes trust in the theology of one's religion regarding the treatment of women as well as trust in one's community to intervene in cases of domestic violence. For example, Koenig and colleagues (2003) found in a study in Bangladesh that being a part of a conservative Muslim community and living away from one's family increased the risk for domestic violence. It is important for survivors to know that within every religion there are variations of beliefs concerning the status of women. It is important to find connection and community with those of one's religion who do not condone violence against women. It is also important for family members who may subscribe to the same religious beliefs to support survivors in their quest for safety and health.

How Might the Survivor's Sexual Orientation Affect the Survivor's Trust?

As a gay, lesbian, or bisexual person, the survivor likely has had to face the challenge of determining whom to trust in terms of disclosing the survivor's sexual orientation. Coming out of the closet is largely about trust. Being able to depend on family and friends to be supportive and being able to trust oneself to deal with others' responses is challenging. The traumatic event may in fact be related to the survivor's experience with disclosing their sexual orientation to others. If those who were supposed to help the survivor with the traumatic event responded with discrimination, disrespect, or dismissal, this may have made it additionally difficult to trust others.

Given the prevalence of hate crimes and harassment, it is especially important for the survivor to find people that can be trusted to share the survivor's experiences, feelings, and needs. Elze (1992) notes that LGBT survivors may have difficulty forging trusting friendships with same-sex peers because of homophobia and rejection. It is essential for LGBT survivors to create connections of support where they can be honest and treated with care and respect.

Why Is Rebuilding Trust Important to Recovery?

Isolation is a scar often caused by traumatic events. The survivor deserves to regain everything that the trauma took from her. The survivor may have been traumatized as a child and have no memory of trusting others or herself. The survivor may come from a cultural background that makes trusting others difficult. As human beings, connection and community are keys to living full lives. It doesn't matter the quantity of friends, but it is important to have someone in the survivor's life who she can trust. It is also important for her to trust herself. When the survivor doesn't trust herself, she cannot fulfill her hopes or dreams. With trust in herself, the survivor can accomplish her goals and take steps to improve her life.

How Can the Survivor Tell If Someone Is Not Trustworthy?

- Does this person consistently lie to the survivor?
- Do they make fun of her?

- Do they put down her dreams?
- Do they steal from her?
- Do they abuse her children?
- Do they hit, punch, push, kick, cut, stab, shoot, or burn the survivor?
- Do they torture her pet?
- Do they put her down when talking with others?
- Are they happy when she is suffering?
- Do they sabotage the survivor?
- Are they dating her even though they are married or in a committed relationship with someone else?
- Do they emotionally or verbally abuse the survivor?

How Can the Survivor Determine If Someone Is Trustworthy?

A trustworthy person:

- Believes in the survivor
- Verbally and emotionally affirms the survivor
- Treats the survivor, her children, her pets, and belongings with respect
- Encourages the survivor and her aspirations
- Tells the survivor the truth
- Gives her the freedom to be herself, to have her own thoughts and ideas
- Values the survivor's feelings
- Is willing to take a stand on her behalf
- Is happy that the survivor is taking steps toward her own recovery

The use of social support involves talking with members of one's community to explore themes and issues raised by the traumatic experience and/or to actively problem-solve conflicts created by the violation (Bryant, 1999). The building and sustaining of community networks serve an integral role in empowerment (Abrahams, 1996). Now that the survivor has been working on her safety and self-care, she can begin to pay attention to building and maintaining trustworthy relationships with herself and others.

Journaling/Poetry

Read and try to remember this affirmation.
Affirmation: I choose to build healthy relationships based
on trust and respect.

Activities:

1. Write a description of a person that you believe may be trustworthy. If you don't know anyone who is trustworthy, write a description of the kind of person you would trust.

2. Write a poem that captures the characteristics of a healthy relationship. If you are not comfortable writing a poem, you may write a description.

3. Write the ways that your traumatic experience affected your ability to trust others. Include the effect of your cultural background on the survivor's capacity to trust yourself or others.

Movement

Read and try to remember this affirmation.
Affirmation: I trust my feelings. I trust myself.

Activity:

Rub your hands together until they feel warm. Place your hands on your face. Breathe deeply three times. Rub your hands together. Place your hands on your chest. Breathe deeply three times. Rub your hands together. Place your hands on your stomach. Breathe deeply three times. Rub your hands together. Place your hands on your lap. Breathe deeply three times. Rub your hands together. Place your hands on your feet. Breathe deeply three times. Stretch up reaching toward the sky as you count to eight. Embrace yourself and breathe deeply three times.

Art

Read and try to remember this affirmation.
Affirmation: I use one's experience, wisdom, and heart
to decide whom to trust.

Activity:

Draw a representation of your heart. Use one color to fill in the parts of your heart that represent the times your trust has been violated. Use a different color to represent the times that you have been able to trust yourself and others.

Drama/Theater

Read and try to remember this affirmation.
Affirmation: I have faith and hope.

Activity:

Think about your favorite book or television show. Which of the characters is most trustworthy? Which one is least trustworthy? Write how you can tell the difference between the two characters. Then write if any of the characters remind you of people whom you know.

Music

Read and try to remember this affirmation.
Affirmation: I enjoy keeping myself company and enjoy the
company of those whom I trust.

Activity:

Trust yourself to write your own song about your feelings today. You can write the words to the song and then make up the melody. Another option is to choose a song you already know and change the words to fit your feelings. After you have sung it to yourself, if there is someone you trust, share your song with him or her. If there isn't another person, enjoy singing it to yourself again.

Spirituality

Read and try to remember this affirmation.
Affirmation: I have faith. My life will improve.

Activity:

Take this time to pray or meditate about the strength and courage that you need in order to address the wounds created by those who violated your trust. Then pray or meditate about your ability to trust yourself, others, and the Creator.

Nature

Read and try to remember this affirmation.
Affirmation: I trust that there is good in me and good in the world.

Activity:

The sun can warm and the sun can also burn. Likewise, people have the capacity to do good or do harm. Write the names below of those who have warmed/nurtured you and then the names of those who have burned/harmed you. Some people may have done both. If so, put them on both lists.

What feelings come up when the survivor reviews this list?

Social Support

Read and try to remember this affirmation.
Affirmation: I only confide in those whom I trust.

Activity:

Pick one person to tell that you are reading this guidebook. You do not have to tell them the details of the trauma you experienced. If you would like to tell them what it is, start off by sharing only a small amount. This will give you a chance to see how they respond before you share every-thing. If they don't seem supportive, you can share less. (If you would like to keep it general, let the person know that you had a difficult experience and are now working through it. You may want to say that in the future you may feel ready to share more, but for now you just want them to know that you are working through some past events.) Record how you feel

before you share with this person and then how you feel after you have
shared. If there is no one you can trust, consider seeking counseling or
calling a help line.

Activism

Read and try to remember this affirmation.
Affirmation: I can be myself in the presence of others.

Activity:

Write a letter to a local government official to lobby for funds and
programs that prevent the type of trauma that you experienced. The letter
may be about the need for sexual harassment prevention, racial justice,
prevention of harassment based on sexual orientation, rape prevention,
domestic violence prevention, promotion of peaceful conflict resolution, or
community violence prevention. Keep a copy of the letter in your
workbook and mail the other copy. If you receive a response, keep a copy
of it in your workbook.

Survivor Case Summary Leah is a white female survivor of intimate partner
violence. She is a high school graduate and works in sales. Leah is in her late
thirties and was in an abusive relationship from her late teens to early twenties.
Her boyfriend was emotionally, sexually, and physically abusive. He would
threaten to kill himself, attempt to kill her, and raped her on multiple occasions. The abuse started gradually and intensified over time.

Leah's trust was damaged on numerous levels. She lost trust in romantic
partners because of her boyfriend's abusive behavior. She also lost trust in
other people. Leah's family saw the bruises on her body but never intervened.
In addition, her boyfriend isolated her from her friends, who remained silent,
and physically abused her in front of his friends, who also remained silent.

Leah's trust in herself was also damaged. Although she didn't have a lot
of dating experience before meeting her boyfriend, she had confidence in
her judgment. This was ruined during the course of her relationship. She lost
trust in her judgment in other people as well as her confidence in her self-
worth.

Leah made the decision to leave the relationship once her boyfriend began
talking about marriage, and she feared raising children in an abusive environment. Leah sought short-term crisis counseling immediately after leaving
the relationship. She later returned for long-term counseling after she began to
notice the extensive impact of the relationship on her work life and her dating
relationships.

At work, Leah was very disconnected from others and felt a lot of anger toward her coworkers. In her new dating relationship she felt very distrustful and found herself often testing her new boyfriend to determine if and when he would hit her. She also found she lacked confidence in her ability to select a healthy partner and to have a healthy relationship. The issue of trust also came up in the counseling relationship. The shame and self-blame made it difficult for Leah to trust telling the details of the abuse to anyone, including her therapist.

By creating a safe environment as well as getting psycho-education about the dynamics of intimate partner violence, Leah was able to begin trusting herself and her therapist. In addition, by beginning to face the memories and the impact of the abuse on her affect, cognitions, and behavior, Leah was able to experience a decrease in shame and self-blame and an increase in her ability to trust others and trust her judgment of others. Leah's counseling also explored economic themes related to the stigma of counseling and the lack of resource access and awareness that created obstacles to her recovery. The gender themes that were explored related to her conception of womanhood and manhood as well as the discrepancies between her ideal notions of gender roles and her actual reality. Leah had to have a vision for not only healthy relationships, but for a healthy model of herself as a single woman. Although Leah and her new boyfriend ended their relationship, she was able to retain a sense of confidence and hope in the future. While she has decided not to talk to her family about the abuse, because she doesn't want them to feel guilty and fears her disclosure will not be helpful to them or to herself, she has however disclosed the abuse to her friends. They have been supportive and affirming, and those who knew her at the time of the abuse stated that they were young and did not know what they should do to intervene. Leah allowed her anger at the silence to motivate her to activism and spoke on a public panel about how friends and family members can support people who are in abusive relationships. She has terminated treatment but continues to actively engage in self-care and use positive coping strategies.

5

Shame and Self-Blame

"I'm seeing a psychiatrist. My job sent me to therapy because they could see it was affecting my work. It's made me a stronger person as far as learning not to always blame myself. I had to learn where to put the blame and I've been going to different therapists for over the past five years. Yeah, it's been really helpful."

—a survivor of sexual assault

"It helps a lot to confront the person that victimized you, (as a child you're helpless but as an adult) being able to say to him, you did this to me, and I told him, "I know it and God knows what you did to me. And you lied and you are still lying and you need to be asking for my forgiveness for what you did to me." If I didn't confront him, I may still have had the feeling like, gosh, maybe I was wrong. Gosh, maybe I did something. But being able to confront him and say "No, it was not my fault, it was your fault"—I think that released a lot of the guilt.

—a survivor of incest

What Is Shame?

Shame is the feeling of an internalized "badness" and general negative self-concept that the survivor has. It is not simply guilt over doing something wrong. Instead, it is the belief and feeling that at the survivor's core that something is wrong. Shame creates feelings of embarrassment and causes the survivor to feel the need to hide.

What Common Thoughts May Survivors Have If They Feel Shame?

- I'm dirty
- I'm bad
- I'm stupid
- I'm evil
- I'm worthless and no good
- Anyone who likes me must not really know me
- If I let others get to know me, they will reject me
- I have to use something (sex, money, submissive behavior, masks, humor) to get people to like me

What Is Self-Blame?

Self-blame is the feeling that the survivor is responsible for a negative event. The survivor feels that they caused the event by their thoughts, words, deeds, or because the survivor is simply evil or bad.

It is the sense that the negative event was the survivor's fault. Self-blame fosters guilt, minimization, and denial (Bratton, 1999). It impedes recovery. Self-blame is a cognitive distortion or negative belief about the self that must be challenged (Foa and Rothbaum, 1998).

How Does Trauma Affect Shame and Self-Blame?

Unfortunately, in society persons who are violated are often made to feel ashamed, as if they are to blame for the violation (Herman, 1997; Warshaw, 1988). This happens with those who are victimized by rape, domestic violence, racism, homophobia, sexual harassment, physical assault, and childhood abuse. Shame and self-blame are root causes of many of the negative automatic thoughts that survivors experience. These thoughts have to be identified and challenged to effectively address the aftermath of traumatic experiences (Foa and Rothbaum, 1998).

What Things Do People in Society Say That Make Survivors Feel Shame and Self-Blame?

- Rape—What was she wearing or why did she go to his home?
- Sexual harassment—Why is she so sensitive? So frigid?
- Racism—He's just being sensitive.
- Homophobia—He shouldn't have thrown his sinful lifestyle in our faces.
- Childhood sexual abuse—She developed early so she looks like a woman; How come she didn't tell until now?
- Physical assault—He was in a gang. It's no big deal he got beat up.
- Domestic violence—Why didn't she just leave?

These messages are repeated in our families, communities, and the media. Eventually we come to believe them and feel shame and self-blame. In cases of acquaintance rape, for example, people often claim the rape was "justifiable" when: the woman invited the man out, the man pays for the date, the woman dresses "suggestively," they go to the man's home instead of going out, or the woman drinks alcohol or uses drugs (Warshaw, 1988). These assumptions shift the blame and responsibility away from the perpetrator of the crime and place accountability on the survivor.

In addition, perpetrators of trauma often tell survivors that it is their own fault. Examples of these comments that the survivor may have heard are:

- Domestic violence—"You make me hurt you. You know I don't want to do it."
- Homophobia—"You're just disgusting and sick."
- Physical assault—"You shouldn't have come around here. You should have kept your mouth shut."
- Racism—"You people are always quick to cry racism. It's just a crutch."
- Childhood abuse—"I do this because I love you and because you're so special."
- Rape—"You were being a tease. You kissed me. You know you wanted it."
- Sexual harassment—"I can tell you like it."

Not only does the survivor have to deal with what people around him say and what the perpetrator says, but also with what the survivor says to himself. We often replay the violation in our minds and wonder what we could have done differently. It is natural to do this, but unfortunately the result is often that we hold ourselves responsible for not being able to prevent the traumatic event. When the survivor plays it over in his head, he may emotionally beat himself up with "if only."

The survivor may say: If only:

- I didn't walk down that street
- I didn't wear that outfit
- I didn't drink that night
- I didn't act friendly
- I had fought harder
- I had screamed louder
- I had noticed sooner

Shame and self-blame keep us stuck. We can never move from surviving to thriving if we continue to hold ourselves responsible for the actions of others.

How Does Disability Status Affect Traumatic Context, Including Shame?

Benedict (1994) notes that key issues for disabled survivors' empowerment include: independence versus dependence, accepting help versus distrust, having already existing survival skills versus needing new skills to deal with an increased sense of vulnerability. The tendency of perpetrators to seek out persons in vulnerable situations makes physical and mental disability a risk factor for sexual assault and other forms of violence (Rounds, 1996; Scott, Lefly, and Hicks, 1993). The social and cultural context of disabled survivors must be taken into account in addressing issues of thriving after a sexual assault. Disabled survivors are often discriminated against in that their ability to know and accurately describe their abuse experience is often questioned. Society's doubts concerning the survivor's ability to know and report what has happened can be an additional source of shame. Most disabled survivors are able to disclose their experience with sensitive interviewing procedures that are aimed at building their confidence and trust as opposed to raising their insecurities and distrust (Pillay and Sargent, 2000).

How Might One's Economic Status Affect Shame and Self-Blame?

If the survivor lives in a neighborhood where violence is prevalent, she may feel that she should have known better. She may blame herself for not being guarded enough. The truth is, we cannot predict everything; this does not make it our fault.

While interpersonal violence occurs across economic lines, practitioners working with impoverished communities should be aware that economic lack increases vulnerability to violence (Vogel and Marshall, 2001; Byrne et al., 1999). Some survivors experience sexual assault and harassment at the workplace, and economic coercion is a factor used for intimidation. In one study of attempted and completed rapes occurring at the workplace, only 21 percent of women complained through appropriate channels and only 19 percent quit their jobs. When women are dependent on their current jobs for the basic necessities of life, they are more vulnerable to those in power at their workplace. It is necessary for counselors to understand the context and conditions under which women are subjected to sexual violence in order to truly address the transition from self-degradation to empowerment. This requires an honest analysis of the systems in which women work, not just the choice patterns of the individual woman.

In terms of treatment, given the confines of managed care guidelines as well as the budgetary constraints of low-income survivors, it is essential to find paths to thriving that are time and cost effective. One of the strengths of cognitive-behavioral therapy for survivors has been its capacity to assist them in attaining growth in knowledge, skills, and a sense of empowerment in a brief number of sessions (Foa and Rothbaum, 1998).

How Might One's Gender Affect Shame and Self-Blame?

Girls and women are often taught that they are responsible for their social interactions. If relationships fail, the survivor may feel that she wasn't smart enough, pretty enough, or fun enough to make the relationship work. In addition, the survivor may have been taught that after a certain point, men cannot control their sexual desire. This type of teaching makes girls and women feel responsible for their own sexual violation.

Weems (1993) also describes the way perceived sexual orientation is used to shame and silence women: "In light of the mindless homophobia that exists . . . , the accusation of being a lesbian is most often a ploy to castrate a woman, to silence her, to scare her into obedience, to undermine her effectiveness before her peers and clients, and to remind her of her place. In some instances, it has been effective. For I've seen friendships terminate; I've seen women denounce other women to win male affection; and I've seen women turn in their placard and withdraw from a movement for fear of being labeled a lesbian. . . ." (p. 100).

Societal lenses of sexism and homophobia result in silence and shame. Because discourse about feminism, women's rights, and violence against women is often equated with "lesbianism" and "male bashing," many women are silenced about their experiences of trauma, especially when the traumatic experience is gender based violence.

Boys and men are taught to value strength. For this reason, if a male is violated, there is an intense feeling of shame and self-blame. Burt and DeMello (2002) found in a study of hypothetical rape scenarios that homosexual and heterosexual males were blamed for being rape victims by a sample of college students, especially homophobic male college students. This is related to feeling as if the incident was the survivor's fault for not being man enough or strong enough, physically or mentally, to prevent the violation. Men would like to believe that they are able to protect themselves from rape, and to believe this requires that they blame male victims for not resisting the attacker. To release blame of male victims requires men to acknowledge their vulnerability to violence. As long as masculinity is equated with invulnerability, male survivors will continue to be blamed.

Female and male survivors need to know that they are not responsible for the behavior of others. Accountability and responsibility for trauma lies with the perpetraor.

How Might One's Migration Status Affect One's Sense of Shame and Self-Blame?

If the survivor is a survivor of sexual violence and comes from a country where sexuality is not discussed and where sexual purity is mandatory for girls and women, she may experience additional shame. In all cultures survivors of sexual violence feel shame, but in some countries there is the additional weight of feeling that the survivor has shamed her entire family or community. The survivor may also be told that she is unworthy of marriage because of the sexual violation she experienced.

In addition, in some countries wife-beating is acceptable behavior for husbands, and divorce is not considered a legitimate option. If the survivor is from a country where this is the case, and she is trying to escape such a marriage, her family and community may cause her to feel additional shame. By trying to leave the marriage, she may be accused of assimilating too much and forgetting her culture. This can create great tension and feelings of self-blame.

The following factors have been found regarding immigrants, particularly Asian immigrants (Kenny & McEachern, 2000):

- They may be underrepresented in trauma statistics because of their reluctance to use mental health services and public agencies

- They may be largely unaware of the resources available to survivors
- The traditional values of the culture are based on solving problems within the family rather than utilizing mental health agencies (Sue and Sue, 1995)
- Underreporting of traumatic experiences may also be related to language barriers and lack of bilingual help professionals

Being violated was not the survivor's fault, and taking steps to protect herself and her children is a good thing to do.

How Might One's Race/Ethnicity Affect One's Sense of Shame and Self-Blame?

Counselors should explore cultural norms that may exacerbate shame and self-blame. For example, Comas-Diaz (1995) notes that Puerto Rican cultural norms require that women remain virgins until they are married; women and girls who have been sexually abused or assaulted are shamed and scorned. In addition, their mothers may also be shamed for parenting a girl-child who is not a virgin. The experience of shame and self-blame has to be seen through the cultural lens of the survivor.

If the client is a survivor of a racist incident, she may feel shame that the incident occurred, however, the person who disrespected her is really the person who should be ashamed. The survivor may wonder what she could have done to cause it or may see race as a factor when it is not. Oftentimes racist incidents are more covert (subtle) as opposed to overt (obvious), so it is not surprising that the survivor may wonder about the intent of the perpetrator. Remember that shame and self-blame takes the place of anger toward the perpetrator. If the survivor feels powerless to take action against the perpetrator, she may resign herself to taking the blame for the incident, although it was not her fault.

If the survivor is a survivor of sexual violence or domestic violence and the perpetrator is a member of her race, she may be made to feel ashamed for reporting the crime. The criminal justice system is seen as racist, and utilizing it is sometimes viewed as betraying the survivor's race or community. The opposite is actually the case. The person who violated the survivor is the betrayer of the race and the community. Taking steps to protect one's self and heal are not shameworthy actions or acts of betrayal.

This sense of racial loyalty is exemplified in the following poem by Malika Mapp.

Shh, Don't Tell

He raped me
But I ain't go tell nobody

His friends were in the next room
And I didn't scream because his friends
   were in the next room
And I had been studying this book
   called, "How to Be: Contemporary
   Etiquette
for African Americans"
So I put on my home training, was ex-
   tremely polite, and I did not scream
I didn't want to embarrass him in front
   of his friends
So ever so quietly, I begged him, I pleaded
   with him
Please Stop
Please No
Please Don't do this to me
Great Manners
Quite polite
Quintessentially correct
'Cause it's so ugly when Black women
   are loud

He raped me
But I ain't go tell nobody

After all I walked right into his bedroom
I gave him a massage on his bed and
   enjoyed it
I walked right into the bedroom,
   ignoring all caution
I can use this mouth for anything
   except to tell a man no in front of his
   pals
'No we ain't goin' into your bedroom,
   what's up wit' dat?'
'No, we can chill right here in the
   living room wit' yo' best friends.'
I walked right into the bedroom
And he raped me

But I ain't go tell nobody

I wanna go home
Please just take me home
Don't don't ask questions
Just take me home
OK, I'm leaving
I will walk
I do know how
Yeah to you it doesn't make sense
Yes, I do have to pick up my children
   but not while you're driving
I can steer my own vehicle thank you
Yep, it's broke down and raggedy and
   I still want to go home and drive it
Do I what?
Do I have a split personality?
Didn't you hear me say, "No"
   repeatedly?
I can not believe that you don't get it
No I did not want this
No I did not enjoy it
I'm not acting like you raped me,
   you did

But I ain't go tell nobody

Because my baby brother was sentenced
   to four years in an Ohio State
Penitentiary for raping somebody
And my mother, when she isn't hiding
   behind the hurt, can recall the details
of that hearing faster than any court
   stenographer
And I don't want to jack up anybody's
   life
Give them any reason to take another
   one of us away
So I lay caught between my people and
   myself
I sacrifice self
'Cause a little poonanny on his penis is
   not worth four years and no future
Besides I had just given it away five
   months prior
So what if this one took it

OK girl, this pain is real
I ain't go tell nobody
But this pain is real
I can try to tuck my tears away behind
   smiling eyes
I can laugh and joke and recall and write
   poetry but the pain is still there
I can lie and pretend and protect and defend
But the pain is the truth
This damned vagina has caused me too
   much pain, too much shame
And I hate it!

That day, that day I was bird
An eagle
That large bird of prey with hooked
   bill and strong wings able to soar in
flight

Ahh, I was the dove
That sweet angelic pigeon that shows up
   in the Bible when God got something
especially symbolic to say

That day the eagle took flight
Bad as she wanna be
Decked out in some sexy strap sandals
Ready to soar
Steppin' out on her first date in a long
   while

She walked in an angelic dove - sweet,
   clean, pure
Ready to show the brother some serious
   symbolism
She walked out a dodo bird and if she
   isn't careful
She too will be extinct

He raped me
Shh, don't tell

Afterward

Yesterday I believed I was the dodo
Today I know I remain the dove

Whose feathers are shedding the crude
   oil of every violation, of every
   untruth told

Today I remain the dove
Whose wings now embrace the air of
   morning healing
Whose beak speaks

Yesterday I believed I was the dodo
Today I know I remain the dove

By Malika Diane Mapp

If the survivor is sexually assaulted or abused, she may also feel shame about reporting the incident. It is likely that the survivor is aware of the stereotypes that exist about her racial group. These biases, such as the belief that women of color are promiscuous or that men of color are animalistic, all serve to silence and disempower survivors.

Rituals from a person's racial, ethnic, and cultural background can be used to combat shame. These may be formal or informal rituals of reconnection, cleansing, or community strength. Rituals and symbols serve to repair disconnections and mobilize healing resources (deVries, 1996). Rituals also serve to regulate behavior, time, emotions, and relationship ties.

It is important to resist the tendency toward shame and self-blame. The path to recovery starts by defeating the pressure to remain silent. Grieving and sadness inevitably connects to survivor shame and self-blame. Survivors may take responsibility for the incident, blaming themselves. Counselors can challenge these cognitive distortions with varying techniques, from cognitive to psychodynamic to eye movement desensitization and reprocessing. Whatever a particular therapist's approach, it is important not to endorse cognitive distortions by remaining silent. No one deserves to be violated. This message must be clearly communicated to every survivor.

Shame and self-blame may begin to manifest in people of color as internalized racism. Survivors may speak negatively about themselves or about their target group, with humor or with intense hatred. Even when presented humorously, counselors must recognize such statements as being self-defeating responses to trauma. Comments that downgrade clients' target groups should be highlighted by therapists and examined by client and therapist together in a nonshaming way. Just as when dealing with other kinds of cognitive distortion, counselors must be careful not to close off the dialogue by silencing clients, but at the same time counselors should not observe self-loathing and ignore it. For all survivors of trauma, a major challenge in the healing journey is empowerment and healing self-esteem. As long as a survivor blames the target group, she will remain disempowered and have a bruised self-esteem. Shame, self-blame, and internalized racism must be addressed to aid recovery from racist incident trauma.

Shame and self-blame are present for survivors of various countries. Hindin (2003), for example, found in Zimbabwe that over half the women surveyed believed that wife-beating was justified in certain situations, including if the wife argued with her husband, neglected the children, or went out without telling her husband. These notions of victim-blaming supported by cultural norms keep women of all races and ethnicities silent and shamed.

How Might One's Religion Affect One's Sense of Shame and Self-Blame?

Turell and Thomas (2001) note that although psychology as a discipline recognized the central role of the intrapsychic, the spiritual beliefs of clients and research participants are often ignored. According to Kennedy (2000), numerous counselors view religion as a form of dependency, and numerous religious persons view use of therapy as a reflection of one's lack of faith. It is important to bridge these two worldviews to work toward the wholeness of healthy people, spiritually and emotionally.

If the survivor's religion teaches that anger is unacceptable or bad, he may find it very hard to be upset with others, even when they hurt him. Instead, the survivor's first response may be to become sad and ashamed. He turns the anger in on himself. The survivor blames himself for the actions of others, instead of holding the perpetrator(s) accountable for their behavior. We will talk about anger later in the book, but try to remember that shame is anger turned inward. The survivor does not deserve to feel shame and self-blame. It was not his fault.

Some spiritual and religious teachings attribute physical and mental illness to God or gods, witchcraft, or the disappointment/anger of one's ancestors (deVries, 1996). These teachings may contribute to self-blame by causing the survivor to feel that he has spiritually been responsible for the violation he experienced.

Shame and self-blame may be particularly salient for women of various religious affiliations. Some religions teach that women should be submissive and silent (Kennedy, 2000). For religious women who are sexually violated, they may have difficulty placing blame on the perpetrator instead of on themselves (Turell and Thomas, 2001). Acknowledging the guilt and error of the perpetrator may cause the survivor to feel guilty herself. It is important for survivors to be supported through the process of releasing themselves from the guilt and responsibility of the perpetrators' behavior. Some religious texts also describe women as tempters of evil and sin (Turell and Thomas, 2001). These teachings may result in the survivor feeling in some way responsible for the behavior of the perpetrator. She may feel that something about her must have attracted or caused the abuse or violation. It is important for these cognitions to be challenged and shown as faulty.

Spirituality and religion must be explored in the context of addressing the shame and self-blame created by traumatic experiences (Bratton, 1999).

How Might One's Sexual Orientation Affect One's Sense of Shame and Self-Blame?

If the trauma the survivor experienced was discrimination or harassment based on the survivor's sexual orientation, shame and self-blame may be particularly alive for him. He may find himself questioning his decision to come out of the closet in general or to share his sexual orientation in a particular setting. Others may also blame him for being public about his relationship, as if he shouldn't have the same rights as heterosexual couples.

Homophobia, ranging from negative stereotypes to exclusion, violence, and denial of legal protections, creates shame and self-blame (Blumenfeld, 1992). These experiences are emotionally, relationally, professionally, and spiritually damaging.

If the survivor is gay or lesbian and the traumatic experience was domestic violence, there may be additional shame involved. Some of the shame may be caused by people in general who think it is the survivor's fault for being in a same-sex relationship. The survivor may also feel shame for coming forward because there are already such negative stereotypes that people hold about same-sex couples that the survivor would feel bad for coming forward to share his experience. The survivor may receive pressure from his community to keep it quiet.

Regardless of the nature of the traumatic event, the survivor is not to blame and doesn't need to feel ashamed. No one deserves to be violated or discriminated against.

What Role Does Shame and Self-Blame Have in One's Recovery?

In order to move from surviving day-to-day to thriving and wholeness, the survivor has to understand that she was not responsible for the traumatic event. It was not her fault. As long as she holds herself accountable for the actions of others, the survivor will continue to feel stuck, depressed, and worthless. I understand the desire to control the environment. If the traumatic event was the survivor's fault, that would mean that she could prevent it in the future. We all would like to be able to have enough control to ensure that others will not hurt us. The truth is, we can guarantee that others will not violate us. There are safety precautions that we can take to reduce the risk of violence, but in the end we can not control the behavior of others. We can control how we respond. We can choose not to blame ourselves, not to walk in shame, and not to be angry at ourselves for the actions of others.

Obviously, this is easier said than done. When I hold group sessions with trauma survivors, and they share their experiences, they can see that others in the group were not responsible for their trauma, but they have trouble seeing that they were not. The exercises that follow are to assist the survivor on the path away from shame and self-blame.

Journaling/Poetry

Read and try to remember this affirmation.
Affirmation: It was not my fault.

Activities:

1. List the reasons why you believe the violation was your fault. What are alternative ways of looking at each of the reasons that you listed?

2. Write a letter to anyone who has violated, disrespected, and/or neglected you. Tell the person that you did not deserve to be mistreated.

You do not have to send this letter. It is for you. If you are considering
sending it, wait until you have completed this guidebook, and then
think about the possible responses of the person. If their denial will set
back your recovery, then it probably is not a good idea to not send it. It
is possible that they will deny it. If regardless of the perpetrator's
response you want this person to know how you feel, then sending it
may be healing for you. Regardless of your decision to send it or not,
writing it will be helpful for the survivor.

3. Write about one thing you did during or after the traumatic experience
that you can be proud of.

Movement

Read and try to remember this affirmation.
Affirmation: I do not blame myself. It was not my fault.

Activity:

Breathe deeply three times. Now imagine being weighted down with
shame. Imagine blaming yourself for the traumatic experience. Now begin
moving around the room weighted down by shame. You may walk slowly
or even crawl. Allow yourself to really connect with your shame. After you
have moved or danced with the shame that you are carrying, begin to start
shedding the shame. Begin moving or dancing with lighter movements.
Begin to feel the weight of shame being taken from your shoulders, back,
and finally from your head. Now begin to walk lighter, dance lighter,
jump, leap, skip, run through the space. Allow your body to breathe and
move without shame. When you have finished, stand still and breathe
deeply seven times.

Drama/Theater

Read and try to remember this affirmation.
Affirmation: I release myself from shame.

Activity:

Place a chair in front of you. Imagine that the person in the chair believes that the trauma was your fault. Tell the person the reasons that it
wasn't your fault. Tell them you are not responsible for the violation.
Tell them that no one deserves to be violated or discriminated against. The
rest of the monologue you can write, or you can just spontaneously
share your thoughts without prewriting them. After you have done

this activity, sit still and breathe deeply. Then write about how you are feeling.

Music

Read and try to remember this affirmation.
Affirmation: I am not angry with myself.

Activity:

Sit in a room by yourself and wrap your arms around yourself. Now begin to hum. It may be a song that you know, or you may make it up as you go along. Rock yourself gently and simply hum to yourself. Do this for as long as you like, but for at least three minutes. After you have finished, write how you are feeling.

Nature

Read and try to remember this affirmation.
Affirmation: I am free as the ocean.

Activity:

If you live near a reservoir, lake, pond, or even swimming pool, go and sit by it. If there is not a body of water nearby, the survivor can run water in the sink or tub. Simply reflect on the water. Think about the sound of water, the feel of water, the smell and taste of it. Thinking about the cleansing power of water, allow yourself to visualize the shame and self-blame being washed off of you. Sit and reflect for as long as you like, but for at least twenty minutes. After you have finished, write your reflections.

Arts and Crafts

Read and try to remember this affirmation.
Affirmation: I walk in light and freedom.

Activities:

1. Draw a representation of shame and self-blame. It may be abstract or an actual representation of yourself.
2. Now draw a representation of yourself that is not weighted down by shame.

Spirituality

Read and try to remember this affirmation.
Affirmation: I am a free spirit.

Activity:

Think of someone whose faith or spiritual life you respect. It may be a minister, spiritual leader, family member, friend, or historical figure. Write what you think this person would tell you about shame.

Social Support

Read and try to remember this affirmation.
Affirmation: My true friends don't make me feel ashamed
that I was traumatized.

Activity:

Think about the people in your life who are supportive and trustworthy. Share with one of them the sketch you did regarding shame. It may be a friend, family member, or your counselor. Discuss the two different pictures, the one that is full of shame and the one that is free of shame. If you don't have someone with whom you can share, think about how you would like a supportive person to respond if you showed them the art.

Activism

Read and try to remember this affirmation.
Affirmation: No one deserves to be violated.

Activity:

Think about someone in your life who has also experienced a traumatic event. It may have been recently or a long time ago. It may have been similar to the trauma that you experienced or different. Consider reminding them that it was not their fault. You may do it verbally or by sending them a card. If you don't know anyone, write an encouraging card or letter to a survivor whom you don't know and share it with a battered women's shelter or rape crisis center. Many of the people who come there would benefit from hearing the words of another survivor.

Survivor Case Summary Kim is a Chinese-American survivor of childhood sexual abuse and sexual assault. She is a first-generation American and her parents are not fluent English speakers. Kim grew up in an impoverished area of Chinatown and was sexually abused by a teacher at her school. In her early twenties she was raped by an acquaintance.

Kim sought counseling when she began to feel that her drinking was out of control as well as her intrusive thoughts about the assault. Shame and self-blame were a large part of Kim's cognitions, as is often the case when someone is a survivor of multiple violations. Kim wondered if there was something about her that drew negative attention from men and if she were somehow internally permanently to blame. She received multiple messages from the perpetrators and her community that blamed her. The teacher at her school was popular, so when she reported the abuse—even though other female students came forward and he was eventually convicted—members of the school community were hostile toward her and felt she was somehow to blame. Parents and students called her and the other plaintiffs "sluts" and "whores," and on a few occasions she was physically attacked by a group of students who defended the popular teacher. Her family displaced their anger at the perpetrator and themselves by blaming Kim for not telling them sooner. Her father's violence toward her mother and the high level of drinking in the home made Kim not feel safe talking to her parents about the abuse during the first few months.

Kim started drinking at home with her parents as a teenager and as a result of long-term drinking she developed a high tolerance for alcohol. After being sexually assaulted as a young woman, her reliance on drinking intensified. She began drinking several times a week to the point of blacking out. When Kim sought counseling, the issues of shame and self-blame were layered with the experiences of witnessing domestic violence, being sexually abused by her teacher, and being sexually assaulted by an acquaintance. By exploring her memories, challenging her cognitive distortions related to the incidents, and getting educated about sexual trauma, Kim was able to emotionally accept what she intellectually knew—that she was not to blame.

Kim's sessions also involved exploring the intersection of her national identity, ethnic identity, and gender identity, in terms of such issues as voice, agency, and empowerment. Kim explored the models in her family and community in terms of women's roles and also depictions in the media about the role and identity of Asian women. By examining these observations as well as her acculturation process, Kim was also able to address the shame she experienced regarding her ethnicity and gender. Through individual and group counseling, Kim was able to come to a place of sobriety and begin to work toward her personal and professional goals. At this point Kim is giving herself a break from dating, but hopes in the future she will be ready to connect with someone romantically.

6

Memories

"I escaped with books—reading will keep your mind off it some. But you can't read a book forever. I used to live in a rural area, which was a blessing. . . . I can just go in the woods, with my gun, I hunt by myself, and just leave everything behind, just peaceful in the woods, with my gun, just sit there and think, you know. That's what I used to do, every day. I'd say it was somewhat helpful, because, well, you know you got to go back home, but at the time it's very helpful, you know, just reading, especially in the woods."

—a survivor of child abuse

"I mean I don't necessarily deal with the, um, violence directly in my writing, you know. . . . But what writing does is make you think. Um, I think I spent some years not thinking because of the violence. You know. 'Cause if you think you may have to feel. Uh, and writing forces you to think and to feel. Yeah, because it helps—I mean, it—I think I have the ability to, uh, disassociate myself from things um, a lot. You know, and just. . . . You know, have that there and not feel. You know. Uh, writing makes me feel . . ."

—a survivor of incest

What Are Memories?

The survivor's memory is her ability to recall events from the past. Most people can remember events in their life from childhood through adulthood. Positive and negative events are usually a part of a person's memory.

How Does Trauma Affect Memory?

Van der Kolk and McFarlane (1996, p. 9) note that "because of the timeless and unintegrated nature of traumatic memories, victims remain embedded in the trauma as a contemporary experience." These vivid memories are often accompanied by feelings of extreme loss, anger, betrayal, and powerlessness. Trauma affects memory through intrusive thoughts and avoidance.

What Are Intrusive Thoughts?

At times when the survivor doesn't want to think about the trauma, memories of the trauma may come to mind. These thoughts of the trauma may be in the form of nightmares when sleeping, flashbacks when awake, or the mental replaying of the event when the survivor wants it to stop (van der Kolk, 1996). The nightmares may be of the actual incident or of a similar incident, or the survivor may not remember the nightmare but wake up feeling afraid and having night sweats. When the survivor has flashbacks, she is awake and actually feels that the event is happening again. Flashbacks may be visual, auditory, tactile, or physical (Bratton, 1999). The survivor may also have intrusive thoughts about the trauma, even though she is aware that it is not currently happening. Triggers such as certain people, places, and things may remind the survivor of the trauma (Bratton, 1999). These triggers elicit automatic negative thoughts and feelings (Foa and Rothbaum, 1998). Examples of triggers include:

- Seeing the person who violated the survivor
- Smelling something that was present at the time of the trauma
- Going to the place where the event occurred or to a place that is similar
- Wearing the outfit the survivor wore at the time of the event
- Seeing someone who looks like the person who violated the survivor
- Having (vaginal, anal, or oral) sex if the survivor were sexually assaulted
- Having someone kiss or touch the survivor in a way similar to the person who violated the survivor
- Seeing or hearing about someone being violated (in person, at the movies, on the news, in the survivor's community, etc.)
- Having someone use the same phrase as the person who violated the survivor

What Is Avoidance?

Avoidance of memory is blocking the recall of traumatic events. It may be a conscious decision on the survivor's part, or she may want to remember but have difficulty doing so. If the survivor has been trying to avoid the memories, she may avoid certain things. Avoidance is a normal response to traumatic experiences (Foa and Rothbaum, 1998).

What Are Indicators That the Survivor Is Actively Avoiding Memories of the Traumatic Event?

• Does the survivor try not to think about it?
• Does the survivor avoid talking about it?

The survivor may try to avoid it because she is afraid of the feelings that will come with thinking about it. The survivor may avoid talking about it because she is afraid that people will blame her or get tired of listening to her. Some of the ways the survivor distracts herself from the memories may be unhealthy for her. These unhealthy strategies include but are not limited to:

• Drinking
• Other drug use
• Excessive shopping
• Casual sex
• Staying busy (cleaning, working, hanging out with friends, etc.)

On the other hand, the survivor may want to remember but cannot. Some factors that may keep her from remembering are:

• The survivor was very young when the traumatic incident happened
• The survivor was under the influence of alcohol or other drugs at the time of the event
• The survivor may have been asleep when the event occurred
• The survivor may have been knocked out or fainted at the time of the incident
• The survivor's mind may have protected her by allowing her to dissociate or black out at the time of the event
• The survivor's mind may be protecting her by not allowing her to remember certain details of the incident

The psychophysiological effects of trauma also effect memory and affect survivors in the following ways (van der Kolk, 1996):

Decreased Hippocampal Volume	Activation of the Amygdala	Decreased Activation of Broca's Area
• Declarative memory loss	• Loss of fear response • Meaningful social interaction lost	• Difficulty putting feelings into words

As researchers have found, difficulty in talking about trauma results not only from fear of social stigma and shame, but also from the physiological effects of the traumatic experience.

What Role Does Memory Play in One's Recovery?

It is important for the survivor to be able to sit with the memories he has without becoming overwhelmed. As long as his memories control him, he will feel intense fear and anxiety at the thought of the event. In addition, he may continue to reenact the trauma through self-destructive behaviors, by reentering dangerous situations in which he can be revictimized, or by causing harm or destruction in the lives of others (van der Kolk and McFarlane, 1996).

To gain control over the anxiety, fear, and shame, the survivor has to be able to recall the parts of the event that he can and sit with them until his distress decreases. Through exposure to the memories, survivors are able to work through the pain and therefore experience a decrease in anxiety (Foa and Rothbaum, 1998). The more the survivor is able to do this, the more he will gain power over the memories. As Herman (1997) notes, remembering the survivor's life before the traumatic incident(s) as well as the horror of the trauma itself is critical to recovery. This remembering transforms the survivor's experience of the trauma, and with the support of allies in a safe context the memory goes from unbearable to bearable. This empowers the survivor to not only remember the event, but also acknowledge the affective response, the context, and the meaning the trauma had for the survivor in the moment and the meaning he ascribes to the event now.

When we try to avoid our memories, they show up in nightmares, increased anxiety and body tension, and irritability. Eventually the survivor should be able to recall the event without feeling as though he is reliving it or in imminent danger. Remembering and speaking the truth of our traumatic experiences is an act of liberation (Herman, 1997). The goal of recovery is for the survivor to overcome the phobia of the traumatic memories and the phobia of life itself (van der Kolk, van der Hart, and Marmar, 1996).

If the survivor is unable to remember the event because of the reasons listed earlier, he can still have a strong recovery. He doesn't have to know the details of what occurred when he was intoxicated, passed out, asleep, or too young to remember. Even without knowing the details of the event, recovery is possible.

Some survivors find the support and safety of therapy helpful when attempting to confront and explore the memories of traumatic experiences. Individual and group psychotherapy have been found effective. In determining the psychotherapeutic needs of survivors, Draucker (1999) found that the primary therapeutic needs are a focus on feelings, problem-solving, and reliance on their own strengths and resources. The survivors in Draucker's (1999) study wanted therapy that would assist them in making use of their "healing power."

A variety of therapy approaches may assist survivors in psychological growth in the aftermath of trauma. These include crisis therapy, supportive psychotherapy, insight-oriented therapy, cognitive-behavioral therapy, dynamic therapy, exposure therapy, EMDR, expressive art therapy, and psychopharmacology (medication). The individual therapies that have been empirically documented as effectively transforming sense of self and sense of power and control are crisis intervention therapy and cognitive-behavioral therapy.

Crisis Intervention

Crisis intervention or debriefing is a short-term intervention that involves working with a survivor immediately after the assault. The initial response survivors receive after disclosing their trauma is key in predicting the long-term outcomes of sexual assault victims. By providing immediate crisis intervention, survivors may be empowered by the normalizing of their response to the trauma, the provision of knowledge on available resources, and basic education on coping and self-care strategies (Muran and DiGiuseppe, 2000). Crisis intervention or psychological debriefing must be done with great sensitivity and only at the request of the participant, as it has been found in some cases to have no effect or even be damaging to the survivor when conducted too soon (Solomon, 1999).

Cognitive Therapy

Cognitive therapy focuses on transforming thoughts and behavioral patterns that are disserving the survivor. Cognitive therapy has been shown to be effective not only in reducing symptoms, it may also assist in the psychological growth of survivors by allowing them to face the memories of their experience and thus take power over their experience as well as their thoughts (Cohen et al.,

2000). Cognitive therapy also helps survivors process and reframe their experience, therefore giving them an opportunity to gain wisdom about themselves, the perpetrator, and the assault. For child survivors, this work is also empowering when it involves parental treatment. It is necessary to facilitate growth in the lives of those who are caretakers of survivors in order to maximize survivors' growth and life appreciation (Leibowitz, Mendelsohn, and Michelson, 1999).

Cognitive therapy also assists in the growth process by teaching the survivor new skills and strategies that allow her to reach specific treatment goals (Weaver et al., 1999). These new skills may be taught through psycho-education for child, adolescent, and adult survivors (Saywitz et al., 2000). By gaining new skills and knowledge the survivor is able to exercise power and control in her life. In assisting survivors' capacity to get in touch with their healing power, cognitive therapy helps provide knowledge and skills related to self-esteem, power, trust, safety, faulty thinking patterns, and intimacy (Westwell, 1998).

Group Therapy

Group therapy provides an opportunity for survivors to gain knowledge about themselves and others. It lets survivors know that they are not alone, that their responses are normal, and that learning to trust others again is a possibility (Foy, Eriksson, and Trice, 2001). Group therapy may follow a variety of approaches, including but not limited to: psychodynamic, psycho-educational, cognitive-behavioral, or support-focused. Wood and Roche (2001) note that feminist groups that focus on the use of narrative and social context can help women gain empowerment after marital acquaintance rape. This is done through support, cognitive reframing, and the use of ritual ceremonies. Groups are helpful with not only symptom abatement, but also with issues of identity that are integral to thriving, such as self-esteem and understanding of the self in relation to others (Morgan and Cummings, 1999; Lubin et al., 1998).

How Does One's Disability Affect Trauma and Memory?

• Physical and mental disabilities can create additional challenges to using the exposure method of facing one's memory. Particular exposure requires one to break the silence, secrecy, and shame of the barrier by communicating the memory, usually by speaking it. If one's disability makes communication challenging, sharing one's memory with another person can be difficult. Our emotions are most tapped into when we use the form of communication that is normal for us. Trying to communicate in a different format or using an interpreter in counseling may result in a loss of some of the affective response of the trauma. It is important to try to find someone safe with whom to communicate the traumatic memories. This support person should be clinically skilled with trauma issues and be educated outside of the therapeutic relationship about the person's disability. In other words, it is not for the client to provide all of the counselor's education about their needs. While the client knows the particulars of their experience more than anyone else, it is still vital for the counselor to research the general dynamics of the client's disability. Important points to consider are:

- Pain associated with the disability (Is the person in constant pain, including during their time with you?)
- The effect of the disability on memory
- The effect of the disability on communication
- Myths and facts about the disability
- Cause of the disability
- Abilities and strengths
- Experiences of the survivor with discrimination and stigma
- Support system
- Self-care activities including activities the survivor currently or formerly found joyful

How Might One's Economic Status Affect One's Memory?

If the survivor has financial constraints, he may feel that he has to avoid the memories in order to focus on working and taking care of financial responsibilities. Even though the survivor has a lot of responsibilities, he has to make himself and his recovery a priority. Avoidance may work in the short term, but in the long run all of those feelings are still under the surface. Also as noted above, some of the strategies that the survivor is using to avoid the memories may not be healthy for him. For many people there is still a social stigma attached to undergoing traditional psychotherapy. Themes that reinforce this stigma include cultural ideology about mental health, lack of financial resources, and past negative experiences with the mental health system. This stigma is particularly relevant for low-income and ethnically marginalized survivors. It is important that recognition be given to the alternative ways in which people have found healing and transformation and, when possible, to include these methods in the traditional therapy provision.

If the survivor is a person of wealth, he has a lot of strategies and resources for avoidance available to him. The survivor needs to fight the urge to distract himself with travel, shopping, or other activities that do not bring him closer to recovery.

How Might One's Gender Affect One's Memory?

Many women are sexually violated at some point in their lives. If this has happened to the survivor, intimate relationships, including sexual intimacy, may be very challenging. Sexual intimacy may be a trigger for intrusive traumatic memories. It is important to begin to distinguish past from present and perpetrator from current partner. Some things that may help decrease the triggering of negative sexual memories are:

- Leaving the lights on
- Being in a different physical position than the survivor was during the violation
- Having the survivor verbalize her feelings during intimacy and asking her partner to verbalize his feelings for the survivor during intimacy as well
- Telling the survivor's partner any phrases or sudden movements that may trigger negative memories
- Gradually increasing intimacy with breathing and feedback, from cuddling to kissing to touching to intercourse
- Silently reminding oneself where one is and who one is with
- Telling the survivor's partner if she needs to stop and asking him to check in with her in case she is having difficulty with an intrusive thought
- Remember that the survivor deserves love and pleasure without guilt or shame

For ethnic minority and racial minority women, the existence of negative stereotypes and oppressive images makes it particularly difficult to face the pain of traumatic memories in the company of another person. The racial minority survivor has to be in a supportive context with someone who is willing to bear witness to the trauma while being sensitive to the increased vulnerability of the legacy of trauma based on historical and contemporary manifestations of racism (Daniel, 2000).

If the survivor is male, he may have been taught to not talk about painful or fearful experiences. If he continues to avoid these memories, he may have intense nightmares and irritability. He will need to work on confronting the memories so they do not intrude on his life by making him feel out of control.

How Might One's Migration Status Affect One's Memory?

Emotional distress has to be named and explored with immigrant survivors. McKelvey and Webb (1995) found in a sample of Vietnamese Americans that 22 percent of males and 18 percent of females reported a having history of physical and/or sexual abuse. In addition, the males in their sample who were abuse survivors reported significantly higher levels of psychological distress compared with their nonabused counterparts. Women's psychological distress, however, was not predicted by their history of physical or sexual abuse; it is possible that the women in the sample who were not survivors of childhood abuse were survivors of traumatic experiences during their adult years.

If English is not the survivor's primary language, the emotions he has connected to the traumatic memories may be mentally stored in his primary language. To truly gain access and control over those overwhelming feelings, it is important for the survivor to talk about his memories and feelings in his primary language. This may be done by speaking with a counselor who speaks the survivor's language, speaking to a counselor with an interpreter in the room, speaking with family or friends who speak the survivor's primary language, or writing/speaking the memories, including feelings, to oneself.

How Might One's Race/Ethnicity Affect One's Memory?

If there is pressure from members of the survivor's race or ethnicity to avoid talking or thinking about the trauma, it may be challenging for her to find a safe, supportive person with whom to discuss her memories. Specifically, the high prevalence of trauma in a racial or ethnic community sometimes leads survivors of that community to minimize and deny the impact and memory of trauma as a way of coping. It is important to let the survivor and her loved ones know that avoidance is not healthy. If the survivor doesn't face her memories, they will come out in other ways such as nightmares, flashbacks, and in irritability. Members of the survivor's support system should be informed that she won't always need to talk about the traumatic event, but when she does need to talk about it, it is important for her to have support. If they are unable to be supportive for various reasons, including the possibility that they also have unhealed traumatic memories, the survivor will need to find other people for support.

If the traumatic event was of a racist nature, the survivor may find that she is constantly vulnerable to triggers of the traumatic event. If she is a minority group member, she is likely surrounded by majority race/ethnicity members for a large part of her day. It is important for her to be able to distinguish safe from unsafe situations and persons. This is done by being able to explore her memories and experiences with racial trauma.

Societal traumas are traumas that arise from racism, sexism, and classism or due to the profound influence of social, economic, and political oppression (Villena-Mata, 2002; Everett and Gallop, 2001). Racism is a potentially traumatizing and terrorizing form of victimization that affects ethnic minority children and adults (Sanchez-Hucles, 1998; Wyatt, 1990). As traumas, racist incidents may result in long-term psychological effects such as post-traumatic stress disorder; as opposed to being a "post" trauma, however, racism is a constant stress to ethnic minorities in the United States (Allen, 1996).

Loo and colleagues (2001) found that race-related stressors accounted for a significant proportion of the variance in post-traumatic stress disorder for Asian-American Vietnam war veterans (Loo et al., 2001). Woodard (2001) found that experiences of racial trauma for African-Americans were significantly associated with increased psychiatric and physical symptoms. The conception of PTSD has been expanded to include not only war veterans, but survivors of domestic and sexual violence as well; the concept should be further broadened to include the trauma of racism (Sanchez-Hucles, 1998).

Some key components of traumatic events are that they are threatening to life or life quality, cause severe harm or injury, and are marked by intense fear, helplessness, or horror (Friedman and Marsella, 1996). Milliora (2000) notes that "racism assaults victims with experiences of being perceived as less than human." While it is obvious that racially motivated physical assaults threaten the lives of target group members; those who experience nonphysical forms of racism have their quality of life threatened by housing discrimination, employment discrimination, and unequal education (Allen, 1996; Wyatt, 1990). Within the United States, targets of racism include members of ethnic minority groups such as people of African or Asian descent, Latinos, and Native Americans. Some target group members may resist being seen as trauma survivors because their psychological functioning is already pathologized (Ridley, 1995). Ethnic minority clients tend to be misdiagnosed with more severe psychopathology; are more apt to be assigned to junior professionals; and tend to receive more low-cost treatment, including medication only, rather than intensive psychotherapy in comparison to white clients (Ridley, 1995). However, denying the traumatic impact of racism does not serve those who are carrying its wounds. The trauma of racism must be acknowledged in order to provide the appropriate service to those who have already been affected by it as well as to prevent trauma in the future (Bryant-Davis and Ocampo, in press). In addressing the potential concern of the "racism as trauma model" as being pathologizing of ethnic minorities, it is important to note that within the trauma framework, traumatic symptomology is not found in every trauma survivor. Traumatic symptoms are possible manifestations that may result in some survivors. In other words, not all rape survivors develop PTSD, and not all survivors of racism will develop PTSD or other trauma-related symptoms.

How Might One's Religion Affect One's Memories?

The survivor's religion may encourage avoidance of negative thoughts, including thoughts of things that have occurred in the past. While it is important to not become stuck in the past, it is also important to face the memory and trauma of the past in order to heal. Engaging in religious rituals can help in regaining control when the survivor is feeling overwhelmed or engaged in worship. It should not be used, however, to avoid taking the necessary steps for the survivor's recovery.

How Might One's Sexual Orientation Affect One's Memories?

If the trauma was related to homophobia, the survivor may find that triggers of the event occur throughout the day. Heterosexist comments made around the survivor as well as media images can elicit traumatic memories. It is important for the survivor to be able to distinguish past from present as well as safe from unsafe environments.

What Should One's Recovery Goals Be in Terms of One's Memory?

- The survivor should not engage in unhealthy avoidance behaviors
- The survivor should be able to think about memories and feelings without feeling in current danger
- The survivor should be able to talk about his memories without feeling that his emotions are out of control
- The survivor should be able to calm himself through breathing, relaxing his muscles, engaging in pleasurable, healthy activities, reaching out for social support, and/or engaging in spiritual/religious rituals

Attaining these goals can be done through practice and persistence, and with the help of supportive family, friends, and/or counselors. Begin working on these goals by doing the exercises that follow.

Journaling

Read and try to remember this affirmation.
Affirmation: I can face the past.

Activity:

Breathe deeply seven times. Write down what you can remember about the traumatic event. When you have finished, rate how distressed you feel on a scale 1 to 100, with 100 being the highest. Breathe deeply seven times and write down the memory again. Rate how distressed you feel. Repeat this activity, until your level of distress has decreased by 20 points. This may take a few minutes, hours, days, or weeks. Take your time and be encouraged. You can gain power over your memories.

Movement

Read and try to remember this affirmation.
Affirmation: I choose not to deny what happened. I remember.

Activity:

Stand up straight and breathe deeply seven times. Think back to what you can remember about the traumatic experience. Now physically begin to symbolically represent how you felt before the incident(s), during, and after the traumatic experience(s). Allow your body to remember and release the physical memories by moving through space. Think about the different feelings that came up for you during the experience both emotionally and physically.

If you don't remember details about the incident, don't worry. You can still express the general memories through movement. If the movements do not flow, you may choose to embody the experience with different poses. Think of ten words that describe your experience and come up with a pose for each word. When you make the pose, stand still and breathe as you count to eight. After you finish the physical journey of the experience, stand up straight, embrace yourself, and breathe deeply seven times.

Arts and Crafts

Read and try to remember this affirmation.
Affirmation: I will not use unhealthy habits to avoid my memories.

Activities:

1. Draw a picture to represent how the perpetrator looked at the time of the traumatic event.
2. Now draw a picture to represent how the perpetrator looks to you now.

Music

Read and try to remember this affirmation.
Affirmation: I can tell my story.

Activity:

Use a tabletop, hardback book, or actual drum if you have it. Drum out a rhythm to represent how you felt right before the incident, during the traumatic incident, immediately afterward, and now. Allow the rhythm, speed, and volume to communicate your feelings and memories. This is your song. There is no right or wrong way to do this activity.

Drama/Theater

Read and try to remember this affirmation.
Affirmation: It is healthy for me to acknowledge one's feelings.

Activity:

Think of a safe person to tell about your traumatic event. Practice telling them what happened to you. You should practice aloud or by writing down what you want to say. You may want to start by saying "I want to talk to you about something that is hard for me. Do you have time to talk?" Then practice saying what happened, how it made you feel, and how the person you are sharing with can be most helpful.

After you have finished, write how this practice made you feel.

Social Support

Read and try to remember this affirmation.
Affirmation: I deserve respect and support.

Activity:

You may be ready to do the activity that you practiced in the previous exercise. Choose someone you think will be supportive and share your experience. If at any point you observe that the person is not being supportive, you can stop sharing your story.

Signs of NOT being supportive are smirking, laughing, changing the subject, asking the survivor blaming questions, or saying, "I can't deal with this." If the person IS supportive, continue to share the survivor's memory and feelings, and ask what, if anything, the person can do to assist in the survivor's recovery. Write a reflection of how you felt before, during, and after sharing the memory.

Spirituality

Read and try to remember this affirmation.
Affirmation: I have faith that I will move from
victim to survivor to thriver.

Activity:

Find one encouraging line from a religious text or other inspirational writing. Fill in the verse or line at each place where you see a blank line below.

Even though I am sometimes afraid, _____

_____.

I was violated but _____

_____.

I may feel depressed, angry, or numb, but I know _____

_____.

Nature

Read and try to remember this affirmation.
Affirmation: The traumatic event affected me, but it
does not define me.

Activity:

Think about the trauma you experienced. After you think about it for a few minutes, begin to visualize an ideal place for you. This place should be somewhere that you find soothing and calming. You may have been there before or only dreamed of going. It may be a beach, a mountain, a park, or anywhere that you choose. Imagine what you would see, hear, feel, touch, and/or taste if you were in that place. Allow this image to relax you. Breathe deeply and remember that you can do this exercise whenever you would like.

Activism

Read and try to remember this affirmation.
Affirmation: I can think about the past without getting stuck in the past.

Activity:

Contact a community agency that works to prevent traumatic events. Find out about any upcoming events that they are having and try to attend. It may be a workshop, seminar, rally, or program. Attend a few of their events and then, if you are comfortable, ask if there is a way you can help out with the next event. They may need help with mailings, setting up chairs, handling refreshments, or giving out handouts.

Survivor Case Summary Louis is a Mexican-American adult survivor of childhood physical abuse by his father. He also witnessed the sexual abuse of his sisters. Louis has a graduate degree and is a high-level administrator. Louis is in his forties and had no prior counseling.

Louis had actively avoided thinking about the abuse of his childhood. His primary avoidance behaviors were eating and pornography. Both of these behaviors had become addictive and led to Louis seeking counseling. The compulsive eating resulted in him being severely overweight. Louis began using eating as a coping strategy as a child. His mother, who felt unable to intervene in the abusive behavior of his father, would attempt to nurture the children with food. Louis experienced eating as a way to relieve his anxiety and suppress his emotions.

Louis' use of pornography had also become addictive. His Christian beliefs and the overwhelming control pornography had on his life created a lot of distress for Louis and he threw all of his pornography (films and magazines) away. Unfortunately, he then became addicted to Internet pornography. He found himself looking at pornography constantly, even at work, and experienced great fear and shame that he would be discovered by his employer.

Louis sought counseling to address his compulsive eating and pornography addiction. He also was concerned because of a recent angry outburst he had toward his parents. Louis went home for the holidays and had an outburst of yelling and throwing things.

During counseling, a safe space was created for Louis to begin exploring and facing his memories. He was able to recount the numerous occasions of verbal, emotional, and physical abuse that he experienced as well as the occasions that he saw his father sexually abuse his sisters. By facing his memories, Louis was able to experience a decrease in his anxiety and anger as well as an increase in his use of healthy coping strategies to replace the role of eating and pornography in his life. He found counseling, reading, and prayer helpful. He attempted to create a healthy connection with one of his sisters, but she was unable to discuss their abusive childhoods and became angry with her brother for introducing the topic. Louis began contemplating talking to a minister at his church or joining a male support group, but at this time has not felt comfortable. He is still working through the shame of his pornography addiction as well as his feelings of shame and powerlessness at not being able to defend himself or protect his sisters. During counseling, cultural notions of manhood and sexuality were explored as well as his religious beliefs. The goal of this process was for Louis to retain and strengthen those factors that led to healthy living decisions and discard those factors that contributed to his emotional restrictedness. By facing his memories within the context of cultural traditions, Louis has begun to gain a sense of self-efficacy, esteem, and freedom.

7

Mourning the Losses

"You have a hard heart, you know, you don't feel anything. Everything is power, I guess. You don't cry, you can't laugh, you know, you don't really show any emotions. When your heart becomes hard, you stay on that level. So in your heart, you know, that's the way you are, not even human, you're not even there. So that's why somebody getting hurt doesn't kill you, cause you're dead already. You don't feel..."

—a survivor of war

"Some people think I'm crazy cause I laugh when things are at their worst. When I'm in the most painful situations or whatever, I grin. Or when I'm in a stressful situation, I smile and grin, and I know that throws people off but that's how I cope and I feel comfortable doing that. I'm always stressed but yeah, I laugh and smile and that's like my norm."

—a survivor of physical abuse

"My friends would tell me, you don't belong out here, you can make it, you know. They always used to say you should be doing stuff. You know, you have a good heart. So that made me try. That's what made me try. If they feel like that, I'm gonna do it. Yeah . . . and when our friends would get killed, we'd talk about it for a minute. We would, you know, sit and cry, you know, they'd find him in a garbage can in an alleyway. And then we'd laugh at that. You know? You know, just to get it out. And I was always saying hey, we're gonna miss the brother. We talked about it and pour some libations, some alcohol for him. And saying farewell, somebody died you know. Show some respect and we would do that every time. Yeah. It was helpful. We were like a family, you know, sort of like losing part of the family. But that was our way of life, you know. We'd accept that type of like, you know, these things will happen."

—a survivor of gang violence

What Is Mourning?

Mourning is experiencing grief for and recognizing the losses one has endured. People mourn in different ways. It requires the capacity to sit with one's feelings of sadness. This begins with an acceptance of the fact that there have been losses.

What Is the Relationship between Trauma and Mourning?

Traumatic events result in loss. Some things the survivor may have lost are:

- Her sense of safety
- Control over her body
- Her health
- Her joy
- Her faith
- Her peace of mind
- Trust
- Her voice
- A sense of power
- Hope
- A relationship
- Her marriage
- A loved one's life
- Her job; a promotion
- Her ability to enjoy sex (Warshaw, 1988)

How Does One Mourn Losses?

- Recognize the losses that one has had
- Allow the one's self to feel the impact of those losses—including sadness and grief

Many survivors try to skip this stage. We want to deny the impact of the trauma because to acknowledge the impact means we recognize the power of the event and the perpetrator. This is painful, but we can heal our wounds only if we recognize that there are wounds. Some of us resist sadness because we are afraid we will get stuck in the sorrow. The survivor may fear becoming overwhelmed by feelings of grief. It is healthy to mourn and to give the survivor space for grief. If the survivor alternates between numbness and intense over-whelming emotion, he will need to work on moderation. Moderation does not mean I turn off my feelings and remain numb. It means I allow myself to feel a range of emotions, and I also learn strategies to soothe and calm myself after I feel the sorrow. Mourning will not be a onetime event. There will be different times in the survivor's life when memories of the losses reemerge and the survivor grieves them again. This is normal and healthy.

How Might One's Disability Affect One's Mourning?

Persons with disabilities often strive to develop skills of self-reliance and in-dependence. Mourning in the presence of another person requires trust, connection, and the capacity to communicate one's feelings. It is important for the survivor not to close off her feelings and for those in her support network to inquire about the emotional experience of the survivor, including feelings of loss and sadness. Along with general psychological distress that can be found in survivors in general, sur-vivors with learning disabilities are more likely to exhibit stereotypical behaviors, such as repetitive rocking (Sequira, Howlin, and Hollins, 2003).

Post-traumatic losses for those with disabilities may have intensified earlier losses. In other words, the survivor may have already experienced losses re-lated to her disability as well as societal stigma and discrimination associated with the disability. Losses due to the traumatic experience may heighten or bring to mind earlier losses. It is important for the survivor to be able to explore and acknowledge the various losses of her life experience. As a source of hope, however, the survivor may be able to recall memories of recovery and/ or adaptation after prior losses or negative experiences. It is important that a reservoir of healthy coping strategies be developed to assist the survivor through the mourning process so that it is growth-promoting and so it does not result in the survivor being stuck in despair. With support, coping strategies, and cog-nitive reframing, this is possible. Cognitive reframing is challenging for those with mental disabilities, but it is possible, and health professionals should con-tinue to communicate healthy cognitions to the survivor.

How Might One's Economic Status Affect One's Mourning?

If the survivor has limited resources, she may feel that she doesn't have time to mourn. She may feel that she doesn't have the time or money for

therapy. The survivor has to work and take care of her family. Unfortunately, trauma does not lessen its impact because of our financial or family ob-
ligations. The impact of the trauma is there, and whether the survivor allows time
and space to grieve now or later, the grieving has to be done for her complete
wholeness. Some people put it off for a while, but eventually the survivor will
come face-to-face with the impact the trauma has had on her life. The survivor has
to mourn in her own time and should try to create a community or relationship
that can be supportive through the process. The survivor's support may be a
relative, a therapist who has a sliding scale and/or provides pro bono services, a
religious support group or prayer group, or a neighbor who is willing to sit with
the survivor.

If the survivor is a person of wealth, people may be less sympathetic to her
losses. Often people who are focused on the survivor's material possessions
have trouble recognizing the emotional pain that person is feeling. Contrary to
popular belief, money does not erase sorrow. It is important to remind survivors of their right to grief. Survivors need to connect with people who will not
dismiss their pain.

How Might One's Gender Affect One's Mourning?

Women are generally given more social permission to mourn. If, however,
the survivor is a mother, people will often pressure her to quickly get over it
and tend to her children's needs. It is important to attend to both the children's
needs and the survivor's own grief. If the survivor doesn't grieve but instead
swallows her pain, her children will experience it as detachment or misplaced
anger at them. If the survivor is having trouble juggling the grieving process
and her role as mother, she may want to seek the support of those around her.
In addition to their family responsibilities, another barrier to mourning for
women are the taboo topics that surround societal expectations of women.
Particularly, some of the losses women may face include loss of enjoyment of
sexuality and loss of faith (Warshaw, 1988). There is often a stigma against
women who articulate these concerns. It is important to have safe spaces and
people in place so women can explore and express their feelings about these
losses as well as find ways to address these losses.

Men are not often given permission to mourn. Blumenfeld (1992) notes
that, as men, "we are taught we must be in control. We cannot get too close to
our feelings, and if we do, we certainly cannot show them. We must keep it all
together; we cannot show vulnerability, awkwardness, doubts. We have to be
on top, in bed and out. To keep us in line, *faggot, pansy, wimp, sissy, girl*, and
homo are thrown at us like spears to the heart" (p. 37).

The survivor may have been taught to swallow his feelings. He may have been taught that tears and grief are signs of weakness. The opposite is actually the case. It takes a courageous person to face their pain. It takes courage to recognize and mourn the losses that the survivor has experienced. The survivor needs to try to connect with people who will encourage him in this process and minimize contact with people who will discourage or shame him.

How Might One's Migration Status Affect One's Mourning?

Mourning for death may be acceptable in the survivor's home country, but mourning for personal losses may not be. Therapy and talking about painful events may be unfamiliar to the survivor. There may, however, be particular strategies or rituals that the survivor is familiar with to help in his mourning. I encourage him to do these things, and I also encourage him to try talking with someone about his feelings.

How Might One's Race/Ethnicity Affect One's Mourning?

Randall Robinson wrote: "No people could live successfully, fruitfully, triumphantly without a strong memory of their past. Yet we as a people have been largely overwhelmed by a majority culture that wronged us dramatically, emptied our memories, undermined our self-esteem, implanted us with palatable voices, and stripped us along the way of the sheerest corona of selfdefinition."

There is much to be gained in exploring racism through the lens of trauma literature. Counselors have to understand that racist incidents can be traumatizing. They can pose a threat or endangerment to one's life and/or integrity. It can create feelings of loss, shock, and despair and in some cases can overwhelm the normal coping mechanisms of the individual.

From trauma literature we understand that a key component in the recovery process is receiving acknowledgment and validation of one's experience. The codes of silence around racism run parallel to the silence concerning rape, incest, and war experiences. The silencing effect is multiplicative when we look at the fact that Jewish, Native American, African, Latino, and Asian survivors of racism often simultaneously endure sexual assault and physical assault as well as war.

When we examine racism through a trauma lens, we are reminded that this society has accepted and expected scripts for victims. Victims are supposed to be sad, sympathetic virgins. When victims of racism are loud, angry, vocal, strong, and complain often, they lose sympathy and thus their status as victims. Now they are merely overly sensitive at the least and paranoid troublemakers at the worst. As with sexual trauma, the script for victims of racism must be erased.

There are examples of individuals and entire nations of peoples dissociating in the face of the trauma of racism. People become shocked, blank, numb, and unable to function. This may last a moment or several generations. As with physical and sexual trauma survivors, this dissociation is effective as a coping tool only in the moment, but in the long run it further endangers the oppressed, leaving them more vulnerable.

Secondary traumatization is a reality. Young people growing up today may have never been in a concentration camp or on an auction block, plantation, trail of tears, or reservation. It does not erase the genetic memory—the knowing that one's people have been subjugated, violated, and nearly annihilated. Knowing that it happened to your people earlier and that it continues today has effects on the knower. People respond to secondary traumatization differently. It may manifest itself in anxiety and panic, in free-floating rage, in shame and self-blame, in depression, or even in denial.

The survivor's racial or ethnic culture may value emotional strength and perseverance. These are important traits, and it is also important to have times and places where the survivor can let down his guard and grieve. Whether this is alone, with a therapist, or with the survivor's family/friends, mourning is important for the survivor's recovery.

If the traumatic event was a racist incident, the survivor may feel unsafe about showing his pain in front of others (Collins, 2000). Even if the survivor has to mourn alone, it is important to give oneself space and time to do so. The survivor should try to connect with others who are supportive and encouraging of the survivor's process (Daniel, 2000). The losses created by racial harassment and racially motivated assaults are numerous and include but are not limited to increases in stress, life dissatisfaction, negative perceptions of health, PTSD, and job dissatisfaction (Valentine, Silver, and Twigg, 1999; Schneider and colleagues, 2000).

Members of privileged racial and ethnic groups also need to acknowledge the emotional and mental costs of racial oppression. While racism dehumanizes its victims, it also "corrupts the humanity" of those who are placed in power by it (Harper, 1992). Members of privileged groups live with anxiety, fear, distrust, insecurity, and unhealthy notions of self and others. In order to motivate oneself to work against racial oppression, people must acknowledge and mourn the negative effect that racial injustice has on society as a whole.

Considering the need for safe places for racially oppressed communities to heal, Hooks (1995) states, "The words we speak mean nothing if we are not creating a cultural context where black pain can speak and be directly attended to. . . . " (p. 136).

How Might One's Religion Affect One's Mourning?

Clinicians and researchers are gradually taking greater notice of the effect interpersonal trauma has on spiritual themes such as loss of faith, difficulty reconciling faith and violation, and a greater immersion in faith-based behaviors (Kennedy, 2000).

Warwick (2001) argues that a person's identity development is influenced by the way she experiences herself in relationships, including her relationship with God. With this in mind, it is important to consider the impact of trauma on the survivor's relationship with God. Along with the relationship to God, a survivor's relationship to their religious leader or local clergy can also be significant to the recovery process.

Regarding sexual violence, Sheldon and Parent (2002) found that many clergy blame rape victims and adhere to rape myths, with the more fundamentalist and sexist clergy being the most likely to blame rape victims. Clergy ranging in age from twenty through eighty were found to attribute blame to the victim when she didn't resist physically and when she wore provocative clothing; many also considered sexual intercourse to be a part of the marital role and therefore did not acknowledge marital rape (Sheldon and Parent, 2002).

Hall (1995) found that Christian women who were sexually abused as children reported lower spiritual functioning compared with nonabused women; specifically, women who were survivors were less likely to feel loved and accepted by God, less likely to feel a sense of community with others, and less likely to trust that God had a plan and purpose for their future. In earlier studies, Papania (1989) and Rodriguez (1989) found that sexual abuse survivors scored lower on a subjective sense of religious well-being scale than their nonabused counterparts. Also, in an early study, Finkelhor, Hotaling, Lewis, and Smith (1989) found that survivors of childhood sexual abuse were less likely to be engaged in a religious faith as adults. Although the research and theoretical work in this area is lacking in quantity, it is clear that sexual assault not only affects survivors emotionally, physically, and relationally, but also spiritually. While most survivors may struggle with the concept of feeling bad, survivors of various religious traditions may have to mourn additional losses and address the additional burden of feeling or being perceived as evil or sinful (Kennedy, 2000). All therapists need to address these important issues.

Additionally, if the survivor's religion emphasizes quick healings or instant miracles, there may be less support for recovery, as this is a journey that takes time. Miracles do happen. The survivor's ability to move from victim to survivor to thriver is miraculous and a sign of healing, but it takes time. Giving the survivor time to recover and mourn does not make her healing any less real or significant.

In any religious tradition, the survivor can find examples of people who had to persevere to find healing and wholeness. It takes time, but it is possible.

How Might One's Sexual Orientation Affect One's Mourning?

If the trauma the survivor experienced was a homophobic incident, the survivor may feel unsupported in his mourning process. He may feel isolated and afraid of reaching out to others. Even if the survivor is mourning alone, he should not skip the process. He needs to treat himself with compassion and allow time to sit with and express the sorrow. The losses he may need to mourn include the scars of invisibility, harassment, assault, damnation, denial of police and judicial protection, discrimination, loss of family, loss of employment, and loss of housing (Thompson, 1992).

One example of interpersonal violence is sexual assault. Sexual assault early in life disrupts the development of identity and intimacy capacities. Lesbian, gay, and bisexual survivors who were raped in adolescence or early adulthood have to find ways to relinquish self-blame, establish the capacity for intimate relationships, and develop a positive identity (Warwick, 1996). Unfortunately, homophobia within counseling personnel may lead them to stereotype lesbian survivors. This is a major disservice to lesbian rape survivors and may dissuade their desire to seek help (Orzek, 1988). Many biases exist in our society, many biases against those who disclose rape histories as well as those who disclose gay, lesbian, or bisexual orientations. These biases may undermine the therapeutic alliance and the goals of treatment. Counselors must address their own homophobic beliefs and values in order to successfully work with lesbian and bisexual survivors.

Lesbian, gay, and bisexual youth are generally at higher health risks than their heterosexual peers (Lock and Steiner, 1998). This discrepancy is due to a number of factors, which include but are not limited to family rejection, homophobia in society, internalized homophobia or self-hatred, and lack of appropriate resources that are sensitive to the issues of lesbian and bisexual youth. These issues must be explored in order to effectively bring about psychological growth with lesbian, gay, and bisexual adolescent rape survivors as well as adult lesbian and bisexual survivors, who are also at greater risk for mental health and physical health difficulties. For these reasons, thriving for lesbian, gay, and bisexual survivors must go beyond symptom abatement; cognitive skills and knowledge of resources must be provided with sensitivity to issues of identity and oppression. Benedict (1994) notes that lesbian, gay, and bisexual survivors, whether assaulted by men or women, have to explore and address issues of: self-blame because of internalized self-hatred for lesbianism, lack of support from family and community because of prior rejection based on one's sexual orientation, feelings about the men in one's life if the perpetrator was a man, feelings about the women in one's life if the perpetrator was female, and sexual intimacy with one's partner regardless of the perpetrator's gender. For self-help, it is important for lesbian, gay, and bisexual survivors to utilize their social networks for support, to utilize the ways one has coped with homophobia in the past to deal with those who discriminate against sexual assault survivors, and to remember that one's sexual orientation does not provide justification for assault, violation, and violence.

How Does the Survivor Know When She Is in a Mourning Period?

- Is the survivor aware of specific losses that she experienced in the wake of the trauma?
- Is the survivor able to feel sadness and sorrow?

If her answers are yes, the survivor is mourning. This is a healthy step in the survivor's recovery process. It may occur again as time passes. This is natural and to be expected.

If the survivor's answers are no, she should take time and energy to connect with her feelings. She may not feel comfortable sitting with her sadness and losses at this particular time. She should not be pushed or rushed, however. When the survivor is ready and feels safe, she will be able to sit with her feelings. The ability to sit with feelings is a skill that the therapist can help the client develop through cognitive strategies. By learning affect moderation, connection, and healthy expression, the survivor can move forward on the path to wholeness.

Whether the survivor has already been in mourning or not, the activities on the following pages will assist her on her journey.

Journaling/Poetry

Read and try to remember this affirmation.
Affirmation: I acknowledge the sadness I feel for the ways the traumatic experience has affected me.

Activities:

1. Write a poem about the consequences the traumatic experience has had in your life.
2. Write a description of the person you were before the traumatic experience occurred.

3. Write a list of the things that you would like to get back, such as your self-confidence or your trust.

Movement

Read and try to remember this affirmation.
Affirmation: I grieve for the impact the trauma had on my body,
my heart, my breath, and my walk.

Activity:

Pick an object to represent the person that you were before the traumatic experience. Make sure it is an object that you can carry. Pick up the object and begin to move around the room carrying it. Walk with it through the depression, through the shock, through the anger, through, the emptiness. Now sit down or lay down and be present with your former self. You may rock with it, lay still with it, caress it, or just look at it. Now stand up and breathe slowly seven times.

Arts and Crafts

Read and try to remember this affirmation.
Affirmation: I have wounds but I am healing.

Activities:

1. Draw a representation of yourself the week after the traumatic event occurred.
2. Draw a representation of how you would like to see yourself in the future.

Music

Read and try to remember this affirmation.
Affirmation: I give myself permission to mourn.

Activity:

Find a song that is usually sung at funerals. It may be from your religion or cultural group, or you may want to find one from another culture. Play the song three times, or if you know it, sing the song three times. Allow the melody and lyrics to fill you. Sit with the feelings of the song. Write a reflection about how you are feeling after the activity.

Spirituality

Read and try to remember this affirmation.
Affirmation: Grieving is a part of the healing journey.

Activity:

Create a ritual for yourself to represent your mourning. You can make
the ritual as large or small as you like. You can do it in your home, your
religious meeting site, or outside in nature. You may want to wear a certain
color to represent your mourning, your past self, or your future self. You
may want to read certain poems or holy texts. You may want to sing certain
songs. You can consider including dance or movement, specifically you
may want to lay down, kneel, walk, run, or dance. Depending on your
preferences, you may want to sit quietly and light a candle. You can even
ask another person to come and bear witness to your ritual. It is your
ritual. Plan it in a way that allows you to express your feelings in a
healthy, safe way.

Social Support

Read and try to remember this affirmation.
Affirmation: Those who care for me acknowledge the sadness of my loss.

Activity:

Ask someone who knows you well if they have noticed any changes in
you since the traumatic event. Sometimes others notice things that we
may not see. Write down their comments. If the trauma happened when
the survivor was a small child, observe a child who appears to be
happy and safe. How do you imagine your childhood was compared
to the child you observed? Share your observations with a friend or
counselor.

Nature

Read and try to remember this affirmation.
Affirmation: My recovery is important. My life is important.

Activity:

Go to the library or look on the Internet at the impact of fire and storm on
trees. Look at the pictures of the trees. Then, write how your experience
is similar and different to the experience of the trees.

Activism

Read and try to remember this affirmation.
Affirmation: My tears fuel my commitment to making a difference in the world.

Activity:

Make a donation of tea, Kleenex, or blankets to a place where people may
be grieving. A counseling center, shelter, crisis center, victim advocates
office in a courthouse, or a religious site. If you don't have money to
purchase items to donate, you can donate your time. Volunteer a few hours
at an agency for survivors.

Survivor Case Summary April is a Jamaican lesbian survivor of sexual harassment, racial harassment, and homophobia. She works as a cook in a restaurant where she was sexually harassed by her white supervisor. Her employer
touched her sexually on multiple occasions and made sexually inappropriate
comments to her when she was alone and around other employees. The comments were both racist and homophobic. April came to America when she was in
her late teens. She enjoys cooking and before the harassment she loved her job.

A few of the waiters in the restaurant began asking April questions about her
sexual orientation, and when she disclosed that she is a lesbian, her coworkers
began making derogatory comments about either "wanting to show her what a real
man can do" or telling female employees to watch out because she may "attack
them." When April complained to her supervisor, he laughed and began to join in
the harassment. He grabbed her sexually on multiple occasions and began making
sexual comments about black women, Jamaican women, and lesbians.

In Jamaica, April experienced isolation and rejection because of her sexual
orientation. When she came to the States, she found support in a community of
lesbian women. This was the first time April experienced sexual harassment
and homophobia at work as well as her first time experiencing racial harassment. April was devastated that her skills as a cook were not enough to grant
her safety and security at work.

She sought counseling when she began crying every morning and night,
after she began dreading going to work. April was considering taking action or
quitting her job, but was unsure of her options. Along with problem-solving related
to the harassment, April was mourning the multiple losses caused by the traumatic
experiences. Her losses included: loss of emotional and physical safety, loss of
confidence, loss of the joy of cooking, loss of happiness with her employment, loss
of a sense of control, loss of trust in her coworkers, loss of trust in her employer,
loss of belief in the "American dream," and loss of confidence related to her
identity as a lesbian, a black woman, and an immigrant. Although April had
experienced verbal abuse motivated by her race and sexual orientation, this was

the first time the harassment had become physical and the first time that it jeopardized her employment.

It was important for April to have a safe place to name and mourn these losses. She also needed a safe place to decide her plan of action given her emotional, physical, and economic concerns. Psycho-education about harassment was also imperative to assist April in resisting the tendency to blame herself for the abusive behavior of others. Along with counseling, April found the support of her mother, her network of friends, and prayer to be helpful in coping with the aftermath of the harassment. Initially, April wanted to try to stay at her job for financial reasons, but she soon found the continued harassment to be unbearable. She filed a formal complaint and is in process of waiting for the case to be resolved. April's process of mourning and psycho-education about the dynamics of sexual harassment, racial harassment, and homophobia were key to her moving from shame to a sense of empowerment.

8

Anger

"I just believe in the ancestors, I think a lot of them come through. I think I always rely on ancestral insight. I think it's just a part of me. I think I'm the grandfather and the baby at the same time. I rely on that because yeah, I believe in karma when it comes to what happened with my dad. The dude had a heart attack at thirty-five. You know, things come to light. I don't use karma as a vindictive factor, I mean, that's just the universe. You know, I just mean that's a—old black folks think that, yeah, they did bad, you got to suffer that. You got to pay. So I be careful and not have to pay for too much. You know what I'm saying (laughs) I got enough bills, I ain't trying to pay no karma, you know, on a doggone karma mortgage, unh unh, it's too heavy. . . . Yeah, he had to pay, you know."

—a survivor of domestic violence

"Reflections of an African-American male survivor who as a child was sexually abused by a white male: In my study of history I can see how, you know, and this may be a broad statement, but my study of history, I can see how that tied into their culture. I mean, you know, so it's expected. So when you have a young African and a young European, there's no telling what can happen. Look at all the countries that's had European colonization, European rule. It's not a mystery. You see my point? Personally, I know that's helped me make sense of it and in my study of history and culture and everything, when I found out about their collective history, I see where he fit in just in the modern state and in the African tradition, in the subculture of hip hop he needs to be dealt with. . . ."

What Is Anger?

Anger is the feeling of annoyance and irritation. It is stronger than the feeling of being upset, but not as intense as rage. Anger may be directed at oneself, at other people, or at situations. People respond differently to anger. When the survivor is angry, she might do any or none of the following:

- Scream
- Cry
- Fight
- Clench her fists
- Grind her teeth
- Run away
- Shake
- Shut down and close into the self

How Does Trauma Relate to Anger?

Anger is a healthy response to traumatic events. Being violated is upsetting. The survivor did not deserve to be violated. When we believe that we did deserve it, we become angry with ourselves or are only able to feel sadness. Getting to a place that allows the survivor to feel anger toward those who violated her and at the violation itself is a step in the recovery process. It is important to feel anger without being consumed by rage that is uncontrollable and/or consuming (Bratton, 1999). It is also important to not get stuck in anger. Roth and Batson (1997) note that one of the consequences of trauma is difficulty with the modulation of anger. Survivors may feel overwhelmed by their anger and therefore try to suppress it or internalize it. It is healthy for the survivor to allow her anger to motivate her to work on healing her wounds and fight against violence and discrimination. The survivor's goal should not be to take on the characteristics of the one who hurt her, but she does want to come to a place of recognizing that as a human being they are worthy of safety and respect.

How Does One's Disability Affect the Experience and Expression of Anger?

Persons with disabilities often have to resist the limitations and stigmas held by people without disabilities. This includes the limited and discriminatory view of persons with disabilities as being childlike or without effective lives. These stigmas are dehumanizing and deny survivors a safe place to express and explore their feelings, including anger. Survivors with disabilities may also have to confront the discomfort of others when they attempt to communicate their anger. Others may attempt to shut down the emotion or punish the survivor for their expression. The survivor should be affirmed that anger is a healthy response and should also receive psycho-education about constructive versus destructive communication of anger. The constructive strategies should be sensitive to the person's capabilities. In other words, to require highly intellectualized and complex articulation of emotions from a person with a mental disability is to mandate them to silence. There are a number of strategies, listed earlier, for a person to express and explore anger, including use of visual and expressive arts. Anger that is silenced is destructive to the survivor; there has to be a safe place to constructively express one's feelings.

How Might One's Economic Status Affect One's Anger?

The survivor may have grown up in an environment where anger was an acceptable emotion to express and one that was expressed often. Now the survivor may be in a context where people do not show their anger or they communicate it differently. It is important to observe these distinctions so the survivor doesn't end up feeling isolated or punished for their affective expression. Anger is a normal response, but the survivor does not want his behavior to result in people isolating him and therefore ignoring the pain that he has experienced. Therapists needs to help him find ways to express his feelings in a way that people can hear. It is, however, important to know that sometimes people cannot tolerate anger, even when it is being expressed in a nondestructive way. The survivor needs to be encouraged so the emotional limitations of others do not cause the survivor to internalize and repress his feelings. Hooks (1995) states that the majority of racial minorities who live in poverty, specifically African-Americans, are rendered invisible to people of privilege, and that "this class-based cultural neo-colonialism" acts to censor and silence efforts to name the pain and heal the wounds of many. Resistance therefore to classism, along with other forms of oppression, is critical for emotional wholeness.

How Might One's Gender Affect One's Anger?

Girls and women are often discouraged from having or expressing feelings of anger. This results in the anger being turned inside as self-blame, shame, and depression. If someone has hurt the survivor, she has a right to feel angry. It is healthy and normal. Feeling anger is a part of the woman's recovery and a part of having a complete, whole life. As long as the survivor doesn't surrender to destructive anger that involves self-destruction or destructive activity toward other people, animals, or property, she should be encouraged to express anger in a healthy constructive way.

If the survivor is male, he may have been taught to express anger physically instead of verbally. This is not healthy and will likely result in the survivor being penalized for seeking revenge and/or displacing his anger. Sometimes displaced anger results in male survivors being abusive toward those they love. The survivor should be taught nonviolent ways of communicating so he does not become a part of a cycle of violence. Masculinity is often defined as social ascendancy and dominance through power, strength, coercion, and violence; a counter social definition of masculinity needs to be encouraged and expressed as being sensitive, nurturing, compassionate, and emotionally expressive (Hanke, 1992). The survivor should be encouraged to practice expressing his feelings with words and not misplacing his anger at those who care about him.

In addition, some racial minority male survivors may use violence as a way to prove themselves, to express their frustration, or to obtain societal rewards that are difficult to obtain due to racism and the cycle of poverty (Majors and Billson, 1992). Racial minority male survivors have to develop safe internal and external resources that allow healthy safe expressions of affect that do not extend to violence, danger, or disregard for the safety of themselves or others (Majors and Billson, 1992).

How Might One's Migration Status Affect One's Anger?

The survivor may have a different way of expressing anger depending on the cultural norms of his country of origin. It may be more acceptable to express anger in the survivor's culture, or he may come from a culture where anger is never openly expressed. It is important to determine healthy ways to express the survivor's anger.

How Might One's Race/Ethnicity Affect One's Anger?

In all cultures, trauma has a significant impact on emotional functioning (Herman, 1997). For example, Haj-Yahia and Tamish (2001) found in a study of Palestinian college students that those who were sexually abused reported higher levels of emotional distress, including hostility. In the United States, Briere and Elliott (2003) found in a multicultural sample of men and women that childhood physical and sexual abuse resulted in a range of post-trauma symptoms, including anger/irritability.

Similar to those who are immigrants, the survivor may come from a culture where the expression of anger is prevalent or where anger is very hidden. Regardless of the survivor's race or ethnicity, she should remember that destructive anger, or rage, hurts her and those around her. Constructive expressions of anger are healthy and normal. Racial and ethnic minorities may have anger and losses to mourn not only about the traumas that they have experienced, but also intergenerational or transgenerational legacies of trauma, such as slavery and the Holocaust (Harper, 1992). These feelings need to be explored and expressed, not silenced or minimized. This requires active resistance of the "collective cultural refusal to assume any accountability for the psychological wounding" of transgenerational traumas such as slavery (Hooks, 1995).

Another challenge the survivor will face, however, is the discomfort of majority group members when they encounter racial and ethnic minority group members who are angry. The survivor has a right to feel angry and to express it in a healthy way. Due to stereotypes about members of her racial or ethnic group, some people may become very afraid and distant when the survivor is angry. As long as she is not being destructive, remember that the survivor has the right to feel angry for the violation she experienced.

She may also experience fear of showing her anger because of the myths that others hold about people of the survivor's race or ethnicity. The survivor may try very hard to be the opposite of what others predict she will be. This may result in the survivor trying to constantly please others and be a perfect person, even if it means hurting herself or denying her feelings. This is not healthy. The survivor has to learn to acknowledge and express anger in a constructive way. While masking of emotions may have been useful in certain situations of racial oppression, it undermines intimacy and makes emotional availability and connection impossible (Hooks, 1995).

In understanding the affective impact of racism, Ocampo (1999) argued that due to the lived, historical, and chronic nature of racism, the racist intentionality of an event is secondary to its perception as a racist incident by targets. In other words, one does not have to agree that a negative incident was racially motivated to understand that it could reasonably be perceived as racism by a target—and therefore produce harmful sequelae. Perceived racist incidents result in negative psychological, social, and physiological effects (Clark et al., 1999).

Harrell, Hall and Tagliaferro (2003) investigated the role of racism as a chronic stressor and contributor to the development of psychophysiological disease such as hypertension and diabetes. Williams and Williams-Morris (2000) published a review of selected U.S. studies conducted between 1965 and 2000 that examined the mental health effects of prejudice and racism in African-Americans and other targeted groups. The mental health effects of racism fell into three general categories: 1) the direct consequences of institutional racism, resulting in unequal access to mental health care (which may be mediated by socioeconomic status); 2) racist experiences that "induce physiological and psychological reactions that can lead to adverse changes in mental health status" (p. 243); and 3) internalization of stereotypes that lower one's positive self-evaluation and psychological well-being.

In terms of category 2, Williams and Williams-Morris reviewed findings of both laboratory analogue and community self-report surveys that linked various kinds of racist experiences with cardiovascular and psychological reactivity, psychological distress, and depressive symptoms among a broad range of groups (African-Americans, gay men in New York, Hispanic women, Chinese immigrants in Toronto, Southeast Asian refugees in Canada, children of immigrants in South Florida and San Diego, and a national probability sample). Williams and Williams-Morris (2000) also found a positive association between internalized racism and increased alcohol consumption, lower self-esteem, lack of socio-emotional de-velopment in children of mothers who feel highly internalized racism, symptoms of depression, and chronic health problems. Kendall and Hatton (2002) propose that racism may contribute to the diagnosis of attention deficit hyperactivity disorder in children. For elderly African-Americans, institutional racism-related stress in particular impairs psychological health (Utsey et al., 2002).

Walters and Simoni (2002) are among the few to conceptualize racism and discrimination as unresolved historical and present trauma among Native American women, contributing to various physical and psychological sequelae such as post-traumatic stress disorder (PTSD) and depression. Racism has also been linked to PTSD in Asian-American populations and increased psychiatric and physical symptoms among African-Americans (Loo et al., 2001; Woodard, 2001).

How Might One's Religion Affect One's Anger?

The survivor's religion may teach that anger is sinful. Destructive anger is negative, but there is a difference between destructive anger and constructive anger. Destructive anger is aimed at hurting the self or other people. Constructive anger is aimed at protecting the self and expressing the survivor's feelings and experiences to others.

Some religions teach that healing or recovery is based on one's faith. In other words, if you have enough faith, you will feel better. This causes a challenge to trauma survivors because recovery is a process that takes time. Kennedy (2000) notes that some religious leaders have blamed survivors for their lack of healing by claiming that the true problem or sin is the survivor's lack of forgiveness. Some religious survivors may feel guilty that they are still struggling with post-trauma symptoms such as depression, PTSD, or eating disorders. They may have heard advice from religious leaders such as "Just get over it"; "Just leave your burdens at the altar"; "Give it over to Jesus"; "If you trust God to handle it, you won't have to worry about it anymore." While it is true that faith is a source of strength, it is also true that recovery from sexual violence takes time. Survivors should be reminded of narratives from the religious tradition in which restoration and healing took time. Recovery from trauma is work over time; it requires wrestling and persevering through the various symptoms such as flashbacks and anxiety attacks. The time required for one's healing is not a negative mark of one's faith; instead, it is a positive sign of one's perseverance.

How Might One's Sexual Orientation Affect One's Anger?

With the prevalence of negative stereotypes about gays, lesbians, bisexuals, and transgendered persons, the survivor may be very hesitant about expressing anger. The survivor may be afraid of feeding into the stereotypes of others or making him or herself vulnerable to further violation. Regardless of the negative assumptions of others, survivors have the right to feel and express their anger in a healthy way.

What Are Destructive Ways of Expressing Anger?

- Fighting
- Being verbally or physically abusive
- Shutting everyone out
- Destroying property
- Destroying the self with unprotected sex, alcohol, or drugs

What Are Constructive Ways of Expressing Anger?

- Telling the support person that the survivor is angry and the reason he is angry
- Sharing with those who support the survivor in his recovery about how he is feeling
- Acknowledging to the self how the survivor feels without self-judgment

Three Things to Remember

- The survivor did not deserve to be violated
- The person(s) who violated the survivor are responsible for their behavior
- Constructive anger is healthy. Destructive anger is not.

Survivors should be reminded of these pointers as they complete the following activities.

Journaling/Poetry

Affirmation: I can feel angry without losing control.

Activity:

Write a poem about your anger. You may feel it intensely or you may not feel any anger. You may be angry with yourself or at those who hurt you. You may usually express your anger with tears or with screaming. Whatever your experience with anger, write it in your poem. If you are uncomfortable writing a poem, simply write a description of your experience with anger.

Movement

Affirmation: I can express my anger without hurting myself or others.

Activity:

Think about the trauma that you experienced and the impact that it has had on your life. Now think of a movement that matches the feeling of the word NO. The movement may be a kick, a punch, a lunge, or any other movement. With each movement say the word NO or another phrase that is meaningful to you. If you try this activity and feel unable to connect with your anger, mark this activity and come back to it later. If you have problems with anger management and are afraid that you may lose control while doing this activity, ask someone to sit with you before, during, and after this activity. If you don't have someone who can be present with you at this time, mark this activity and come back to it when you have someone who will be present with you. After the activity, sit down and breathe deeply seven times. You may want to journal or talk with a trusted friend after you have completed the deep breathing.

Arts and Crafts

Read and try to remember this affirmation.
Affirmation: I have the right to feel angry about being violated.

Activity:

Draw a picture that represents your anger. It may be abstract or specific representations of people and places. Your picture may have words written in it or it may be all symbols. Just think about the anger that you feel, and if you do not feel connected to anger, imagine what anger would feel like and draw what comes to mind. There is no way to do this activity wrong. This is for you.

Drama/Theater

Read and try to remember this affirmation.
Affirmation: If I am not safe or happy, I do not have to mask my feelings.

Activity:

Put an empty chair in front of you. Pretend the person who violated you is seated in the chair. Tell him or her about your anger. You can say as much or as little as you want. You may want to stand over the chair or sit eye-to-eye. You may want to scream or cry. Whatever you want to do or say to the empty chair is okay. You may want to kick the chair. As long as you don't hurt yourself or someone else, it is okay. If you do it the first time and don't feel anything, take a few breaths and try it again.

Spirituality

Read and try to remember this affirmation.
Affirmation: I choose to be constructive and not destructive.

Activity:

Pray or meditate about your anger. Focus on the need to be constructive
and not destructive. Spend at least fifteen minutes on this prayer or in
meditation.

Nature

Read and try to remember this affirmation.
Affirmation: I can feel anger without becoming stuck in my anger.

Activity:

Sit outside and look at birds or butterflies. Observe them flying or sitting.
Listen to see if they are silent or singing. Whatever you observe of the
birds' behavior, think about how it may relate to your anger. Write your
observation and thoughts.

Social Support

Read and try to remember this affirmation.
Affirmation: I can tell those I trust about my feelings.

Activity:

Tell a family member, friend, or counselor about your relationship
with anger. Tell them if you lose your temper quickly or if you have
trouble feeling and expressing anger. Tell them if there are ways
you have been destructive and about your plans to be more constructive.

Activism

Read and try to remember this affirmation.
Affirmation: My anger at injustice makes me work to eliminate it.

Activity:

Go to the library or a bookstore and get a book about trauma prevention.
It may be about sexual harassment, rape, domestic violence, physical

assault, racism, or homophobia. Read about how people in society can work
to eliminate these traumas. After you have read the book, write your
reflections. If you have trouble reading, see if there is a book tape available
at the library or bookstore.

Survivor Case Summary Patience is a thirty-year-old West African Muslim
woman. She came to America for college. Patience came in for counseling with an
intense amount of anger. At the time of assessment, Patience's anger was displaced on anyone she encountered. Her attributions regarding her anger were
that "either everyone is crazy or I'm a magnet for drama." Patience would become
enraged by incidents that most people would consider minor.

While Patience was concerned that her anxiety was high, it was difficult
for her to disclose to herself or to the counselor the source of her anxiety
and anger. During the initial assessment, Patience gave very few details about
her childhood, repeatedly describing her upbringing as "normal" or "un-
eventful." After a few months, however, Patience felt safe enough to disclose a
history of childhood trauma. Patience had been physically abused by her
mother on a regular basis. Additionally, her father had sexually abused her
from age eight until eighteen. Patience has memories of her mother walking in
while the abuse was occurring and not intervening. When she tried to tell her
mother the first time, her mother ignored her, and when she tried again a
second time, her mother became physically abusive. When Patience was sixteen, her mother came to the States, leaving her behind with her father and her
father's other wives. The sexual abuse became more regular and her other mothers were emotionally, verbally, and physically abusive. At eighteen her mother
had saved enough money for Patience to come to the States, and she was able to
get a scholarship to a local community college. Patience and her mother rarely
spoke, and within five months of coming to the States, Patience moved out and
began renting a room in an elderly couple's home.

Patience completed college and lives a very isolated life. Her job does not
require social connections to others and she does not have close friends. During
counseling, as Patience began to recount the physical and sexual abuse of her
childhood, she was able for the first time to express the anger she felt: anger at
her father, her mothers, herself, her country of origin, and Allah. She was
angry at her parents for abusing her, angry at herself for not being able to stop
it, angry at her country because she felt abuse of children, especially girls, was
accepted, and angry at Allah for not rescuing her.

By creating a safe place to explore all of these themes, Patience was able
to gain power over the memories, connect with her sense of loss, and release
the self-blame that was consuming her. After working through these issues,
Patience decided to write her mother a letter. Although her mother did not
respond to the letter, Patience felt closure and a sense of accomplishment
for facing the past and telling her mother the impact the trauma has had on her

life. Patience was also able to distinguish her faith and her country from the abuse, which enabled her to connect with other Muslims and gain a sense of pride in her country and culture. She also became more comfortable with herself and as a result was better able to make social connections. A number of acquaintances acknowledged the change they noticed in Patience's demeanor, and this gave her a great sense of accomplishment and growth.

9

Body Image

"I would say that praying was probably the most helpful because there's just Someone so benevolent and so loving that's really listening to you, that's helping you work these things out, and it helps you to sort things out in your own mind, because even though he, she, they can't talk back to you, it's giving you room, an area to think about them, sorting them out, to understand that touching your body doesn't mean touching your soul."

— a survivor of sexual assault

What Is Body Image?

Body image is the regard the survivor has for their physical appearance. It includes the survivor's thoughts and feelings about their weight, features, hair, and complexion. Body image can be positive, negative, or a combination of both. Body image is shaped by messages from the media, family, peers, and the self.

Comments that reflect negative body image include:

- I'm ugly
- I'm too fat
- I'm too skinny
- I'm weak
- I have horrible skin, thighs, hair, etc.

How Does Trauma Affect Body Image?

Some survivors who experience sexual violence develop a self-loathing of their bodies and blame the physical body for the assault. Some sexual abuse survivors, on the other hand, develop with the feeling that their body is all that they have to offer.

If the survivor experienced domestic violence or other physical violence, she may have injuries that cause her to feel ashamed of her body. Survivors of domestic violence often work constantly to hide the bruises and scars.

Some survivors of racial or ethnic discrimination develop internalized racism and begin to wish they looked more like those who are in power. Mainstream media images of beauty often do not reflect the survivor's beauty and may leave her questioning her beauty and value.

Some adult survivors of childhood sexual abuse worry that they developed too soon and therefore blame their physical development for the violence perpetrated against them.

A major component of trauma recovery is for the survivor to come to a place of respect, appreciation, and love for their body. The survivor's body is not her enemy. Her physical body deserves the survivor's care and compassion. It is a part of the survivor, yet it is not the full definition of her. There is more to the survivor than the physical self, but the physical self does deserve care and respect.

How Might One's Physical Disability Affect One's Body Image?

Living in a society where beauty standards are set on notions of able-bodyism, it is challenging for persons with disabilities to develop and maintain positive body esteem. Creating a positive body image in the face of media and social campaigns that promote beauty ideals that oppose one's natural physicality is a major challenge. One that can be met through positive socialization messages from one's support systems as well as products and media that utilize a range of body types and disabilities. The experience of interpersonal trauma for survivors with disabilities then compounds the challenge of positive body image development by creating new sources of shame and feelings of body betrayal. These are additional and multiplicative factors that survivors with disabilities must face.

How Might One's Economic Status Affect One's Body Image?

Healthy foods are often expensive. If the survivor lives in a low-income area, there may not be a local supermarket but instead small corner stores that don't always have fresh fruits and vegetables. Even though it may take more effort, it is important to find ways to nurture the body and cultivate an appreciation for one's health.

How Might One's Gender Affect One's Body Image?

Girls and women are often taught to idealize body types that are unrealistic. This makes hatred and shame over the survivor's body a regular part of her thinking. Images in magazines, movies, advertisements, and videos promote beauty ideals that are not healthy physically or emotionally. Although it is hard to do, it is important to resist the messages of the survivor's family, peers, the media, and the perpetrator. The survivor's body is not disgusting or bad.

Weems (1993) provides the following reflection on body image and sexuality: "Sex is the one aspect of our being that we express the most, but know the least about. Very few of us ever become comfortable with our own bodies, even fewer of us ever become comfortable with our sexuality (p. 97).

A growing number of males are also developing eating disorders and a negative body image. The ideal for male bodies is very muscular and unrealistic for anyone who doesn't spend hours at the gym every day. While it is hard to resist the messages around us, the survivor's body is worthy of respect and care.

How Might the Survivor's Migration Status Affect the Survivor's Body Image?

In the survivor's country of origin, very thin may be the ideal, or a fuller bodied woman may be the ideal. It is important for the survivor to unpeel the layers of messages from her current country's culture and her former country's culture in order to find an appreciation for her body. Rituals that incorporate movement can also repair body image; through community rituals, stress can be alleviated and anxiety can be replaced with comfort and confidence (deVries, 1996). When a survivor is away from her community, it is important that variations of these rituals or substitutions for them bring wellness to the survivor's sense of self, including her physical self.

How Might the Survivor's Race/Ethnicity Affect the Survivor's Body Image?

The survivor may have received negative messages about her body depending on how much her looks differ from the ideal beauty image promoted by the racial/ethnic majority where the survivor lives. A part of the myths about people of the survivor's race or ethnicity may even be that they are hypersexual and incapable of being sexually violated (these myths exist about African-American women and Latinas) or that they are sexually submissive and enjoy being dominated (this myth exists concerning Asian women). All of these myths are damaging and place the responsibility of the violation on the woman's body instead of on the perpetrator. However, Collins (2000) notes that racially marginalized women attempt to define themselves outside of stereotypical images of mammies, welfare mothers, matriarchs, work mules, and sexually immoral women. Their self-definition includes a resistance to society's myths and a radical move toward self-acceptance based on identity markers such as self-reliance, work ethic, connection to family and community, spirituality, sexuality, independence, and empowerment (ability to effect change).

People may believe that members of the survivor's race are violent, and therefore they do not take the violence against her body seriously. The historical devaluing of racial minorities' bodies creates barriers to outrage and justice when it comes to the violation of women of color's bodies.

When racial violence is articulated, Tillet (2002) notes that it usually is focused on police brutality and lynching of African American men's bodies, while violence against African American women, interracial and intraracial or largely made invisible and inconsequential. Combating the racial injustice and violence against the bodies of racial minority men, has led to a lack of protection of racial minority men (Tillet, 2003). There is a need for space and freedom to fight racial and sexual violence simultaneously. Another challenge concerning body image is the myth of minority group members being physically strong and athletic. This being the case, people may assume that if the survivor had fought harder, she would have been able to avoid being violated.

Regardless of others' beliefs about the survivor's body, she is beautiful and her body is worthy of respect and care. Coming to believe this requires active resistance of societies' myths and active acceptance of a positive sense of self, including one's racialized and gendered self. Resistance of internalized racism in relation to beauty requires that people love themselves, and this self-love is a "radical political agenda" (Hooks, 1995, p. 119). To find beauty in one's African, Latina, Asian, Native American, or Arab reflection requires a rejection of society's perception of one as ugly, undesirable, animalistic, and monstrous. This is radical self-love that requires active resistance and positive racial socialization.

How Might One's Religion Affect One's Body Image?

The survivor's religion may teach her that sexuality, even when it is against her will, is dirty and stains the survivor. It is important for the survivor to know that she is not evil, marked, dirty, bad, or unlovable. Her body is a gift of creation. Consensual sexual intimacy is a beautiful gift. The violation the survivor experienced in the past does not define her or her body. It was not her fault. The survivor did not deserve it.

Many religious communities can go many years without ever providing a sermon, homily, or study lesson on rape or molestation. Sex in general is a subject that is often silenced in many religions. If the survivor has depended on her religious community for support and education, she may interpret the silence of the community on these issues as evidence that they are not significant or that she should be ashamed of them and not discuss them. Kennedy (2000) notes that there is a pervasive myth in religious communities that children and women are safe within the boundaries of social interactions with other members of the community; this is clearly not the case, as violence and trauma affect all communities regardless of religion.

The therapeutic relationship may be the first opportunity for clients to discuss their sexual history and concerns with another person. It is important to provide a safe forum for these discussions as well as for any education that may be required on such issues as physical arousal that may occur during child sexual abuse, even though the child emotionally and mentally may be upset, confused, or afraid. A possible example to use to describe this physical response that some survivors may have experienced is the fact that even when people don't want to be tickled, if someone tickles them they will laugh. It is a physical reaction, not an emotional sign of happiness. It is important for the physiology of the body to be understood to understand the response to trauma, including arousal, shock, freezing, and dissociation.

How Might the Survivor's Gender Identity Affect the Survivor's Body Image?

If the victim is a transgender survivor, this person already has a very complicated relationship with their body. The survivor feels disconnected from the body they were born with or even betrayed by it. It is important to recognize that the body is a part of the survivor and a part that deserves care and compassion.

How Can Survivors Improve Their Body Image?

- Make positive statements to themselves about their body
- Eat healthy foods
- Exercise in moderation (not excessive)
- Respect their body and their life enough in their choices regarding sexual activity
- Reject beauty myths and ideals that do not include the survivor
- Find aspects of the survivor's body to celebrate in terms of both beauty and strength

Finally, to continue working on their self-image, survivors can be encouraged to try the following activities.

Journaling

Read and try to remember this affirmation.
Affirmation: My body deserves respect.

Activities:

1. List as many things as you can that you like about your body.
2. Write a description of the impact the traumatic experience had on your body and/or your body image.
3. Write a description of anything that you do that is not good for your body.

4. Write a letter to yourself expressing appreciation for your body and
   detailing the ways you will honor your body better.

Spirituality

Read and try to remember this affirmation.
Affirmation: I am amazed by the creation of my body temple.

Activity:

Write a prayer concerning your body image, or use this prayer
written by Reverend Bryant (1995) in her book *I Dance with God*: "God,
this is my body. She is an expression of your genius. Give birth in my
body to a spirit of exaltation, wonder, reverence, praise, and
hope...Amen" (p. 35).

Movement

Read and try to remember this affirmation.
Affirmation: I am beautiful.

Activity:

Stand in front of a long mirror or a large window that allows you to see
your reflection. Breathe deeply three times. Start with your head. Move
your head in your own way as you count to eight. Then say "Beautiful.
Absolutely beautiful." Then proceed through each body part, moving it for
the count of eight and then saying the affirmation. Go from your head all
the way to your feet. After you have finished with your feet, move your
entire body for eight counts and declare "Beautiful. Absolutely beautiful."
Stand still and breathe deeply seven times.

Arts and Crafts

Read and try to remember this affirmation.
Affirmation: My body deserves respect and appreciation.

Activity:

Get one or a few magazines. Choose a magazine that has pictures of diverse
body sizes and racial backgrounds. Create a collage with the different

pictures and words. The collage may represent a positive or negative body image or a combination of both.

Music

Read and try to remember this affirmation.
Affirmation: My body is a part of me.

Activity:

Write a song and then sing it. Words to include in your song are: beautiful, body, strength, and respect. If you have trouble writing a song, find one that is affirming and encouraging.

Drama/Theater

Read and try to remember this affirmation.
Affirmation: I will compliment myself and encourage myself.

Activity:

You are going to play the part of two characters. First, play the role of the part of you that usually says and/or feels negative things about your body. What are the discouraging messages you tell yourself about your body? Say those comments aloud. Then sit still and breathe deeply seven times. Now take on the role of the part of you that wants to feel good about your body. Say all of the things that person would say to you. Say it as if you believe it. When you have finished, sit and breathe deeply seven times. Finally, write your reflections on the activity.

Nature

Read and try to remember this affirmation.
Affirmation: I choose affirmation over negativity.

Activity:

Take a walk outside. Notice all of the beauty that is around you. Find beauty in things that you may not always notice. Look for beauty in the clouds, grass, flowers, trees, birds, and even insects. Look for beauty and you will find it.

Social Support

> *Read and try to remember this affirmation.*
> *Affirmation: I can give and receive affirmation.*

Activity:

Think of one nonsexual but physical compliment that you can give to a friend or family member. It may be that they have a nice smile, beautiful eyes, a nice hairstyle. Practice giving affirming messages about body image to others and also being able to receive those messages as well.

Activism

> *Read and try to remember this affirmation.*
> *Affirmation: I want to be a part of positive change in the world.*

Activity:

If you can afford it, donate a culturally diverse magazine subscription to a public service area that works with survivors. If you don't have money for a subscription, you may want to donate one magazine that features models of different body types and cultures. If the magazine is not in your budget this month, don't worry. There is no timeline for this activity. There will always be survivors who would benefit from affirming images and words.

Survivor Case Summary   Ebony is a twenty-year-old African-American female. She will be the first member of her family and first person from her community to graduate from college. Everyone is proud of her, including her four younger siblings, who consider her a role model. Ebony is very popular on campus and is very active in various student organizations.

Ebony was recently devastated by another student on her campus who sexually assaulted her. After the rape, Ebony developed an eating disorder. She began engaging in compulsive exercise, binging, and purging. She didn't want to upset her family, disappoint her community, or let down the members of the various student groups she led. As a result, Ebony kept the assault a secret. She coped by focusing on her schoolwork and her extracurricular activities. From the outside Ebony looked very successful.

Under the surface, she was crumbling emotionally and physically from the shame, self-blame, negative body image, and eating disorder.

Ebony's insecurity was rooted in the belief that something about her appearance had caused the assault. The semester after the assault, she began to work out constantly, wear baggy clothes, no longer do her hair or wear makeup, and began bathing less frequently. The drastic change in her appearance led some of her friends to encourage her to seek counseling.

During counseling, Ebony was initially very shut off emotionally. Once she began talking about the assault, however, she began sobbing for the first time since the attack. Along with facing the memories, shame, and anger, she also began to acknowledge and mourn the effect the assault had on her mind and body. She realized how she felt betrayed by her body, both because she froze during the assault and because she felt her body had attracted the attention of the perpetrator. She also confronted a sense of powerlessness for the first time in her life. Ebony had always excelled academically and socially, so the assault was the first time she felt she had failed herself. Through exploration of the memories of the trauma as well as psycho-education about sexual assault, Ebony was able to stop blaming herself and stop blaming her body. She was able to cut down on her binging and compulsive exercising, and stopped her purging behaviors. She was able to stop purging after she trusted herself and her parents enough to disclose the assault to them. They responded with incredible support, and this helped Ebony regain her self-confidence.

During counseling, her identity as an African-American female on a predominately white college campus was explored. Specifically, she discussed two major barriers to her taking action against the perpetrator. One was the fear of rejection from the already small African-American student population. The perpetrator is also a popular member of the African-American community, and Ebony feared that people would side with him in the matter. In addition, the experiences with racism and racial profiling by the police in her neighborhood created a great sense of distrust of the judicial system. As a result she feared that the police, judges, and lawyers wouldn't believe her. Although her parents wanted her to disclose the name of the perpetrator, she refused. She preferred to wait for the end of the year, when the perpetrator was graduating. During the year she advocated to get a change in dorm residence to minimize the chances of seeing the person who violated her. She also sent the student an e-mail requesting that he cease all communication with her; he complied with her request. With counseling and the support of family and friends, Ebony was able to create a sense of safety and self-esteem for herself.

10

Sexuality

Poetic reflection of a sex abuse survivor:

UNTITLED

My daddy is the greatest man in the whole wide world
    A coward, you say
My daddy kisses hurt away and makes it all better
    Your developing breasts are not hurt
My daddy cuddles me
    And squeezes me
And takes out all the fears
    A choken cuddle
A cuddle choken
    How can you breathe?
My daddy is a wonderful man
    My daddy is an awful man
My daddy loves me
    My daddy loathes me
But covers me in a sweet scent

What Is Sexuality?

Sexuality is intimacy and attraction. In its holistic form, sexuality can be a physical, emotional, and spiritual connection. Sexuality is both the attraction and the expression of that attraction.

What Are Healthy Forms of Sexual Expression?

- Sexual intimacy based on honesty and respect
- Sexual communication concerning one's safety, history, needs, desires, and concerns
- Emotional connection
- Spiritual connection
- Physical intimacy ranging from holding hands to sexual intercourse

What Motivates Some People to Become Sexually Active?

Elze (1992) notes a number of factors that motivate people to have sexual intercourse, which include but are not limited to:

- Fun and pleasure
- A sense of duty related to marriage or relationship expectations
- Rebellion, to defy parents and authority figures
- Disinhibition resulting from alcohol or other drugs
- For attention
- For affection
- For love
- For money
- For status with peers
- To prove "normalcy"

Elze (1992) writes that some LGBT youth feel pressure to engage in heterosexual sex in order to prove to themselves or others that they are straight.

There are also nonconsensual instances of sexual activity resulting from

1. Manipulation
2. Coercion
3. Physical force
4. Threat of force or punishment
5. Trickery or deception
6. Use of drugs and alcohol

How Does Trauma Affect Sexuality?

Traumatic experiences can have a number of effects on survivors. The stress of the traumatic experience can result in both loss of interest in sexuality for some survivors and hypersexuality in other survivors. The reasons some survivors lose interest in sexuality are: recovery can be overwhelming and mentally consuming; sexual trauma can result in intrusive thoughts of the trauma during sexual intimacy; negative body image from trauma can make physical intimacy extremely shameful. Also, in terms of lack of interest and/or fulfillment from sexual intimacy, some survivors were violated as children and developed with a negative sense of their bodies, others' bodies, and intimacy in general.

On the other hand, some survivors become hypersexual after the traumatic experience. Compulsive sexual activity is a form of hypersexuality. Reasons some survivors become hypersexual include: sexual abuse/assault survivors internalize the message that sexual activity is the only thing they have to offer; use of sexual activity for comfort; use of sexual activity as a distraction; unsafe sexual practices to punish themselves; conceptualizing sexuality as a form of power and control; use of sexual activity to resolve issues of insecurity and low self-esteem; and use of sexual intimacy as a substitution for emotional intimacy. When survivors of sexual violence blame themselves for the violation, they are more likely to remain silent about later violations and to have difficulty maintaining voice and self-efficacy in future decisions about relationships and sexuality (Wyatt, 1997).

What Are Unhealthy Forms of Sexuality?

- Obtaining sexual contact through harassment, threats, coercion, physical force, and/or deception
- Adult sexual attraction to children
- Sexual arousal that is based on violence, torture, and dehumanization
- Sexual addiction
- Addiction to pornography
- Inability to have sexual contact without terror and flashbacks
- Inability to be present during sexual intimacy/being emotionally detached
- Poor body image that results in shame during sexual intimacy
- An association of all sexuality with feelings of guilt

- An inability to discuss sexual concerns with sexual partner
- Extreme fear of sexual intimacy

How Does Having a Disability Affect One's Sexuality?

People with both mental and physical disabilities are often stereotyped as asexual. Along with the general deficit of media images of persons with disability is the particular absence of persons with disabilities in romantic roles. Often persons who have disabilities have to combat the myths about their sexuality, particularly myths of lack of interest and myths of lack of ability. It is important for all people, including persons with physical and mental disabilities, to explore and claim their sexuality in a healthy self-affirming manner.

Etaugh and Bridges (2004) provide the following review of research findings concerning sexuality and women with physical disabilities:

- Women with disabilities have spoken out about the lack of adequate counseling and medical attention related to sexuality and sexual health
- Women with disabilities report less satisfaction with their sex lives than able-bodied women
- Women with disabilities report not getting enough physical touching
- Most individuals with disabilities have the same sexual desires as able-bodied persons
- Women with disabilities report being less satisfied with their dating life and report having trouble attracting dating partners
- Their ability to perform sexually depends on the physical limitations of their disability and the availability of a helpful partner
- Able-bodied persons falsely assume that the disabled are asexual

How Does Economic Status Affect Sexuality?

Survivors who are impoverished may find themselves and their sexuality more vulnerable to abuse. Specifically, low-income neighborhoods have higher community violence crime rates. Additionally, low-income women are more vulnerable to sexual harassment in the workplace. Due to their economic dependence on the job, the employer makes this violation more difficult to escape.

Living on a low income can also make it more challenging to obtain quality sexual health care. Oftentimes, health care agencies that serve low-income neighborhoods are understaffed and underresourced. This results in a lower quality of care than that available to survivors who can make use of private doctors.

It should also be noted that poverty creates stress. When people are facing multiple stressors, they often experience a decrease in sexual drive. Survivors should know that this is a normal reaction to a stressful life situation. By developing coping strategies and social support networks and obtaining support from community agencies, counselors, or employment agencies, survivors can experience a decrease in their stress level.

It is important for impoverished survivors to know that their bodies are worthy of safety and protection. In addition, sexual expression is a healthy aspect of life.

Survivors who are wealthy experience the challenge of trust when it comes to sexuality and intimacy. Particularly, it may be challenging to determine if a person is interested in the survivor because of their wealth or because of who they are as a person. It is important for survivors to be able to develop trusting relationships in which there is mutual respect and acceptance. Sexuality is a healthy aspect of intimacy and emotional connection.

How Does Gender Affect Sexuality for Trauma Survivors?

Girls and women in U.S. society as in many societies are socialized to be the gatekeepers of sexual purity. This means that there is a greater social pressure and expectation for women to be more sexually restrictive than men. When women do not follow this social prescription, they are penalized. In the United States that penalty or consequence is usually one of verbal and emotional abuse through derogatory labels, such as "slut" or "whore." In some countries the consequence can be burning, other forms of physical assault, and even death. The murder of women who have sexual contact outside of marriage, even when that contact is nonconsensual, is called "honor killing." It is based on the perception that the female's sexual purity is a source of honor for her family, and women who are no longer "pure" have to be punished or killed in order to redeem the honor of the family. While "honor killings" are not common in the United States, there is the emotional and verbal attack of girls and women who either embrace their sexuality or are sexually violated.

Simultaneous to the pressure for sexual innocence is the pressure on women and even girls in our culture to be sexy. Family, peers, and the media communicate this expectation through socialization. Clothing and music in popular culture as well as the pervasiveness of pornography in our culture speaks to the demand for female sexual availability. These images and expectations are often not of healthy empowered sexuality, but instead objectification. The dangers of this objectification include the subduing of women's voices within the sexual realm concerning their needs, desires, and safety. While women and girls receive messages that make them responsible for male sexuality (blame for arousing men sexually if the woman is not willing to engage in intercourse) and for the issue of contraception, they are also given the message that they should not speak about sexual matters. This doublespeak of female responsibility and silence leaves many women disempowered sexually. There is then an ongoing cycle of silence in that women who were never given voice about sexual matters pass on this silence and shame to their daughters.

In addition, sexuality for survivors of sexual violence may now evoke feelings of dread, anger, or disgust (Warshaw, 1988). Women survivors may have difficulty for a number of reasons, including but not limited to loss of trust, physical injuries, emotional worries, inability to relax, diminished arousal, sexual discomfort, and intrusive thoughts (Warshaw, 1988).

Women of color in the United States have particular sexual social myths to combat. These myths are based in the sociocultural historical experiences of the treatment of racial and ethnic minority women. There is the myth of the asexual matriarch; the woman of color who takes care of others but has no sexual identity. There is also the notion that women of color are sexually promiscuous and animalistic and therefore incapable of violation. Another sexual stigma of women of color is that of the exotic being who is not quite human but is skilled in sexually pleasing her partner. Finally, there is the notion of some women of color as being sexually prone to submission and again incapable of violation. In pornography, many of the depictions of women of color are ones of violence and abuse. These myths serve to silence and control ethnic minority women's bodies and voices. By resisting these myths, women of color can reclaim and even celebrate their sexuality.

The challenge many men confront in the socialization of male gender role identity is being linked to their sexual ability and activity. The sexuality that many males are socialized to embrace through peers, family, and especially the media, including pornography, is one that is absent of emotional connection and intimacy. The disconnection between body and emotion is a barrier to holistic intimacy. To develop healthy sexual relationships, men have to resist societal norms and expectations of sexuality that are based on notions of power. The additional experience of trauma can intensify the emotional distance some survivors experience from their sexuality.

For men of color there is the additional challenge of racist myths concerning manhood and sexuality. There are two polar stereotypes of ethnic minority men. The first and most prevalent is the notion of ethnic minority men as sexually animalistic. This leads to the objectification of ethnic minority men as well as the false assumption that more ethnic minority men are sexual predators. The second stereotype is the asexual ethnic minority male who is seen as emasculated and invisible. These myths serve to both demonize and neutralize ethnic minority men. By resisting these myths, ethnic minority men can reclaim their sexuality.

Women and men have to develop a healthy sexuality that is based in communication, connection, and safety.

How Does Migration Status Affect Sexuality for Trauma Survivors?

Immigrants experience many components of culture shock. For some this cultural discrepancy includes the commodification of sexuality in the United States. The sexualization of children, the use of sexuality to sell objects, and the expression of sexuality in dress, music, and public can be quite disturbing to some immigrants. Additionally, recent immigrants may experience being eroticized by members of their new community. This erotization, while masked as affirmation, is actually objectification in which the survivor is not seen as a whole person but instead a fantasy of the observer. Along these lines, coming from a place where one is a majority member to a place where one is a minority requires the trauma survivor to reestablish their sense of self in relationship to the way the world around them perceived them.

For some survivors the source of their trauma was central to their migration. The trafficking and enslaving of people is an ongoing crisis that is causing trauma in the lives of millions. For persons who were trafficked for sexual slavery, either for an arranged marriage or forced prostitution, the issue of sexuality is particularly challenging. Reclaiming their sexuality involves addressing safety, shame, self-blame, trust, and intrusive thoughts. This work can best be done in the safety of a counseling relationship. A challenge, however, remains language barriers. The use of translators can be particularly difficult when speaking about experiences of sexual violation; the translator represents one more person in whom the survivor has to risk shame in sharing their experience. It is important for the counselor to proceed at a gradual rate and to assure confidentiality, especially when using a translator.

What Role Does Race Play in Recovering Sexuality for Survivors?

As described earlier within the gender section, racial and ethnic minority survivors have to combat the myths that exist about their sexuality. The awareness of these myths as well as cultural socialization of silence can serve as barriers to disclosure in counseling, in terms of sexuality concerns. The survivor may have been socialized with the notion that discussion of sexuality is inappropriate, or they may be concerned that the counselor or support group members hold certain biases regarding them and their sexual behavior. This relates to the notion of "healthy paranoia" among racial and ethnic minorities.

Particularly, psychologists have found that due to the pervasiveness of racism in our culture, it is a healthy response for minority group members to have a certain level of caution and concern with self-preservation. It is the role of the counselor, through honest discourse and cultural competence, to over time create a safe atmosphere where sexuality as well as other themes can be explored. (Some minority group members who have internalized stereotypes about their own group members may also hesitate to work with a counselor from their background because of the fear of that person's beliefs. For example, due to the role of religion and spirituality in the lives of some minority group members, the survivor may feel concern about sharing explicit sexual experiences with a counselor of their ethnicity or race.) It is important for survivors to find a safe place to discuss, explore, and embrace their sexuality, resisting the myths and stigma that others may place on them.

What Is the Role of Religion in Sexuality for Trauma Survivors?

Many religious traditions and teachers focus on sexuality as a negative entity. Specifically, some survivors struggle with the notion of sexuality as being sin, shameful, bad, dirty, and guilt-ridden. Sexuality for some is seen as something to resist or subdue, a part of the person that is a source of evil temptation. On the contrary, while sexual manipulation, violation, and abuse are negative, these things should not be a source of shame or guilt for the survivor; violation should be the shame of perpetrators, not survivors. Survivors should be informed that being violated does not mean they are stained, dirty, or ruined. This in fact is a wonderful opportunity to integrate the teachings of many faith traditions concerning hope, transformation, growth, love, and resurrection.

While the perpetrator does in fact harm the survivor, if the survivor is still alive, she has the opportunity to truly embrace life, including having healthy and safe experiences and expressions of her sexuality. While sexuality can be used as a tool of violence, to reduce sexuality to only negativity loses sight of the beauty it holds. Just as there is more to religion than religious wars, more to race than racism, and more to gender than sexism, there is more to sexuality than sexual degradation.

It is important for survivors who are a part of particular faith communities to be able to explore and appreciate the teachings of their faith in relationship to the development of healthy sexuality. Sexuality is a beautiful gift and one that can foster intimacy; true intimacy is a spiritual connection that is absent of manipulation, deception, or abuse. Williams (1992) notes that sexuality is not sinful but a spiritual gift; "both the spirit and the flesh are sacred" (p. 263). It is important for survivors to come to a place of celebration and affirmation regarding positive healthy sexuality.

Many religions teach their followers to value sexual purity and virginity (Kennedy, 2000; Weems, 1993, p. 110) and to not engage in sex outside of marriage. Sex outside of marriage is considered a sin. For this reason, many religious survivors who are violated sexually suffer from additional feelings of dirtiness, shame, guilt, disgust, and fear of damnation. Survivors may feel unclean and less worthy of the Creator's love or the love of other people as a result of being sexually violated. Survivors may feel stained and unclean, not only physically but also spiritually. They may feel that their souls are damaged. This pressure for sexual purity serves to further silence survivors of sexual abuse and assault (Kennedy, 2000).

It is important for survivors to understand two concepts related to this issue: (1) sexual violation is not their fault and is not a reflection of who they are or their worth as a person and (2) they are not beyond recovery, restoration, or healing. These concepts can be addressed through insight-oriented eye movement desensitization and cognitive behavioral approaches of cognitive restructuring, including challenging the evidence concerning one's self-concept. Supportive group psychotherapy can also be an effective context for survivors to challenge the cognitions they have adopted about themselves. Finally, use of the expressive therapies, such as visual art, creative writing, and movement, can be incorporated to address issues of shame and guilt.

What Role Does Sexual Orientation Have in Addressing Sexuality Themes with Trauma Survivors?

One of the challenges for LGBT survivors is the homophobic attitude of those around them. These attitudes include the tendency to define LGBT survivors solely as sexual beings. This exclusivity serves to dehumanize and eroticize and therefore disempower. Additionally, gay men face the stigma that they are pedophiles and sex addicts. These stereotypes serve to reinforce homophobia by instilling and maintaining a culture of fear and distrust. For lesbian and bisexual women there is minimization, objectification, and attempts to infiltrate and thus conquer their sexual expression. This serves to promote fear, hostility, and violence. Elze (1992) notes that some LGBT survivors engage in heterosexual sexual activity "to mask their sexual orientation or to attempt to force themselves to change." LGBT survivors have to resist internalized homophobia, including the myths concerning their own sexuality, on order to forge a healthy sense of self that is truly whole, including mind, emotion, body, and spirit.

Threats of "outing" someone as lesbian or gay also serve to silence LGBT survivors' sexuality.

Why Is the Development of Healthy Sexuality an Important Aspect of Recovery?

Moving from surviving to thriving requires integration and functioning of the entire being. This means that the survivor not only addresses her cognitions, but also her emotions, behavior, spirituality, sexuality, physical health, and social network. The expression of healthy sexuality is a component of total well-being. To aid the survivor in developing a healthy sense of sexuality, these activities can be utilized.

Journaling

Read and try to remember this affirmation.
Affirmation: I am capable of enjoying emotional
and physical intimacy.

Activities:

1. Write a description of the first consensual sexual encounter that you can remember. After you have written the description, write how you feel about the experience.

2. Write a description of the most recent consensual sexual encounter that you can remember. After you have written the description, write how you feel about the experience.

3. Write a description of your ideal vision of sexual intimacy. What are the characteristics that you feel are necessary for a healthy and fulfilling sexual experience.

4. Create a hierarchy of sexual activities that you would like to be able to do. Make sure the items on the list are not merely what other people want you to do, but activities that you truly would like to be able

to enjoy. List them from least anxiety-provoking to most anxiety-provoking. Then next to each item, write a check for things you are already comfortable with. For those things you are not comfortable with, write a projected time frame for when you would like to be comfortable with each activity. For the activities you are not comfortable with, write what specifically makes the activities uncomfortable and what you think may help you to be more comfortable. Helpful strategies may be: taking it slow, having your companion talk you through it, having the lights on, being in a different position, talking with your partner more to explore the issue and to increase a sense of intimacy and connection, or getting support and guidance from a counselor.

Arts and Crafts

Read and try to remember this affirmation.
Affirmation: I am connected to my body and to my feelings.

Activity:

Create a poster board that celebrates your senses. If you don't have use of one or more of your senses, complete the board using your other senses. Draw a representation of sounds that you find pleasing. It may be certain instruments, the sound of rain, the sound of your companion's voice, or any other sound. Now on the same poster board or sheet of paper, draw a representation of the things that are pleasing to the touch (examples include satin, bubble bath, or lotion), then things that are pleasing to you visually (examples include a sunset or the beach), things that are pleasing scents to you (examples include flowers, incense, and perfume), and finally things that are pleasing to your taste. Getting in touch with your senses is a way of learning to be present with yourself and with your surroundings. Healthy sexuality requires you to reconnect your body to your mind, heart, and spirit.

Movement

Read and try to remember this affirmation.
Affirmation: I move from shame to celebration.

Activity:

Imagine how you feel when you are ashamed of your body and/or yourself as a sexual being. Begin to move around the room carrying that shame

and discomfort. Let your body represent the feelings that you connect
with this shame. After you have moved in this way for a few minutes. Stand
still with your hands over your heart. Take seven deep breaths. Now
image what it feels like to be comfortable with your body and with
your sexuality. Begin to move around the room with a sense of celebration and freedom. Continue to move in this way for a few minutes.
Finally, stand still as you embrace yourself and breathe deeply seven
times.

Drama

Read and try to remember this affirmation.
Affirmation: I am comfortable with my sexuality.

Activity:

Put a chair in front of you and imagine the person who sits in
the chair believes sexuality is dirty, shameful, sinful, and/or anxiety-
provoking. Talk to the person in the chair about the beauty of
sexuality. If you have difficulty, you can write what you want to say
first and then read aloud your reflections. Once you are finished, reflect on
this exercise. Was it difficult, easy, confusing, or upsetting? If it was
difficult, you may want to try it again when you have completed the
book and again a few weeks later, once you have digested more of the
material.

Music

Read and try to remember this affirmation.
Affirmation: Sexuality can be safe and healthy.

Activity:

Find a love song that you enjoy. It may be instrumental, country,
soul, or any form of music. Get into a comfortable position and close
your eyes as you listen to the song. When the song is over, stand
up and stretch. Then listen to the song again in your comfortable
position. After listening to the song twice, write a reflection of the
thoughts and feelings that came up for you while you listened to
the song.

Nature

Read and try to remember this affirmation.
Affirmation: I celebrate the beauty of sexuality.

Activity:

Take a walk, preferably in a park. While you walk be sure to take deep breaths. Also be sure to observe nature around you. Take notice of the breeze, trees, flowers, birds, grass, and anything else you see during your walk. As you walk, think about your connection to the universe. Begin to take notice of yourself. Become aware of any tension in your muscles and try to relax as you walk or as you sit in the park. Relax. Relaxation is a gift to your body, mind, heart, and spirit. It centers you. If distracting thoughts come up, try to release them from your mind. This takes time and practice, but eventually you can be more comfortable with your presence in the world around you.

Social Support

Read and try to remember this affirmation.
Affirmation: I can talk about my sexuality in a healthy way.

Activities:

1. If you are sexually active with someone currently, think about a part of your sexuality you would like to talk with the person about. Possible things you may consider sharing are something you enjoyed the previous time you were intimate, something that you makes you uncomfortable sexually, issues of sexual safety (sexual history, contraception, etc.), or something you would like to try sexually. After you have shared, ask them if there is anything they would like to share with you. After you or both of you share, reflect on this activity. How difficult was it? Is it something you would like to continue to do? If you were to try it again, what might you do differently or the same?

2. If you are not sexually active with someone currently, think about a safe friend who you can try to talk with about sexuality. A good person to try this activity with is someone who you are not interested in becoming sexually active with and whom you feel certain is not interested in you sexually. This person should also not be in a relationship with another person because you don't want your conversation to be misinterpreted. Examples of possible people may be a safe long-term friend, family member, or therapist. Decide what you would like to share with the

person. It may be a concern that you have about sexuality, an experience that you have had, or simply the fact that you are reading this guidebook and trying to get more comfortable with your sexuality. After you have shared with the person, write a reflection about this activity.

Spirituality

Read and try to remember this affirmation.
Affirmation: I celebrate my spirituality and sexuality.

Activities:

1. Read through a spiritual text and try to find an affirming verse about sexuality. The text may be from your faith tradition or may be a poetic or inspirational poem from another text. After you have read the text, write your reflections.

2. Write a prayer concerning your sexuality or use the following prayer. Reverend Bryant (1995) in her book *I Dance with God* provides this prayer for making love: "Lord, we belong to you. Open us to each other's desire. Take the longing and joy to deeper realms than we have known before. Explode the boundaries of our imagination. In each other's arms, let us go to Heaven before we die. Pour down oils of passion in our bodies and then ignite us with eternal fire" (p. 37).

Activism

Read and try to remember this affirmation.
Affirmation: Everyone has the right to safety.

Activity:

Write a letter or call your local school or religious institution. Ask the school or institution to invite the local rape crisis center to come and conduct a free presentation for the local children about "safe touch"—a workshop to help children by describing the difference between "good" and "bad" touch.

Survivor Case Summary Jen is a middle-aged Filipino-American survivor of incest. Her father and older brother sexually abused her during her pre-adolescent years. They touched her breasts on multiple occasions and forced her to touch them sexually. Jen sought counseling as an adult because of her inability to relate to men romantically. She was attracted to men, but the thought of spending time with a male caused her great anxiety. Her treatment goal was to reduce her anxiety about men and to be able to gain comfort with emotional and physical intimacy.

As a young woman she confronted her brother, and he minimized the abuse and told her it was not significant and that she was overreacting. Since that time she tried to minimize the abuse herself, but has been unable to have a romantic relationship throughout her life.

During counseling, Jen was able to explore her feelings about the incest, including her sadness, shame, and anger. By exploring the shame she felt, she also began to explore the shame she experienced as a result of internalized racism and internalized classism. As an impoverished Asian woman who was abused as a child, Jen felt inferior to other women. To heal her self-esteem, the cognitions feeding her sense of shame had to be challenged. This included cognitions that were based in messages she received from the media, her peers, and her family.

In addition, to improve her comfort with her sexuality she developed the capacity to distinguish her father and brother from men in general. Jen was introduced by a mutual friend to a man she found attractive. They began spending time together and Jen went on her first date. She felt very comfortable and safe spending time with her new friend. Jen required a lot of psychoeducation and general health education about dating and sexuality—both of which she had never received information about. After a few months of developing coping strategies and relaxation training, Jen was able to enjoy emotional intimacy and physical affection. Jen has since terminated treatment and has been in a stable fulfilling relationship for over a year.

11

Coping Strategies

"I think about that moment and I learn how to prevent it from happening, and it's just basically being a better judge of character. Not being so casual, just going anywhere with—even someone you may know well, and their friends. And so in that situation it makes you more cautious but not unnecessarily so. Rightfully cautious. It makes you a better communicator. You cope because you're more understanding and sympathetic to other people's baggage because you realize that you have an issue. And you just . . . you just move on, because you, you know, sometimes you cope cause you got to, because you know, life is still going. I know it's not my fault, but I also have to make wiser choices, and also learn how to deal with this constructively so it does not affect my relationships."
                                        —a survivor of sexual assault

"Anything that I deal with, I always look for—actually, what I do now is I look for the good in it. So anything that I deal with, I'm like, there's some good in there somewhere. Where is it? So I try to pick it apart, find the good in it. Whereas before, I may not have done that. Dealing with problems, I'm like, well, I see the bad, I can't even see the good for looking, you know . . . looking at the bad. But now, I'm like, there's some good in there somewhere, I may not can see it now but I know God has something good in store for me. I may not can see it now [but I really feel like His plan is], He won't lead me wrong."
                                        —survivor of physical abuse

What Are Coping Strategies?

Coping strategies are cognitions and behaviors that are used to manage stress. There are both healthy and unhealthy coping strategies. These strategies can be learned from various people, including but not limited to: the coping patterns of our family and friends, strategies we observe in the media, strategies we learn in therapy, and strategies you learn through reading or taking courses.

How Is One's Use of Coping Strategies Affected by Trauma?

People first respond with the strategies that they are accustomed to using, particularly the strategies that have brought them relief in the past. Unfortunately, traumatic experiences can overwhelm our usual coping strategies. For example, the family member who is usually a source of support may not be comfortable talking about an abusive relationship or an experience of sexual assault. Also, some people who found prayer helpful in some situations may experience a challenge with how or what to pray in the aftermath of interpersonal trauma. As a result people sometimes turn to more destructive strategies to numb or distract them from the emotional pain. It is important for survivors to move from unhealthy to healthy coping strategies.

What Are Unhealthy Coping Strategies?

Unhealthy coping strategies compromise the survivor's safety, health, functioning, and well-being. Coping strategies that compromise the health and safety of others are also unhealthy. Examples of unhealthy strategies are:

- Self-medicating with alcohol and other addictive substances
- Compulsive sexual activity
- Avoidance
- Compulsive shopping
- Isolation
- Dissociation (disconnection from the self and the environment)
- Abuse of others (children, partner, pet, etc.)
- Eating disorders (overeating, starvation, binging and purging)
- Cutting
- Excessive exercise
- Poor boundaries (either very rigid boundaries that keep others out or very loose boundaries that do not allow time and maturation of the relationship before intense sharing of personal information)

While dissociation may have been helpful during the crisis in that it allowed the survivor to physically and emotionally disconnect from the horrors being enacted upon them (Bratton, 1999), it can become uncontrolled, unhealthy, and a predisposing factor in the development of post-traumatic stress disorder (Herman, 1997; McFarlane and Yehuda, 1996).

What Are Healthy Coping Strategies?

Healthy coping strategies are strategies that either assist in affect regulation, providing insight, or problem resolution. The survivor's ability to cope is essential, both in terms of her ability to cope with the post-trauma symptoms as well as the trauma itself (McFarlane and Yehuda, 1996). They can provide emotional relief and/or guidance for the future. Strategies that some survivors have found helpful include:

- Talking with friends or family
- Journaling
- Prayer or meditation
- Use of the expressive arts: drama, music, and dance

Drama or role-playing, as with a number of the strategies, can be helpful alone or in the context of therapy as a strategy to teach survivors assertiveness skills and to have them practice these skills in social interactions (Foa and Rothbaum, 1998).

- Visual artistic expression
- Relaxation (muscle relaxation and breathing exercises)
- Therapy (individual, family, and group)
- Medication when needed
- Humor
- Exercise in moderation
- Problem-solving
- Confrontation when it is safe (letting the perpetrator know the impact of his behavior)
- Seeking assistance from the justice system (pressing criminal charges, obtaining a restraining order, filing a lawsuit, pursuing restorative justice strategies such as community intervention and perpetrator accountability, etc.)
- Self-help books and Internet research
- Self-defense and/or assertiveness courses

• Group therapy or informal support groups
• Speaking with a spiritual leader
• Connecting with nature
• Engaging in fun, safe activities such as going to the movies or to a museum
• Activism when one has worked through the issues of the trauma

Regarding activism, while oppression has the power to enforce a particular worldview, to deny equal access, and to physically, emotionally, and mentally harm, the survivor has the power "to risk, to resist, to love, and live, with a fierceness of integrity and dignity despite and (unfortunately) at great costs" (Pelligrini, 1992, p. 54). It is important for survivors, beneficiaries of oppression, and bystanders to be empowered and motivated to work for change in society.

Culture plays a critical role in trauma recovery as well as in the efforts of society to promote or combat interpersonal violence. "Culture plays a key role in how individuals cope with potentially traumatizing experiences by providing the context in which social support and other positive and uplifting events can be experienced. The interactions between an individual and his or her community play a significant role in determining whether the person is able to cope with the potentially traumatizing experience ... Thus PTSD reflects the sociocultural environment in which it occurs" (DeVries, 1996, p. 400).

Coping refers to efforts to master conditions of harm, threat, or challenge (Monet and Lazarus, 1977). Folkman and Lazarus (1980) asserts that coping is the totality of physiological, cognitive, and behavioral processes through which the individual deals with the stressful situation. Coping strategies are responses whose purpose is to reduce or avoid psychological stress and negative emotions. Coping strategies include both cognitive and behavioral activities. There are coping activities designed to regulate the emotional reaction to the stressor, such as religious belief, denial, and optimism; there are also coping strategies that are direct, problem-focused activities such as information-seeking and resource generation (Lazarus, 1980).

While these well-accepted, general notions of coping are widely applicable across different cultural contexts, the influence of cultural context is nevertheless essential to consider. For example, the general tendency for children to feel safe and invulnerable does not apply to everyone. Several groups of people, often those with the fewest resources and the least ability to control their lives, feel vulnerable prior to their personal encounters with victimization. These persons include the elderly, women, and ethnic minorities. Recognizing the influence of cultural context, the importance of exploring the dynamics and recovery from violent experiences becomes evident.

How Do Mental and Physical Disabilities Affect Coping Strategies?

Survivors with disabilities have to find accessible resources for the coping strategy of their choice. Depending on one's location this can be a challenge. Some agencies are not wheelchair accessible, and this communicates a lack of awareness for the needs of survivors. In addition, many agencies do not have counselors who sign or interpreters for deaf survivors. Counseling is supposed to be a place of safety and acceptance, and agencies need to assess their accessibility and attractiveness to survivors with disabilities; "tolerance" is not an acceptable standard of care. When people feel they are a burden to an agency, healing is hindered. The access to care should be at a level where the dignity and respect of the survivor are not compromised.

For survivors with mental disabilities, use of expressive arts can be very helpful. There are biological and social barriers to disclosure for all trauma survivors; this is intensified with survivors who have mental disabilities. Use of the movement, music, and art activities in this guide can be quite helpful. In addition, expressive arts can be quite powerful with survivors with physical disabilities, so their ability to participate should not be discounted. For example, two of the most powerful uses of expressive arts with survivors that I have seen are the use of dance and movement with survivors who are wheelchair bound and the use of drama and poetry with survivors who are deaf. It is important for counselors and advocates to work with clients to ensure a high quality of mental health care.

Whether survivors choose to use professional services, social support, or internal resources for coping, every survivor needs to explore and embrace healthy approaches to coping.

What Role Does Economic Status Have in Coping Strategy Choices?

For impoverished and wealthy survivors there are barriers to use of the criminal justice system as a tool of coping. For impoverished survivors there is distrust of the criminal justice system, lack of resources for quality representation, and lack of awareness of the affordable options available to them. For wealthy survivors there is the fear of loss of privacy as well as loss of one's current standard of living.

Regarding counseling as a mental health coping option, there are two main barriers for impoverished survivors. The first is the economic barrier. Survivors may not be able to afford counseling and may not be aware of or have access to free or sliding scale services. The second barrier is the stigma of going to counseling. For many people, speaking with a counselor is outside of their experience and assumed to be for people who are "crazy" or without friends or family. This requires more public mental health education about the nature of counseling as well as its affordability. For those who choose not to use professional support, there are strategies that can be helpful as described previously.

What Is the Impact of Gender on Coping Strategies?

A positive for women is the social acceptance of the use of social support as a coping strategy. The encouragement of social support networks is important to prevent the internalization and isolation often experienced by survivors. This is often a challenge for men and boys who are taught that manhood requires constant emotional strength or detachment and an ability to handle your problems alone. When social support networks are available and healthy, they can be an important resource for survivors.

It should be acknowledged, however, that unfortunately sometimes members of the social support network may also be overwhelmed or may be insensitive to issues of trauma, either because it reminds them of their own trauma history or because the topic generally overwhelms them. It is important that community members be educated about issues of trauma as well as appropriate responses. Members of support networks can be most helpful when they are sensitive and compassionate listeners who communicate belief and support. It is also important for concerned family or friends to be informed by the survivor of what would be most helpful to them. For example, some survivors prefer for a support person to listen and become a source of emotional support while other survivors prefer an action response such as problem-solving, transportation, child care, or other resource assistance.

What Is the Experience of Immigrants in Terms of Coping Strategies?

Immigrants may face many challenges when it comes to choosing the appropriate coping strategies. The first challenge is the separation from their social support network (deVries, 1996). They may not have family and friends in their new country of residence, and developing these networks can be particularly difficult in the aftermath of trauma. In addition, use of counseling may be difficult both because of the language barrier and need for translators as well as the cultural stigma of counseling that may not have been common in the survivor's country of origin. Use of the judicial system may also feel impossible, depending on the legal status of the survivor. For survivors who are in the country illegally, there can be intense feelings of vulnerability because of fear of deportation and lack of legal protection from perpetrators. It is important for agencies to engage in outreach within communities of immigrants. Survivors who are recent immigrants should explore a number of strategies until they find one that works well for them, whether it is spirituality, building support networks, or journaling.

What Role Does Race Play in the Utilization of Coping Strategies?

Racial and ethnic minorities may have a distrust of psychology (Neville and Pugh, 1997). This is connected to the history of medical and mental health professionals' abuse of and tendency to pathologize racial minorities. There is also a stigma attached to counseling based in the belief that counseling is for people who are weak or friendless. Combating these myths and rebuilding trust in the mental health profession requires community outreach and education.

The history and contemporary reality of racism in the criminal justice system also serves as a barrier to use of the justice system as a source of coping. This has resulted in a distrust and fear of police officers and the legal system. This barrier can be addressed only by community connection and active resistance to racial discrimination within the criminal justice system.

An additional issue with the criminal justice system is the false belief that survivors who utilize the criminal justice system are betraying the race. It is important for community members to be educated about trauma such that it is understood that the perpetrators of violence are the persons who are "betraying the race," not the survivors who are seeking safety and/or justice through the criminal justice system. By not holding members of the community accountable for violating other members of the community, everyone is disserved.

The intersection of racism and sexism also affects survivors by making disclosure of trauma to professionals and nonprofessionals difficult for racial minorities due to the fear of not being taken seriously (West, 2000; Wyatt, 1992).

For many racial and ethnic minority males there is a barrier to the use of social support. The realities of racism serve to block economic and educational opportunities for the majority of racial majority members. As a result of this reality and frustration, some men look for alternative expressions of manhood outside of the traditional role of provider. Majors and Billson (1992) developed the concept of "Cool Pose" or hypermasculinity in which men rely on posturing and emotional toughness as a way of proving manhood. This impedes the use of social support and the disclosure of traumatic events. This mandated silence, however, has left a few options for disclosure for racial minority men. One of which is the use of hip-hop lyrics. Hip-hop is a complicated coping outlet because, while it serves as a socially acceptable way for men who are often silenced to speak about the challenges they face, when not channeled as a healthy resource it can also be used as a way to communicate and support misogyny and violence. It is important for those who use hip-hop as a positive source of communication and therapeutic expression to be supported and encouraged as they continue to resist violence and express their realities.

There are a number of additional strategies, however, that racial minorities can and do utilize. African-American trauma survivors, for example, have been found to use social support, activism, spirituality, humor, the arts, and safety measures (Bryant-Davis, in press; Hill and colleagues, 1995; Wolfer, 2000).

While Folkman and Lazarus's (1988) Ways of Coping Questionnaire (developed on middle-aged Caucasian participants) has been widely used, Smythe and Yarandi (1996) conducted a factor analysis of the measure with 656 African-American women, and the factors that emerge suggest the need for attending to the intersection of culture and coping. Folkman and Lazarus's dataset has sixty-six items and eight factors: confrontive coping, distancing, self-controlling, seeking social support, accepting responsibility, escape-avoidance, planful problem-solving, and positive reappraisal. In Smythe and Yarandi's dataset of 656 African-American employed women, only thirty-five out of the sixty-six items loaded on a three-factor model: active coping (largely social support), avoidance coping, and minimization of the situation. The total variance explained by the three factors was 67 percent as compared to 46.2 percent explained by eight factors by Folkman and Lazarus. In an earlier study with 191 African-American women, only two factors emerged, and they were social support and positive reappraisal (Smythe and Williams, 1991).

It is of both scholarly and clinical importance that a systematic descriptive understanding is gained concerning the coping strategies of racial minorities. Many people of color do not seek therapy because it is not part of their repertoire of strategies. If therapists begin to gain a respect and an understanding of the strategies used by racially diverse survivors and find ways to incorporate them into traditional techniques, the therapeutic process may be more attractive to and effective for diverse survivors. Highlighting culturally relevant ways of coping is one way of understanding the strength and resilience of all survivors.

Overall it is important for racial minorities to be encouraged to use self-care, social support networks, activism, and other expressive, artistic, spiritual, or counseling resources. Silence, shame, and minimization have to be resisted in order for healing to occur.

How Does Religion Affect the Use of Coping Strategies?

Along with the impact of sexual violence on spirituality, more attention has been given to the use of spirituality and religiosity as coping strategies (Holzman, 1994). Religiosity has been associated with increased general life satisfaction and decreased distress; for African-Americans, religious coping has also specifically been associated with lower ambulatory blood pressure (Steffen et al., 2001). Specific behaviors include prayer, meditation, reading spiritual texts, attendance at services, and counseling or advising by spiritual leaders (Bryant-Davis, 2003).

Elliott (1994) found that the severity of adult symptoms for Christian survivors of childhood sexual abuse were mediated by the religious practices of the adult survivor. The use of religious ritual has long been documented as therapeutic for many persons of Eastern and Western religions (Galambos, 2001). Mattis (2002) found that religion/spirituality was used as a coping strategy to help (1) interrogate and accept reality, (2) gain insight and courage, (3) confront and transcend limitations, (4) recognize purpose and destiny, (5) achieve growth, (6) identify and grapple with life lessons, (7) define character and moral principles, and (8) trust in the viability of transcendent sources of knowledge.

Survivors who are believers in a particular religion may find various religious and spiritual strategies helpful, including but not limited to prayer, mediation, reading of texts, community worship experiences, and speaking with a religious leader (Few and Bell-Scott, 2002). This can be a positive source of coping, inspiration, and hope.

The challenge is to ensure that four pitfalls do not occur. The first is the equation of mental health with faith. By that I mean, post-trauma symptoms are a normal reaction to a stressful experience and should not be used as indication of a person's lack of faith or spiritual maturity. Depression and anxiety are not a result of lack of prayer or connection to God, and survivors who experience these symptoms should not be discouraged.

Second is the discouragement of other strategies. Therapy, journaling, the arts, and support groups are other helpful strategies for religious and nonreligious survivors. Survivors should be encouraged to use every resource available to them. Third, sometimes religious leaders who are trying to be helpful may suggest that the trauma was sent by God as a test of the survivor's faith. It should be taught and understood that it is not God's will or desire for rape to occur, for incest to occur, for domestic violence to occur. We can not teach a theology of God as a God of love and justice and then imply that God desires the physical and sexual violation of people. This is unsound theology and very damaging to humanity. Finally, as members of religious communities we have to resist the tendency to focus on forgiveness without any mention of repentance, remorse, accountability, or justice. Oftentimes there is pressure on the victim to forgive and forget without any attention being paid to the continuation of violence in our homes, communities, and institutions. There is a place for forgiveness, but recovery, healing, and thriving of individuals and communities take many more steps before reconciliation can be considered. These steps include safety, truthtelling, education, restoration, and accountability.

Holzman (1994) notes that religion can be both a source of comfort and conflict for survivors. While some religious principles may serve as challenges to the therapeutic process, religion can also provide a source of strength for some survivors. Five of these sources of strength are described below.

All-knowing.

Some religious survivors describe the relief they get from believing in the Creator's omniscience. As a result of the Higher Power knowing everything, survivors have the assurance that there is someone who believes them and understands the magnitude of the violation they experienced. Even if the perpetrator denies it, or if the survivor doesn't feel safe disclosing the violation to another person, she knows that the Creator knows. This can decrease feelings of isolation and self-doubt. There is One who has been a witness to her experience and knows that it is true.

Unconditional love.

Some survivors talk about the positive effects of knowing that the Creator loves them. Even if the survivor feels that no one else will love her or truly know her, she believes that the Creator knows and loves her, and this brings about peace and a better sense of self. It is important for survivors to strive to love themselves just as God loves them. With the blame and shame that is often associated with traumatic experiences, it is powerful for the survivor to believe or strive to believe in God's love. This also works against the belief that the violence was a punishment by the Creator or evidence that the Creator does not care about her. Belief in the Creator's love is a source of emotional and spiritual strength for the survivor and serves to destroy shame and self-blame.

Justice.

Many religious texts teach that justice prevails. Specifically, teachings include principles such as things that are done in the dark will come to light, the wealth of the wicked is stored up for the righteous, people reap what they sow, vengeance belongs to the Creator, and the first shall be last and the last shall be first. Religious survivors may find relief in the belief that even if perpetrators have not done time in the criminal justice system, they will be held accountable to the Creator for their behavior. A belief in justice can bring peace of mind and alleviate anxiety and anger.

Healing.

Most religions teach that restoration, transformation, and/or healing is a real possibility. A belief in healing and transformation is key for any survivor recovering from a traumatic experience. It also supports the foundation of counseling, which is based on the belief that recovery or healing is possible. Religious texts give many examples of those who are burdened, sick, wounded, oppressed, and even dead being healed. These examples are a source of strength to survivors, especially during periods when they are feeling stuck in the recovery process. A belief in the possibility of healing and recovery provides encouragement to religious survivors.

Ever present.

Some survivors express relief and strength from the belief that the Creator is always present. Believing that the Creator was with her through the violation and in her difficult moments after the violation gives the survivor a sense of protection, nurturance, and safety. Some attribute the presence of God as the protective factor that kept them from committing suicide or having a psychotic break. While the concept of God's presence can cause a challenge for some survivors who question the Creator's decision not to intervene or stop the violation, many survivors also attribute the presence of God during the violation as the protector of their sanity. It is important for the counselor to provide space to explore both the survivor's questions about God's action or inactivity during the violation as well as the client's gratitude for God's presence during and after the violation.

How Does Sexual Orientation Affect Use of Coping Strategies?

Due to the prevalence of homophobia, LGBT survivors may feel impeded by using coping strategies that involve counseling or the judicial system. Survivors may legitimately fear the biases of those with whom they come in contact. These biases include blaming the victim or not taking the violation seriously. These responses from those who are supposed to be in health and safety professions, such as police officers, counselors, judges, and administrators, are retraumatizing to the survivor. LGBT survivors, including those who face the additional oppressive forces of classism and racism, fear disclosure of the trauma as well as "outing" if their sexual orientation will result in the loss of emotional and financial support as well as possible violence from homophobic members of society (Robinson, 2002). It is important for LGBT survivors to find support and resources that are respectful and emotionally safe.

LGBT survivors may fear use of spirituality or religion as a coping strategy because of homophobia, rejection, hostility, and intolerance (Blumenfeld, 1992). Survivors should know the core principles of most religions include respect and love. There are some religious groups and teachings that do not promote hostility and hatred (Blumenfeld, 1992). It is important to find a safe place and people with whom one can explore and build upon their faith and spiritual development.

How Can a Survivor Develop the Use of These Coping Strategies?

These strategies can be developed by utilizing the exercises provided in this guidebook and with the support and guidance of a counselor. Below are some additional activities for the survivor.

Arts and Crafts

Read and try to remember this affirmation.
Affirmation: I use coping strategies that are safe and healthy.

Activity

Get an empty shoe box or other small box. Decorate the outside of the box with representations of the unhealthy coping strategies you are moving away from and decorate the inside of the box with representations of the healthy strategies you are going to use starting today.

Journaling

Read and try to remember this affirmation.
Affirmation: I can face the challenge of this day.

Activities:

1. Write a list of the unhealthy coping strategies you have used and a reflection on how those strategies have been negative for you and for those around you.
2. Write a letter to yourself reminding yourself of all of the reasons it is important for you to practice healthy coping.

Music

Read and try to remember this affirmation.
Affirmation: I chose to turn away from destructive habits.

Activity:

Find a song that you find soothing. For the next week start each day by playing the song and/or singing it. Consider the impact on your day of starting the morning with the centering and inspiration of this song.

Movement

Read and try to remember this affirmation.
Affirmation: I can acknowledge and explore my feelings safely.

Activity:

Think about how you are feeling right now. You may be feeling sad, angry, confused, numb, afraid, bored, happy, excited, hopeful, or pleased. Whatever you are feeling, begin to express it in your body. Move and dance in such a way that you express your feelings. Make sure you use your entire body to express your feelings. This may mean lying down, kneeling, spinning, running, jumping, or crawling. Feel free to express yourself and your feelings. If you felt very self-conscious when doing this activity, you may want to take a few breaths and try it again.

Drama

Read and try to remember this affirmation.
Affirmation: I am capable and creative.

Activity:

Pretend to be someone who usually uses destructive coping strategies. Take on that person's mannerisms and feelings. Now begin to talk as if you are this person who feels stuck relying on unhealthy strategies. The person you pretend to be may be addicted to drugs, alcohol, sex, food, or shopping. Really connect with the character and talk about the difficulty involved in giving up these unhealthy strategies. When you have finished, write a reflection of your dramatic expression.

Nature

Read and try to remember this affirmation.
Affirmation: I am able to experience peace and relief.

Activity:

Look at flowers. They may be in your home, in a park, or in pictures. Think about their color, shape, size, fragility, strength, scent, and petals. Think about how they reach toward the sun and take in life-sustaining water. How are you currently similar or different from the flowers you observe? What are you reaching toward? What sustains you?

Social Support

Read and try to remember this affirmation.
Affirmation: I am not alone.

Activity:

Ask someone to join you in a healthy activity such as exercising, going for a walk, going to the movies, eating, drinking tea, dancing, drawing, or going to a spiritual service. If the person is your therapist, instead of asking them to go with you, you may want to discuss your coping strategies and self-care activities with them during your next session.

Spirituality

Read and try to remember this affirmation.
Affirmation: Love and light are present within me.

Activity:

Talk with a friend, family member, or counselor about your spirituality. Share with them your religious or spiritual history and your current thoughts and practices related to spirituality. You can also share with the person the aspects of your spiritual life that you are happy about and the areas of concern or uncertainty that you have as well.

Activism

> *Read and try to remember this affirmation.*
> *Affirmation: I am using the resources and skills available to me. I am no*
> *longer a victim. I am empowered.*

Activities:

1. Pay attention to the media you come in contact with this week. Media includes commercials, television shows, radio, video games, newspaper advertisements, and magazines. Take notice of which media outlets encourage positive coping strategies and which outlets encourage negative coping strategies. Write a letter to the newspaper or magazine editor or to the radio or television station both commending them on any positive work they are doing and raising concern about any encouragement of negative strategies.

2. Acknowledge and appreciate institutions and people who are taking action to reduce violence and oppression.

Survivor Case Summary Miriam is a Jewish teenage survivor of stalking and gang rape. A teenager from her school began stalking her. He started by bringing her candy, stuffed animals, and flowers at school. Miriam told the student that she was not interested in him. He then escalated to sending her ten to thirty e-mails a day and waiting outside of her classes. Miriam then told him not only was she not interested, but that she was not allowed to date. The male student obtained her number from a mutual friend and began calling and hanging up on her parents. One day after school, the student and three of his friends followed Miriam home, pulled her into an alley, and raped her. They said they were getting her back for being a tease and "acting too good" for their friend.

Miriam immediately told her parents, and they were supportive and took her to obtain medical assistance and police involvement. Not long after the assault, Miriam had a miscarriage before she even realized she was pregnant. A few months after the miscarriage, Miriam began having sex with casual acquaintances. She felt her body was her way to communicate to people, to get them to care about her, and by initiating sex she felt empowered. Her parents found her journal in which she listed her sexual activity, and they brought her in for counseling.

During counseling Miriam was initially emotionally disconnected; she minimized the impact of the rape, the miscarriage, and the subsequent unfulfilling sexual encounters. With patience and normalization of Miriam's responses, she was able to confront the feelings related to the assault and the stalking. With the support of her parents as well as her decision to transfer schools, Miriam was able to work through her shame, losses, and eventually connect with her anger.

Miriam was able to learn to utilize a number of positive coping strategies including problem-solving (the decision to transfer schools), religion, journaling, talking with her parents and one friend, visual art, and dance. Her religion gave her a belief that hope is possible regardless of the current situation. In addition, Miriam feels that her dance classes have saved her feelings of connection to and appreciation of her body. She also acknowledges that journaling and talking to her support system have allowed her to acknowledge and regulate her affect. Miriam was able to replace the unhealthy strategy of emotionally and physically unsafe sex to more healthy self-affirming strategies.

12

Thriving

"I think what the difference is, I was able to distinguish my life from those other things around me. I recognized where I was but I didn't feel like I was trapped in it. I had goals, so I knew that this was a temporary thing for me.

I began to realize that that's something I wouldn't have to live with all my life, that eventually there would come a day that I could be able to make a decision and have choices, then violence would not be a part of my life."
—a survivor of child abuse

"I think that when I think about how I want to give back, I inevitably end up focusing on young women, primarily on African-American women that I see somewhat of myself in, you know what I mean? And so I really strive to connect with young women that I feel may be going through some of the things that I went through as a child. I'm here to be a resource in that way and I think that it helps me to just kind of think about all the possibilities, all the ways that I could have ended up, not to say that the way I chose makes me better than anyone else, but it helps me focus on the importance of really thinking about multiple pathways and determining the pathway I will take."
—a survivor of sexual assault

"Through my job, I work with young brothers everyday. I went to school . . . But all along my scope was always to help people . . . It's like it's like you try to minimize all of the negative things in your life and you supplement the negatives with doing more good things. That's what I did. I work with the young brothers, we teach them cultural esteem, history, abstinence . . . It's rewarding. It's a motivator for me. You know, probably the reason that I didn't make decisions to go on and deal with that individual is because I got people here I need to help, you know. And to a degree it would be selfish, you know. If I get arrested or whatever cause I'm still a young brother who grew up in the ghetto and you hear some people glorify it. I don't glorify it. It's one of the worse places on this earth. But I seen a lot within the space of four inches, you know, right between these two little eyes. I don't have to go that route. I made it a lot farther by just avoiding that type of confrontation and stuff and increasing the positive instead."

—a survivor of sexual abuse

What Is Thriving?

Thriving is post-trauma growth that the survivor may experience as a result of making healthy choices during recovery. It is important to know that trauma is not the source of the growth; therefore we do not attribute any positive outcomes to the trauma itself, but to the survivor's hard work in the recovery process. Rape does not make you strong; domestic violence doesn't make you wise; racism doesn't give you a sense of empowerment. However, some survivors approach their recovery and self-care in such a healthy way that they begin to develop strengths emotionally, cognitively, socially, and spiritually. Areas of growth may include increased self-esteem, self-efficacy, self-awareness, coping skills, support system, knowledge, spiritual practices, sense of empowerment, activism, and purpose. Beyond a cessation of symptoms, the goal of thriving is to live an abundant life that is one of purpose, self-esteem, and empowerment. Another component of thriving is the acknowledgment that the survivor may have periods of distress and setbacks, but that he or she now has the skills to cope with these periods. As Bratton (1999) notes, thriving takes time; "healing is a process not an event" (p. 263).

Thriving refers to more than a return to equilibrium following a challenge; a return to one's former state is better defined within the concept of "resilience" (Ickovics and Park, 1998). Thriving instead refers to the ability to go beyond survival and recovery from a stressor to actually using the challenge as an impetus for personal positive outcomes through psychological growth. These areas of growth include: skills and knowledge, improved interpersonal relations, transformation, utilization of personal and social resources, and meaning-making capabilities (Massey et al., 1998).

Thriving as it is related specifically to trauma can result in perceived growth in three domains: changes in perception of self, changes in relationship with others, and a changed philosophy of life that includes a deeper appreciation for life, along with new life directions and priorities (Calhoun and Tedeschi, 1998). "Thriving can be many different things: focusing on one's own needs for the first time, seeing future possibilities, getting actively involved in social movements, becoming critically aware of oppressive forces, and making decisions to recreate one's life" (Massey et al., 1998, p. 47).

The rationale for growth or thriving not being predictably related to adjustment is explained by Calhoun and Tedeschi (1998), who note that well-being and distress are not necessarily opposite ends of the same pole; as a result, distress and growth can coexist. Massey et al. (1998) go on to note (p. 352) that "discourses of thriving and despair are braided, interwoven into the words and daily lives of men and women coping with the strains of contemporary urban life. Their stories resonate back to us, the researchers, as we search for a pure discourse of thriving. . . . Yet when we are honest, when we listen most carefully, when we dare to hear what they dare to say, we hear whispers within thriving of despair, of fear, of anxiety."

Massey et al. (1998) also explain the lack of correlation between thriving and adjustment by noting that thriving is a process and not an end point; persons can have periods of growth followed by periods of setbacks. A qualitative look at recovery in this sense gives a picture that is much more resonant with the human condition in terms of the path to wholeness.

There has been an important broad-based movement to alter the identity of those who experience interpersonal violence from "victims" to "survivors." To document the possibility of moving from victim to survivor, much research has addressed the effectiveness of various treatment approaches in the abatement of post-trauma symptoms. Less attention, however, has been paid to the ways in which survivors become thrivers, that is, the way people move from overcoming symptoms to obtaining psychological growth and transformation in the aftermath of trauma. This chapter attempts to show the ways in which traditional therapy and nontraditional therapeutic techniques may assist people in finding greater voice, power, and wisdom in the wake of traumatic experiences.

Violence, including sexual violence, is at its root about power, force, and dominance (Aimer and Abbink, 2000). With this is mind, any survivor of violence must regain his or her personal power to thrive. The thriving paradigm is empowering for those who have been violated in that it creates room for the human dual experience of growth and struggle. The real-life recovery experiences of those who have been violated include periods of transformation, stagnation, and setbacks. This reality is not captured by the notion of recovery that connotes a static state of being symptom-free. Thriving on the other hand is a process that leaves room for the true growth and despair that characterizes the short-term and long-term aftermath of sexual assault. It acknowledges the ways in which people are forever changed by violence and how some of these changes, with work, can include growth and transformation.

Thompson (2000) notes that all survivors have the potential to have a positive outcome and sense of empowerment after working through the issues of loss, power, and identity. In a randomized controlled study of patients with post-traumatic stress, researchers found that symptom presentation had to improve before there were any changes in negative belief patterns about the self and others (Livanou et al., 2002). While the reduction of symptoms, through therapy, medication, and personal work, is essential to the recovery process (Bryant and Friedman, 2001), therapists, researchers, and survivors themselves must also attend to strategies that facilitate growth and positive transformation of the fundamental beliefs about the self, the other, and the world. It is not enough to "medicalize" survivors' unhappiness (Wright and Owen, 2001); holistic approaches to healing must address individual empowerment and systemic transformation. True healing or recovery for thrivers must include coming to a place of self-reliance, strength, and power over one's body and life (Ledray, 1994). Whether traditional or nontraditional, the paths to thriving have to address the empowerment, psychological growth, and social connection of survivors.

An important aspect of thriving is resistance. Once clients have acknowledged, shared, and grieved, learned safety and self-care, connected with anger, and developed coping strategies, they should develop resistance strategies. Resistance strategies encompass positive social activism that works to eradicate oppression and violence such as safe confrontations with perpetrators, lobbying for antiracist policies, circulating and/or signing petitions, voting, educating others, or, when appropriate, filing charges against perpetrators. Survivors can also read and educate themselves about the racist experiences of others. Survivor empowerment is enhanced when clients discover ways to utilize their power and voice to address the very trauma that harmed them, whether as individuals or in an organized effort (Bryant-Davis, 2003). In terms of encouraging the use of resistance strategies, mental health professionals should adopt a human rights perspective that acknowledges and works to eradicate oppression and violence.

What Makes Thriving Challenging?

Some survivors' symptoms remit over time without professional intervention. This can result from the survivor's social support network, coping strategies, responsiveness of others, and additional cognitive factors. Additionally, for survivors who do seek professional assistance, cognitive-behavioral interventions as well as other interventions have been proven effective in treating post-trauma symptoms. While relief from symptoms such as dissociation, flashbacks, and hypervigilance is extremely important, addressing the survivor's core sense of self is critical as well. It is an additional challenge to address the survivor's self-esteem and sense of empowerment and purpose. Purpose can mean activism and social connection as one works toward justice (Herman, 1997). This requires the survivor to release feelings of self-blame as well as feelings of powerlessness. It requires that the survivor comes to believe that she is a person of value, worth, and ability. Herman (1997) explains that the goal of perpetrators is to enslave and control the survivor. To dismantle the agenda of the perpetrators, survivors must be empowered to thrive, to walk in freedom. This means shedding the victim identity and drawing on the aspects of identity that one wants to shape for herself (Herman, 1997).

How Does Culture Play a Role in the Process of Moving from Surviving to Thriving?

Culture shapes the way we:

- Define recovery
- Approach healing and recovery
- Conceptualize possibility after a trauma
- Cultivate hope, self-esteem, and purpose
- Approach prevention, intervention, and justice

How Does Disability Affect Approaches to Thriving?

Ablebody-ism and discrimination against the disabled is pervasive. It is important for survivors who have mental and physical disabilities to resist internalizing the negative messages of society. Resistance is key for those who want to move from merely surviving the day-to-day to thriving with a sense of purpose, self-esteem, and self-efficacy. One helpful strategy is to become familiar with role models who have faced similar traumatic experiences. While it is unfortunate that trauma is so pervasive in our society, it also means that there are many survivors among us, and some are even thriving with a renewed sense of self and purpose. It is important for us to remind ourselves that wholeness, strength, and self-esteem are possible.

How Does Economic Background Affect Approaches to Thriving?

For those who are wealthy and those who are impoverished, it is important to recognize that money does not define thriving or health. The presence of wealth does not ensure mental health, and the absence of wealth does not preclude mental health. Emotional well-being is based in safety, respect, connection to others, and self-awareness. While resource access is very helpful, mental health is the right of every survivor. When we think of human rights, they include not only physical safety and well-being but mental health as well.

How Does Gender Affect Approaches to Thriving?

Women are unfortunately sometimes socialized with the belief that striving for success or thriving is selfish or makes women "too aggressive." Self-care, self-esteem, and purpose are not selfish. It is the responsible approach to taking care of yourself and utilizing the gifts, opportunities, and skills that you possess.

For men and women, preparation should be made for occasional periods of symptomology that do occur. Thriving leaves room for growth and distress. Certain life events will remind the survivor of the traumatic experience. These moments of despair and pain do not mean that the survivor is back where they started or that they have not worked hard enough. It is normal for certain reminders or triggers to cause the survivor to reflect and sometimes reconceptualize the trauma and the impact it has had on his or her life. Depending on the trauma, some of the life events that can cause renewed distress are: entering a new intimate relationship, becoming pregnant, having a child, having a child turn the age the survivor was when the trauma occurred, returning home or to the place of violation, seeing a film or television show that depicts a similar trauma, starting to work with a new therapist, and intrusive medical procedures. Thriving does not mean that one experiences only constant joy; it means that when there are periods of despair, one has the resources internally and externally to cope with those feelings and to have hope for the future.

How Does Migration Affect Approaches to Thriving?

Discrimination, social isolation, and feelings of cultural disconnection are challenges facing immigrants, but thriving is also a real possibility. By simultaneously learning and exploring one's new context and continuing to celebrate one's culture of origin, the survivor can utilize new and old resources, including community, spirituality, and professional support. By utilizing these strategies, survivors can increase their sense of self-efficacy as well as their skills and capabilities.

How Does Race Affect Approaches to Thriving?

Racism and discrimination are pervasive in our society and serve to disempower racial minority survivors. Internalized racism attacks the very core components of thriving: including self-efficacy and self-esteem. However, with positive racial socialization, support and acknowledgment of discrimination, role models, and coping strategies as well as resistance strategies (activism), persons who experience traumatic events can move from surviving to thriving. As Hooks (1993) reminds us, for transformation to occur, it requires not only self-actualization and personal will but also resistance and organized activism to address institutionalized racism and patriarchy. While more research needs to be conducted on resilience and thriving among racial minority trauma survivors, one study looked at resilience within a sample of African-American survivors of childhood sexual abuse and found that high school graduation, being reared in stable homes, having parents who were not addicted to drugs, and having strong social support predicted resilience or high levels of functioning (Banyard and colleagues, 2002).

Racism is a reality that requires confrontation and dismantling. At the same time, those who continue to experience racism must be supported and encouraged. Racial minority survivors should take inspiration from the historical and contemporary survivors of their racial background who have been exemplars of thriving.

Resisting racism requires interventions for the perpetrators and the victims. We also understand the imperative for a paradigm that includes prevention along with intervention. An important key that should not be ignored is that most trauma recovery work is done after the incident. Most effective clinicians will not accept a couple for couples 'therapy if the husband is currently battering the wife. Yet we hope and expect that victims of racism will recover while still on the battlefield of racism. As clinicians and researchers, it is imperative for us to be conscious of what we are asking of survivors. Building persons' capacity to cope is important, but more important and effective is the need to psychologically, socially, and culturally dismantle racism. To do this we must resist silence, resist self-blame, and, most important, resist complacency.

The task of addressing racism may seem overwhelming, but Robinson notes at the end of his book *The Debt*: "We must do this in memory of the dark souls whose weary broken bodies endured the unimaginable. We must do this on behalf of our children whose thirsty spirits clutch for the keys to a future. This is a struggle we cannot lose, for in the very making of it we will discover, if nothing else, ourselves."

How Does Religion Affect Approaches to Thriving?

Religious survivors should remember that thriving takes effort and perseverance. Thriving and emotional wholeness is not instant or easy; it requires daily commitment and effort. For some people mental health is a struggle that benefits from professional mental health support to support other strategies such as prayer. With faith, hope, and courage, thriving is possible. Survivors should be encouraged to develop their purpose and sense of self-esteem.

How Does Sexual Orientation Affect Approaches to Thriving?

The prevalence of homophobia can be overwhelming. LGBT survivors however should remember that thriving is possible. While surviving is important, survivors deserve more. LGBT survivors have to resist shame, silence, secrecy, isolation, and internalized homophobia to reach a place of thriving, a place of purpose, empowerment, and self-esteem. By using healthy coping strategies, including the development of a supportive network, LGBT survivors can thrive. LGBT survivors have to move from feelings of deviance and inferiority to a place of affirmation and self-esteem (Blumenfeld, 1992).

To move toward a place of thriving, survivors can utilize the following activities.

Journaling

Read and try to remember this affirmation.
Affirmation: I am growing emotionally, mentally, and spiritually.

Activities:

1. Write a reflection of where you feel you were a year ago, a month ago, and where you are today. Include both where you are in terms of your symptoms and where you are with your sense of self.

2. Write a description of where you would like to be six months from now, including emotionally, physically, cognitively, socially, and spiritually.

Drama

Read and try to remember this affirmation.
Affirmation: I believe in myself. I have the power to make a difference.

Activity:

Pretend that you are a confident public speaker. Stand up and speak with passion about any issue that you would like. First, decide the nature of your audience and what you hope to communicate to them. After you have finished your brief presentation, write a reflection of how it felt.

Music

Read and try to remember this affirmation.
Affirmation: I am moving from victim to survivor, from surviving to thriving.

Activity:

Write a song about thriving or create a melody for the following words:
I am growing
Moving from surviving to thriving
My wings are broader
My back is stronger
Yes I am growing
I know who I am
I have the power to land
On my feet again
I am reaching higher heights
Deeper depths
My mind is clear
My companions near me
Each round goes higher and higher
I dance to my own drum
Sing my own song
The sun is rising and so am I
The sun is rising and so am I

Movement

Read and try to remember this affirmation.
Affirmation: I live with purpose.
My life is important.

Activity:

Find a song that inspires you. Play it and dance freely to the music. Allow
yourself to move without shame and anxiety, but instead with joy and
creativity. This is your dance and only you can do it. It is a dance of your
journey—embrace it.

Nature

Read and try to remember this affirmation.
Affirmation: My skills are growing.
My light is shining.

Activity:

Watch a bird or butterfly. Notice the wings, the motion, and the
stillness. Write a reflection about the ways your journey is similar to that
of the bird or butterfly that you observe.

Social Support

Read and try to remember this affirmation.
Affirmation: I have courage and wisdom
to face today.

Activity:

Think of one person who has been helpful to you in your journey. They
may or may not be aware of the inspiring role they have played in your
life. It could be a relative, friend, religious leader, therapist, or neighbor.
Write the person a letter of appreciation. Let them know how their
presence, words, or support have been helpful to you. A part of growing is
the capacity for appreciation and the ability to communicate. Send the
letter to the person or, if you prefer, give them a call and share your
appreciation.

Spirituality

Read and try to remember this affirmation.
Affirmation: My soul is soaring. The past has not killed me.
I am alive with possibility.

Activity:

Say a prayer of appreciation for your life and for the many steps you have taken forward. Ask the Creator to give you strength to continue on this journey. If you are not comfortable with prayer, meditate on your progress and imagine yourself growing wiser and stronger each day.

Activism

Read and try to remember this affirmation.
Affirmation: The state of the world around me motivates me to move forward.
I am not stuck. I have hope for the future.

Activities:

1. Your story could inspire someone else who has experienced a similar trauma. Write a poem or essay about the trauma you experienced and how you have survived. Include the strategies that have been helpful to you as you move from victim to survivor and from surviving to thriving. You can anonymously or with your name attached give your testimonial to an agency that assists people who are facing similar issues. Such agencies may include domestic violence shelters, rape crisis centers, LGBT support centers, NAACP chapters, or the trauma center of a local hospital. You have come a long way. Let your light shine, and as you grow, continue to be a source of encouragement to others who are just beginning their journey.

2. Challenge heterosexist, sexist, classist, and racist jokes as well as jokes against persons with disabilities.

3. Initiate serious discussions or coordinate an anti-oppression or antiviolence workshop.

4. Read a book about a form of trauma with which you are unfamiliar.

5. Research your state's policies concerning trauma survivors, civil rights, or the criminal justice system. You may also want to explore the policies of your school, job, or religious institutions. If you feel the policy is strong, write a letter of support, and if you would like to recommend some changes, write to the appropriate persons about your concerns.

Survivor Case Summary Carla is a Puerto Rican deaf survivor of community violence. She used to work nights in a factory, and one night as she was walking home, she was shot by a stray bullet. The shooter was never identified. A community advocate from the police department came to the hospital and recommended counseling for Carla.

Carla was experiencing hyperarousal, flashbacks, and nightmares when she came in for counseling. She had to wait two weeks after the shooting for the counseling agency to locate an interpreter. Through exposure therapy to confront the memory of the shooting as well as systematic desensitization to help Carla defuse the anxiety related to walking through her neighborhood, she was able to experience an alleviation of her post-trauma symptoms. A part of her anxiety and anger was related not only to the shooting, but to the lack of resources and service sensitivity for deaf survivors, including the local police, ambulance, and trauma unit of the hospital. She had to wait for a long time going without someone she could speak with. Carla explored her feelings related to feeling disserved on three levels. She felt that being Latina, impoverished, and deaf, she and women like her were more likely to receive inferior medical, counseling, and judicial services. It was important for Carla's healing and empowerment to acknowledge and explore the role of racism, sexism, classism, and discrimination against deaf survivors.

A year after the shooting, Carla became a public spokesperson addressing both community violence and services for deaf survivors of violence. Carla started by writing letters to various local agencies and received her first invitation from the school where her sister teaches. Since then she has helped start a community watch program and made presentations for grassroots Latino organizations and deaf associations. She is most proud of the opportunity she recently had to share her story with the local police department. Carla feels that she has taken her recovery in her hands and become empowered to make a difference in her community.

Afterword

If the house is to be set in order, one cannot begin with the present, (s)he must begin with the past.
—John Hope Franklin in Q. Eli (1997)

I am an endangered species but I sing no victim's song.
—Sung by Diane Reeves

This book is a response to the call issued by Roth and Batson (1997) for researchers to obtain information that fully "celebrates the resiliency, heroism, and richness" embodied by survivors. It is the intention of this work to combat the silence in the literature by providing an opportunity for the cultural context of survivors to be acknowledged and the voices of diverse survivors to be heard.

I mean to knock pods off chestnut trees and bring the guilty to justice, the indifferent to attention, and the needful to safe harbor. The way out is to tell: speak the acts perpetrated upon us, speak the atrocities, speak the injustices, speak the personal violations of the soul. Someone will listen, someone will believe our stories, someone will join us . . .
—Charlotte Pierce-Baker (1998)

Pierce-Baker penned these words in her silence-shattering book on the trauma of rape in black women's lives. While trauma has been associated with war veterans and more recently with survivors of domestic physical and sexual acts of violence, there has been less attention paid to the traumatizing effects of societal traumas or the cultural context of truama. In addition, there has been even less attention paid to survivors of the multiplicative effects of societal traumas as well as domestic, community, and war-related violence.

Historically, the benefits of traumatizing an entire group of people have been the ability to control and dominate. During the mid-atlantic slave trade as well as during the genocide against Native Americans and the Holocaust, it was common practice to utilize tactics to mentally and emotionally dominate and control. These tactics included but were not limited to: (1) separating persons who spoke the same language, (2) publicly lynching those who attempted to gain freedom, (3) cutting out the tongues of those who spoke up, (4) cutting off the genitalia of those who exerted their own will, (5) repeatedly raping young girls, (6) selling family members to different plantations, (7) branding, (8) banning the use of one's native language, religion, or instruments, and (9) rewarding those who were willing to tell of plans the enslaved captives had for obtaining freedom. These tactics served the purpose of controlling the behavior of the marginalized through feelings of fear and vulnerability.

Few people committed to serious thought and reflection would debate the traumatizing effects of interpersonal violation, including homophobic and racist hate crimes. One must take into account both (1) the contemporary emotionally traumatizing effects of societal traumas as well as (2) the effects of collective memory—being a member of a group that has historically been devalued and subjugated. We have to confront and contemplate the prevalence of police brutality, racial profiling, hate crimes, harassment based on sexual orientation, disenfranchisement of the impoverished, and codes of community, legal, and police silence concerning attacks on women's bodies and spirits. Disability, gender, socioeconomic status, sexual orientation, religion, race, and migration status are among key cultural variables that affect the experience of trauma as well as the recovery process.

Where is the justice? Where is the safe place? What does it mean to come of age when one is vulnerable both walking in one's own community and walking in the communities of others? Where is the justice for children of African descent, of Asian descent, of Arab descent, of Latino descent, of indigenous descent—those living in ghettos or suburbs, in public school majorities or private school minorities, in church houses before they burn or crack houses before they burn? What about those who are impoverished, gay, disabled, shamed into silence?

Let us be clear that physical violence is not the only way to pose a threat to a group of people. What about the threat of a doomed future due to low-quality education and rumors of your inherent inferior intellectual ability or your assumed genetic predisposition to fail? What about the threat of walking around in a society that believes you are promiscuous because of your race even though you are only thirteen? What about the threat of walking around in a society where, because of your ethnicity, people are afraid to get on elevators with you or walk past you or sit next to you or talk to you? Would not this experience leave you discouraged, anxious, or maybe, just maybe a little angry?

Interestingly enough, just as people have difficulty extending sympathy to a rape survivor who copes with trauma by staying busy or utilizing humor, so people have difficulty sympathizing with survivors of societal trauma who respond with anger. Often people outside of the marginalized community don't see the tears, frustration, and utter sadness that are also part of the varying responses to traumatic experiences.

Research on the effects of interpersonal trauma, including societal traumas, have found associations with increased PTSD, aggression, depression, high blood pressure, irritability, anxiety, isolation, and distrust. Survivors are taught by perpetrators and by the silence of society that they are inferior, that their futures are uncertain, and that their present is unsafe due to emotional if not physical wounding.

Survivors of racism, sexism, classism, homophobia, and widespread community violence are often continuously bombarded with ongoing stressors and wounds. This gets to the issue of the multiplicative effects of injustice based on membership in multiple oppressed groups. There are black women who are recovering from rape and who within this trauma recovery process as well as outside of it are left to battle racism in their daily lives. There are Latino men who are survivors of homophobic attacks while simultaneously facing racism in their professional lives. Numerous immigrant children endure the hardship of poverty and xenophobia while growing up in a society that tells them their current state is a result of their parents' laziness and ignorance.

Where does the key to fighting injustice lie? We have tried to legislate it and we need to continue to try. We have tried to march about it and we need to continue to march. But along with ballots and billboards, the reconciling process is found in the changing of the hearts and minds of communities and individuals, privileged and oppressed alike.

As we move toward cultural competence, we have to understand that we are not seeking to make an anticulture society, but an anticultural oppression society. In other words, we are not seeking to become color blind and culture-free. An appreciation of culture requires that we take into account the richness of diverse peoples. As we move toward appreciating and recognizing the cultural context of trauma, we have to simultaneously work to eradicate oppression and violence. Essentially, we must resist silence and complacency to actively participate in the struggle against oppression. We have to be radical enough to believe that every human being deserves safety, justice, and equality.

We also have to be radical enough to acknowledge the countless people who have experienced traumatic violations and yet chose life, growth, and recovery. There are many survivors among us and they should be celebrated for the ways they survive and, in some cases, thrive. Survivors have used a number of strategies, including but not limited to racial socialization, social support, activism, the arts, spirituality, and humor. The stories of survival must continue to be told. It is the power of survivors' testimony that refreshes hope in the midst of despair.

> We must tell our truths
> We must tell how we continue to make it
> In the telling there is danger
> So first our telling may be whispered
> But even our whispers will have power
> Even our whispers will begin the stitching, sewing, mending, building that
>   must be done
> Together
> For the aftermath of war leaves not only unburied bodies but
> Broken spirits
> And to mend them
> That, my people, is the true war
> This is war and we will win it
> Step by step
> We will win it

To win the war against trauma, there must not only be effective interventions but also prevention. Prevention requires resistance to oppression and internalized oppression. To fight internalized oppression we have to simultaneously name and combat the forces working against us while we work against those activities within our own communities that lead to our self-destruction. This includes the corruption, poverty, gun violence, sexual assault, addiction, homophobia, discrimination, racism, and divisiveness manifested in ethnic wars and gang violence. We have to be fed up enough with the internalized self-hatred within our communities to break the codes of silence that are killing people all over the globe. This is the season for a new generation of leaders to emerge, take note of the cost of oppression, and vow to do it differently. We have to stop identifying with the myths that have been perpetuated about us. We are neither destined nor deserving of hunger, death, ignorance, or cruelty.

The transition into a positive self-identity is critical. Through anti-oppression strategies, survivors have resisted and continue to do so. I would like to encourage us to not only recover from the wounds of trauma but to press toward a place of thriving. In the trauma literature, the term recovery has alluded to the returning of a place of homeostasis or returning to the place of functioning one held before the trauma. On the other hand, thriving refers to the ability to grow from the experience and end up at a higher level of functioning than the survivor had prior to the experience. We need an active resistance to injustice, racial and otherwise. We need to educate, motivate, legislate, and press toward the mark of equality in tangible ways. Survivors are not asking for special treatment; in fact the call and need of survivors is for justice and equality for every person.

While survivors have to invest time and energy into the recovery process, it is also important that bystanders, members of the dominant community, and passive recipients of the benefits of oppression play a critical role in resisting violence, trauma, and oppression. It is essential for people who are educationally and economically privileged, white, heterosexual, able-bodied, born citizens, and/or male, to systematically work to eradicate oppression within themselves, those in their circles, and in the institutions in which they have membership. The first step in transforming a society begins with the socialization process of those who have benefited from the status quo.

Some multicultural scholars have offered "tolerance" as the ending goal point for a just society. Tolerance does not equal justice because it does not incorporate one of the fundamental ingredients of justice, which is mutual respect. Tolerance is the mere following of laws and social norms required to be politically correct. It means not allowing your dislike for a person to keep you from being polite in their presence. An unspoken but understood part of tolerance is the fact that you really wish the person was not there, but since you cannot get rid of them, you learn to bear the nuisance of their presence. Tolerance for human beings falls short of standing in as a viable solution for justice. To tolerate women, gays, lesbians, people of color, persons with disabilities, persons of diverse faiths, and impoverished persons is only one step away from accepting discrimination and violation of those who are different. When it comes to trauma, neutrality is not an option. By remaining silent, we support violence and condone trauma. Resistance requires active participation.

Gardiner, Mutter, and Kosmitski (1998) propose that tolerance is an intermediate stage of growth in cross-cultural interaction, but that there is another stage that requires critical thinking, personal growth, cross-cultural sensitivity, and engaging in new experiences. I believe their model is more appropriate with majority cultures because it puts forth a goal of multicultural interdependence, which is defined as sharing your culture and exploring new ways of experiencing and viewing the world as a result of engaging with other cultures. "Minority" children, particularly children of immigrant parents who do not speak English, begin this process very young. It is a part of survival as a minority member of a majority culture.

As a society that proclaims a love of justice and a profession that proclaims a commitment to all people, we have to say to the perpetrators of rape, murder, genocide, humiliation, harassment, and dehumanization: *never again*. We will allow not one more silenced survivor.

SOUL ON ICE

It's the year 2000 and I want to know who caused the puddles in my brother's eyes
  Who made him sit here opening and shutting his fists?
    fighting to stop the cascade of tears recklessly balancing on his
  lashes
It's the year 2000 and my brother's soul is on ice

Don't look them in the eye
Step
Don't let them hear your accent
Step
Don't tell them you live in special housing
Step
Don't don't don't crash
Step
Don't remember
Step
Don't get mad
Step
Don't don't don't step out of the lines
Step
Dress nice
Step
Be polite
Step

It's the year 2000 and my sister takes careful steps
    but is still shot daily with discrimination
and the gun holders and bullet providers say
    It's her imagination

It's the year 2000 and my sister is my elder and I want to know
who put the shame in his shoulder,
who took the lava from her eyes,
who surrounded her feet with ice

It's the year 2000 and I wonder if the icemakers know that black souls on ice,
that brown souls on ice, that red souls on ice, that yellow souls on ice
Don't melt
I wonder if the icemakers know there will be no more water but fire next time
I wonder if the icemakers know that when the smoke clears
My brothers and sisters will have learned that the secret to surviving on ice
        Is to dance
Wonder if the icemakers will recognize these professional ice skaters
Gliding through space

Carry my briefcase with a dip in my stride
Glide
Look you in the eye with secrets in my shoulders
Glide
Flow effortlessly between my tongue and the king's English
Glide
Triple somersault, loop to loop and glide, glide, glide
Just long enough, just long enough
For me to teach my sons and daughters
And the icemaker's sons and daughters
How to break the ice
Just a little bit longer
Glide
Just a little bit longer
Glide
A little bit longer
Glide

And we'll break the ice
We'll break
The ice

As we break the ice of oppression, the table is set for us to break bread together in equality of mutual respect, resource allocation, and civil rights. In the wake of trauma, our vision and dreams may change but they do not die. As Mark Twain wrote: "The rumors of my death have been greatly exaggerated." Our dreams are simply reality in the making. This vision for justice transcends individuals and lives in the very souls of humanity. As society changes, as global policies come and go, as the face of oppression creates new masks, the need for revised revolutions are ever present. We have marched and must continue, we have cast ballots and must continue, and we have educated and must continue. Simultaneously, we must go about the business of changing hearts and minds. We have to resist oppression within others and ourselves. This revolution must start with the rewriting of our internal scripts—our scripts of culture, trauma, justice, and the possibility of change.

We have to write scripts that shatter the silence of racism, sexism, classism, able-body-ism, religious intolerance, and homophobia
We have to write scripts that salute our cultural resiliency
We have to find words, people, and sites of resistance
That push us out of the ritual of complacency
Into the winds of thriving
Take up your pens my sisters and brothers
As we write ourselves,
Will ourselves

Work our way
To Holy Ground

I remain hopeful. I see communities of survivors working, pressing, praying, striving toward recovery, abundant living, and thriving. I see communities of people resisting the normalization of violence and trauma. I see resistance in educators, policymakers, community advocates, counselors, police officers, nurses, doctors, lawyers, community educators, politicians. Each day we are growing in number and courage. As I conclude in the poem below, we have been awakened by the midnight reality that we have nothing left to lose. As Audre Lorde taught us, even when we are silent we are still afraid, so we might as well speak, knowing that "we were never meant to survive" and yet we're still here.

HERE WE GATHER AND HERE WE STAND
Reflections from the Association of Women in Psychology Conference 2000

Survivors are crawling out of sleeping bags
Unzipping insecurity
Kicking off oppression
And wiping the crust of complacency from their eyes

Survivors are waking up and creating campgrounds of difficult dialogues
where flames of our children's futures can be fanned

Granddaughters of the Holocaust and Grandsons of Slavery
Are sitting in jungles of blood shed
And opening wolf wombs and eagle wings
And chanting to the galaxy
"I will be heard and yes I will listen."
Women lulled to sleep by silence
those knocked unconscious by beauty myths
those given sedatives of ignorance
those taken off the life support of sisterhood
Survivors are waking up after comas of division brought on by the heart
failure of racism, sexism, classism, homophobia, and able-body-ism

The demon of sleep thought these survivors would inherit legacies of weakness, but their hibernation has left them hungry—craving connection and seeking sound waves

The moon knows full well that hungry women will be fed—not by might or by power but by the spirit
Spirit women are waking up with community in their hearts, policies on their minds, truth on their tongues, and healing in their souls

Welcome to the campground where the night is full of song
The harmony of sign language with the melody of uncloseted symphonies
The drumbeat of impoverished survivors in duet with trumpets of wealth
This crescendo followed by Native American whole notes
And trills of the Latina
This war song accented by the bass line of women whirling through the woods
of life in wheelchairs
And the high-sounding cymbals of men who have migrated by need
And the low-sounding cymbals of women who have migrated by force

Welcome to the campground where the dance of the sacred
is a duet between sensuality and spirituality—intellectualism and activism
the dance of ghettos and villages
temples and alleyways
institutions and open fields

Welcome to the campground where women and men feast on the banquet of
experiences
Where Asian grandmothers stir the stew of struggle
Where Arab fathers add the seasoning of shattered silence
Where daughters sauté the shared strength of sisterhood
And where brothers help summon the soup of survival

Survivors are waking up and the awakening is no easy road
It is an underground trail of tears
It is a daily commitment to fighting sleep
It requires the shock therapy of hearing the reality of our sisters' wails
Through the trees of our truths
Across the mountains of privilege
By way of oceans of histories and her stories
But the pain of our hunger is greater than the comfort of complacency
So survivors are waking up in courtrooms and clinics and colleges and crack
houses

Welcome to the campground where the collage consists of unedited uncensored
women's wails
Women awakened by the midnight hunger that refuses to be quieted by
fear
Women awakened by the midnight reality that we have nothing left to lose

Welcome to the campground of awakened hungry survivors
Where silence is no longer a viable option
Where the only choice is to awaken peacefully or to be awakened by the wail
of these woods

Here we gather and here we stand
This campground is no vacation

It is work and discomfort and denial and tears and frustration and anger and
uphill journeys

This campground is no end point
But a crossroad to reframe and refuel for the journey ahead

Here we gather and here we stand
At this campground
Under this moon
By these flames
In this moment

Here we gather and here we stand
Calling the roll
Africa and her daughters
And Europe and her sons
Daughters of silenced wombs
And daughters of many births
Sons of oppression
And sons of privilege
Daughters who see with walking sticks
And daughters who walk on wheels
Sons in academic battlegrounds
And sons in community trenches
Daughters of fame
And daughters who remain nameless
Daughters with barrettes
And daughters with gray hair
Those who read books
And those who read between the lines
Those who walk in order
And those whose dance mystifies the wind
Those who have known the fulfillment of intercourse
And those who have known the satisfaction of abstinence
Sons who pray with words
And sons who pray with deeds
Daughters of the One who knows all
And sons of the One who sees all

Here we gather and here we stand
Amidst this nation of naysayers
Echoing to the empty spaces
Yes We Can
And Yes We Will
For we have been awakened by the midnight reality that we have nothing left
to lose

References

Abernathy, A. (1995). Managing racial anger: A critical skill in cultural competence. *Journal of Multicultural Counseling and Development 23*, 96–102.

Abrahams, N. (1996). Negotiating power, identity, family and community: Women's community participation. *Gender and Society 10*(6), 768–96.

Ackard, D., and D. Neumark-Sztainer (2002). Date violence and date rape among adolescents: Associations with disordered eating behaviors and psychological health. *Child Abuse and Neglect 26*, 455–73.

Adisa, O. (1997). Undeclared war: African-American women writers explicating rape. In L. O'Toole and J. R. Schiffman, eds. *Gender violence: Interdisciplinary perspectives.;* 194–208; New York, NY: University Press.

Aimer, G., and J. Abbink (2000). Meaning of Violence: A Cross Cultural Perspective. New York, NY, US: Berg Publishers.

Ainslie, R., and K. Brabeck (2003). Race murder and community trauma: Psychoanalysis and ethnography in exploring the impact of the killing of James Byrd in Jasper, Texas. *Journal for the Psychoanalysis of Culture and Society 8*, 42–50.

Allen, I. (1996). PTSD among African Americans. In A. Marsella, M. Friedman, E. Gerrity, and R. Scurfield, eds. *Ethnocultural Aspects of Posttraumatic Stress Disorder: Issues, Research, and Clinical Application*, 209–38. Washington, DC: American Psychological Association.

American Psychiatric Association. (2000). *Diagnostic and Statistical Manual of Mental Disorders, IV-TR*. Washington, DC: Author.

Atlani, L., and C. Rousseau (2000). The politics of culture in humanitarian aid to women refugees who have experienced sexual violence. *Transcultural Psychiatry 37*(3), 435–49.

Backos, A., and B. Pagon (1999). Finding a voice: Art therapy with female adolescent sexual abuse survivors. *Art Therapy 16*(3), 126–32.

Balogh, R., K. Bretherton, S. Whibley, T. Berney, S. Graham, P. Richold, C. Worsley, and H. Firth (2001). Sexual abuse in children and adolescents with intellectual disability. *Journal of Intellectual Disability Research 45*(3), 194–201.

Bandura, A. (2002). Selective moral disengagement in the exercise of moral agency. *Journal of Moral Education 31*(2), 101–19.

Banyard, V., L. Williams, J. Siegel, and C. West (2002). Childhood sexual abuse in the lives of black women: Risk and resilience in a longitudinal study. *Women and Therapy 25*(3/4), 45–58.

Baranowsky, A., M. Young, S. Johnson-Douglas, L. Williams-Keeler, and M. McCarrey (1998). PTSD transmission: A review of secondary traumatization in Holocaust survivor families. *Canadian Psychology 39*, 247–56.

Bell, C., and E. Jenkins (1994). Effects of child abuse and race. *Journal of the National Medical Association 86*(3), 165–232.

Benedict, H. (1994). *Recovery: How to Survive Sexual Assault.* New York: Columbia University Press.

Berrien, F. B., G. Aprelkov, T. Ivanova, V. Zhmurov, and V. Buzhicheeva (1994). Child abuse prevalence in Russian populations: A preliminary report. *Child Abuse & Neglect 19*(2), 261–64.

Bertone, A. M. (2000). Sexual trafficking in women: International political economy and the politics of sex. *Gender Issues*, Winter, 4–22.

Blaine, B., and J. Crocker (1995). Religiousness, race, and psychological well-being: Exploring social psychological mediators. *Personality & Social Psychology Bulletin 21*(10), 1031–41.

Blumenfeld, W. J. (1992). *Homophobia: How We All Pay the Price.* Boston: Beacon Press.

Boeschen, L., B. Sales, and M. Koss (1998). Rape trauma syndrome experts in the courtroom. *Psychology, Public Policy, and Law 4*, 414–32.

Branscombe, N., M. Schmitt, and R. Harvey (1997). Perceiving pervasive discrimination among African Americans: Implications for group identification and well-being. *Journal of Personality and Social Psychology 77*, 135–49.

Bratton, M. (1999). *From Surviving To Thriving: A Therapist's Guide To Stage II Recovery for Survivors of Childhood Abuse.* New York: Haworth Maltreatment and Trauma Press.

Brener, N., P. McMahon, C. Warren, and K. Douglas (1999). Forced sexual intercourse and associated health risk behaviors among female college students in the United States. *Journal of Consulting & Clinical Psychology 67*(2), 252–59.

Briere, J., and D. Elliott (2003). Prevalence and psychological sequelae of self-reported childhood physical and sexual abuse in a general population sample of men and women. *Child Abuse & Neglect 27*, 1205–22.

Bryant, A. Y. (1992). A legacy of survival: Environmental oppressors and the resources of African-American female students. *Dissertation Abstracts International 53*(4-B).

Bryant, C. (1995). *I Dance with God.* Dallas: Akosua Visions.

Bryant, R., and M. Friedman (2001). Medication and non-medication treatments of post-traumatic stress disorder. *Current Opinion in Psychiatry 14*(2), 119–23.

Bryant, R., T. Sackville, S. Dang, M. Moulds, and R. Guthrie (1999). Treating acute stress disorder: An evaluation of cognitive behavior therapy and supportive counseling techniques. *American Journal of Psychiatry 156*(11), 1780–86.

Bryant, T. (1999). The path to wholeness: Effective coping strategies of African-American adult survivors of childhood violence. *Dissertation Abstracts International.*

Bryant-Davis, T., and C. Ocampo (2004). Racism as trauma: Informing clinical responses. Presented at the American Psychological Association Convention, July 31, 2004, Honolulu.

Bryant-Davis, T. (in press). Coping strategies of African American adult survivors of childhood violence. *Professional Psychology: Research and Practice.*

Bryant-Davis, T. (2003). Thriving after sexual assault. In L. Slater, J. H. Daniel, and A. E. Banks, eds. *The Complete Guide To Mental Health for Women.* Boston: Beacon Press.

Buchanan, N. (2004). Racial and sexual harassment: Which predict psychological harm? Presented at the American Psychological Association Convention, July 28, 2004, Honolulu.

Burt, D., and L. DeMello (2002). Attribution of rape blame as a function of victim gender and sexuality, and perceived similarity to the victim. *Journal of Homsexuality* 43(2), 39–57.

Byrne, C., H. Resnick, D. Kilpatrick, Connie Best, and B. Saunders (1999). The socio-economic impact of interpersonal violence on women. *Journal of Consulting & Clinical Psychology* 67(3), 362–66.

Caceres, C. F., B. V. Marin, and E. S. Hudes (2000). Sexual coercion among youth and young adults in Lima, Peru. *Journal of Adolescent Health* 27, 361–67.

Calhoun, L., and R. Tedeschi (1998). Beyond recovery from trauma: Implications for clinical practice and research. *Journal of Social Issues* 54(2), 357–71.

Campbell, D. W., P. W. Sharps, F. Gary, J. C. Campbell, L. M. Lopez (2002). Intimate partner violence in African American women. *Online Journal of Issues in Nursing* 7(1), 4.

Campbell, R., T. Sefl, H. Barnes, C. Ahrens, S. Wasco, and Y. Zaragoza-Ddiesfeld (1999). Community services for rape survivors: Enhancing psychological well-being or increasing trauma? *Journal of Consulting & Clinical Psychology* 67(6), 847–58.

Carter, R., J. Forsyth, S. Mazzula, and B. Williams (2005). Racial discrimination and race-based traumatic stress: An explanatory investigation. In R. T. Carter, ed. *Handbook of Racial-Cultural Counseling and Psychology: Training and Practice.* Vol. 2. Hoboken, NJ: Wiley.

Carter, R., and J. Helms (2002). Racial discrimination and harassment: Race-based traumatic stress. Presented at the American College of Forensic Examiners Conference, September 28, 2002, Orlando.

Castillo, R., H. Waitzkin, Y. Ramirez, and J. Escobar (1995). Somatization in primary care, with a focus on immigrants and refugees. *Archives of Family Medicine* 4(7), 637–46.

Centers for Disease Control. (2002). Hate Crimes Statistics, Table 1, "Incidents, Offenses, Victims, and Known Offenders by Bias Motivation, 2002," p. 9, and Table 9, "Race of Known Offenders, 2002," accessed on November 23, 2003, at http://www.fbi.gov/ucr/hatecrime2002.pdf.

Clark, R., N. B. Anderson, V. R. Clark, and D. R. Williams (1999). Racism as a stressor for African Americans: A biopsychosocial model. *American Psychologist* 54, 805–16.

Cohen, J., A. Mannarino, L. Berliner, E. Deblinger (2000). Trauma focused cognitive behavioral therapy for children and adolescents: An empirical update. *Journal of Interpersonal Violence* 15(11), 1202–23.

Cohen, M. (2003). The affirmation of a religious (not merely spiritual) orientation in clinical treatment. *Journal of the American Academy of Psychoanalysis & Dynamic Psychiatry 31*(2), 269–73.

Coker, A. L., P. H. Smith, L. Bethea, M. R. King, and R. E. McKeown (2000). Physical health consequences of physical and psychological intimate partner violence. *Archive of Family Medicine 9*, 451–57.

Collins, P. (2000). *Black Feminist Thought: Knowledge, Consciousness, and the Politics of Empowerment.* New York, NY: Routledge.

Comas-Diaz, L. (2000). An ethnopolitical approach to working with people of color. *American Psychologist 55*, 1319–25.

Comas-Diaz, L. (1995). Puerto Ricans and child sexual abuse. In L. Fontes, ed., *Sexual Abuse in Nine North American Cultures*, 31–66. Thousand Oaks, CA: Sage.

Cunningham, M. (1999). The impact of sexual abuse treatment on the social work clinician. *Child and Adolescent Social Work Journal 16*, 277–90.

Daley, A., J. Jennings, J. Beckett, and B. Leashore (1995). Effective coping strategy of African Americans. *Social Work 40*(2), 240–48.

Daniel, J. H. (2000). The courage to hear: African American women's memories of racial trauma. In L. Jackson and B. Greene, eds. *Psychotherapy with African American Women: Innovations in Psychodynamic Perspective and Practice*, 126–44. New York: Guilford Press.

Dawsey, D. (1996). *Living to Tell about It: Young Black Men in America Speak Their Piece.* New York: Doubleday.

Denmark, F. (1998). Women and psychology: An international perspective. *American Psychologist 53*(4), 465–73.

DeRubeis, R., and C. Crits (1998). Empirically supported individual and group psychological treatments for adult mental disorders. *Journal of Consulting & Clinical Psychology 66*(1), 37–52.

deVries, M. (1996). Trauma in cultural perspective. In B. A. van der Kolk, A. C. McFarlane, and L. Weisaeth, eds., *Traumatic Stress: The Effects of Overwhelming Experience on Mind, Body, and Society.* New York: Guilford Press.

Diaz, R. M., G. Ayala, E. Bein, J. Henne, and B. V. Marin (2001). The impact of homophobia, poverty, and racism on the mental health of gay and bisexual Latino men: Findings from three U.S. cities. *American Journal of Public Health 91*, 927–32.

Donovan, R., and M. Williams (2002). Living at the intersection: The effects of racism and sexism on black rape survivors. *Women and Therapy 25*, 95–105.

Draucker, C. (1999). The psychotherapeutic needs of women who have been sexually assaulted. *Perspectives in Psychiatric Care 35*(1), 18–28.

Drieschner, L., and A. Lange (1999). A review of cognitive factors in the etiology of rape: Theories, empirical studies, and implications. *Clinical Psychology Review 19*, 57–77.

Duran, E., B. Duran, M. Yellow Horse Brave Heart, and S. Yellow Horse Brave Heart-Davis (1998). Healing the American Indian soul wound. In U. Danieleli, ed., *International Handbook of Multigenerational Legacies of Trauma*, 341–54. New York: Plenum Press.

Dykman, R., B. McPherson, P. Ackerman, J. Newton, D. Mooney, J. Wherry, and M. Chaffin (1997). Internalizing and externalizing characteristics of sexually and/or physically abused children. *Integrative Physiological & Behavioral Sciences 32*(1), 62–83.

Eli, Q. (1997). *Many Strong and Beautiful Voices: Quotations from Africans throughout the Diaspora.* Philadelphia: Running Press.

Elliott, D. (1994). The impact of Christian faith on the prevalence and sequelae ofs sexual abuse. *Journal of Interpersonal Violence 9*(1), 95–108.

Elze, D. (1992). "It has nothing to do with me." In W. J. Blumenfeld, ed., *Homophobia: How We All Pay the Price*, 95–113. Boston: Beacon Press.

Etaugh, C., and J. Bridges (2004). *The Psychology of Women: A Lifespan Perspective.* 2nd ed. Boston: Pearson.

Everett, B., and R. Gallop (2001). *The link between childhood trauma and mental illness: Effective interventions for mental health professionals.* Thousand Oaks, CA: Sage Publications, Inc.

Feagin, J. R. (1991). The continuing significance of race: Anti-black discrimination in public places. *American Sociological Review 56*, 101–16.

Feagin, J. R., and M. P. Sykes (1994). *Living with Racism: The Black Middle-Class Experience.* Boston: Beacon Press.

Feinauer, L. L., and D. A. Stuart (1996). Blame and resilience in women sexually abused as children. *American Journal of Family Therapy 24*, 31–40.

Feldhaus, K., D. Houry, and R. Kaminsky (2000). Lifetime sexual assault prevalence rates and reporting practices in an emergency department population. *Annals of Emergency Medicine 36*(1), 23–37.

Few, A., and P. Bell-Scott (2002). Grounding our feet and fears: Black women's coping strategies in psychological abusive dating relationships. In C. West, ed. *Violence in the Lives of Black Women: Battered, Black, and Blue*, 59–78. New York: Haworth Press.

Firth, H., R. Balogh, T. Berney, K. Bretherton, S. Graham, and S. Whibley (2001). Psychopathology of sexual abuse in young people with intellectual disability. *Journal of Disability Research 45*(3), 244–52.

Fischer, A., and C. Shaw (1999). African Americans' mental health and perceptions of racist discrimination: The moderating effects of racial socialization experiences and self-esteem. *Journal of Counseling Psychology 46*, 395–407.

Foa, E., and B. Rothbaum (1998). *Treating the Trauma of Rape: Cognitive-Behavioral Therapy for PTSD.* New York: Guilford Press.

Foa, E., and E. Meadows (1997). Psychosocial treatments for posttraumatic stress disorder: A critical review. *Annual Review of Psychology 48*, 449–80.

Folkman, S., and R. Lazarus (1988). Coping as a mediator of emotion. *Journal of Personality & Social Psychology 54*(3), 466–75.

Folkman, S., and R. Lazarus (1980). An analysis of coping in a middle-aged community sample. *Journal of Health & Social Behavior 21*(3), 219–39.

Fonagy, P., and M. Target (1995). Dissociation and trauma. *Current Opinion in Psychiatry 8*(3), 161–66.

Fox, J. (1997). *Poetic Medicine: The Healing Art of Poem-Making.* New York: Jeremy P. Tarcher/Penguin Putnam.

Foy, D., C. Eriksson, and G. Trice (2001). Introduction to group interventions for trauma survivors. *Group Dynamics: Theory, Research, & Practice 5*(4), 246–51.

Freedner, N., L. H. Freed, Y. W. Yang, and S. B. Austin (2002). Dating violence among gay, lesbian, and bisexual adolescents: Results from a community survey. *Journal of Adolescent Health 31*, 469–74.

Friedman, M., and A. Marsella (1996). Posttraumatic stress disorder: An overview of the concept. In: A. Marsella and M. Friedman, Matthew, eds. *Ethnocultural aspects of posttraumatic stress disorder: Issues, research, and clinical applications.* Washington, DC: American Psychological Association, 11–32.

Futa, K., E. Hsu, and D. Hansen (2001). Child sexual abuse in Asian American families: An examination of cultural factors that influence prevalence, identification, and treatment. *Clinical Psychology: Science & Practice 8*(2), 189–209.

Galambos, C. (2001). Community healing rituals for survivors of rape. *Smith College Studies of Social Work 71*(3), 441–57.

Garbarino, J. (1996). The spiritual challenge of violent trauma. *American Journal of Orthopsychiatry 66*(1), 162–63.

Gardiner, H., J. Mutter, and C. Kosmitski (1998). *Lives across Cultures: Cross-Cultural Human Development.* Boston: Allyn & Bacon.

Gay, P. (1999). Slavery as a sexual atrocity. *Sexual Addiction and Compulsivity 6*, 5–10.

Goodill, S. (1987). Dance/movement therapy with abused children. *Arts in Psychotherapy 14*(1), 59–68.

Hafer, C. (2000). Do innocent victims threaten the belief in a just world? Evidence from modified Stroop task. *Journal of Personality and Social Psychology 79*, 165–73.

Haj-Yahia, M., and S. Tamish (2001). The rates of child sexual abuse and its psychological consequences as revealed by a study among Palestinian university students. *Child Abuse & Neglect 25*, 1303–27.

Hakanen, E. (1995). Emotional use of music by African American adolescents. *Howard Journal of Communications 5*(3), 214–22.

Hall, T. (1995). Spiritual effects of childhood sexual abuse in adult Christian women. *Journal of Psychology and Theology 23*(2), 129–34.

Hanke, R. (1992). Redesigning men: Hegemonic masculinity in transition. In S. Craig, ed., *Men, Masculinity, and the Media*, 185–98. Newbury Park, CA: Sage.

Harper, P. B. (1992). Racism and homophobia as reflections on their perpetrators. In W. J. Blumenfeld, ed., *Homophobia: How We All Pay the Price*, 57–66. Boston: Beacon Press.

Harrell, J., S. Hall, and J. Taliaferro (2003). Physiological Responses to Racism and Discrimination: An Assessment of the Evidence. *American Journal of Public Health 93*(2), 243–48.

Harwell, T. S., K. R. Moore, and M. R. Spence (2003). Physical violence, intimate partner violence, and emotional abuse among adult American Indian men and women in Montana. *Preventive Medicine 37*, 297–303.

Heggen, C., and V. Long (1991). Counseling the depressed Christian female client. *Counseling & Values 35*(2), 128–35.

Henning, K., and C. Frueh (1997). Combat guilt and its relationship to PTSD. *Journal of Clinical Psychology 53*, 801–8.

Herman, J. (1997). *Trauma and recovery.* New York: Basic Books.

Hernandez, J., M. Lodico, and R. DiClemente (1993). The effects of child abuse and race on risk-taking in male adolescents. *Journal of the National Medical Association 85*(8), 593–97.

Hill, H., M. Levermore, J. Twaite, and L. Jones (1996). Exposure to community violence and social support as predictors of anxiety and social and emotional behavior among African American children. *Journal of Child & Family Studies 5*(4), 399–414.

Hill, H., S. Hawkins, M. Raposa, and P. Carr (1995). Relationship between multiple exposure to violence and coping strategies among African-American mothers. *Violence and Victims 10*, 55–71.

Hindin, M. (2003). Understanding women's attitudes towards wife beating in Zimbabwe. *Bulletin of the World Health Organization 81*(2), 501–8.

Holloway, K. (1995). *Codes of Contact: Race, Ethics, and the Color of Our Character.* New Brunswick, NJ: Rutgers University Press.

Holzman, C. (1996). Counseling adult women rape survivors: Issues of race, ethnicity and class. *Women and Therapy 19*(2), 47–62.

Holzman, C. (1994). Multicultural perspectives of counseling survivors of rape. *Journal of Social Distress and the Homeless 3*, 81–97.

Hooks, B. (2004). *Rock My Soul: Black People and Self-Esteem.* New York: Washington Square Press.

Hooks, B. (1995). *Killing Rage: Ending Racism.* New York: Henry Holt.

Hooks, B. (1993). *Sisters of the Yam: Black Women and Self-Recovery.* Boston: South End Press.

Hooks, B. (1989). *Talking Back: Thinking Feminist, Thinking Black.* Boston: South End Press.

Howard, A. (1993). Victims and perpetrators of sexual abuse. In K. Dwivedi, ed., Group work with children and adolescents: A handbook.; 220–32; Philadelphia, PA: Jessica Kingsley Publishers, 220–32.

Hughes, R. (1998). Rape! The violation of integrity and will. In M. Rees, ed. *Drawing on Difference: Art therapy with people who have learning difficulties,* 111–29.

Ialongo, N., B. K. McCreary, J. L. Pearson, A. L. Koenig, B. M. Wagner, N. B. Schmidt, J. Poduska, and S. G. Kellam (2002). Suicidal behavior among urban, African American young adults. *Suicide and Life-Threatening Behavior 32*, 256–71.

Ickovics, J., and C. Park (1998). Paradigm shift: Why a focus on health is important. *Journal of Social Issues 54*(2), 237–44.

Imber-Black, E. (2003). Secrets in families and family therapy: An overview. In: E. Imber-Black ed., Secrets in families and family therapy. New York, NY: W. W. Norton, 3–28.

Jackson, J. S., T. N. Brown, D. R. Williams, M. Torres, S. L. Sellers, and K. Brown (1996). Perceptions and experiences of racism and the physical and mental health status of black Americans: A thirteen-year national panel study. *Ethnicity and Disease 6*, 123–38.

Jacobson, N., and J. Gottman (1998). *When Men Batter Women: New Insights into Ending Abusive Relationships.* New York: Simon & Schuster.

James, Sherman (1994). John Henryism and the health of African-Americans. *Culture, Medicine & Psychiatry 18*(2), 163–82.

Jenkins, E. (2002). Black women and community violence: Trauma, grief, and coping. *Women & Therapy Special Issue: Violences in the lives of Black women: Battered, Black, and blue. 25*(3–4), 29–44.

Jessor, R. (1996). Ethnographic methods in contemporary perspective. In R. Jessor, A. Colby, and R. A. Schwader, eds. *Ethnography and Human Development: Context and Meaning in Social Context*, 3–15. Chicago: University of Chicago Press.

Jewkes, R., J. Levin, N. Mbananga, and D. Bradshaw (2002). Rape of girls in South Africa. *The Lancet 359*, 319.

Johnson, V. (1995). *Restoring Broken Vessels: Confronting the Attack on Female Sexuality*. Detroit: Dabar Publishing Company.

Jones, E. D., and K. McCurdy (1992). The links between types of maltreatment and demographic characteristics of children. *Child Abuse & Neglect 16*, 201–15.

Jones, J. (1997). *Prejudice and Racism*. 2nd ed. New York: McGraw-Hill.

Joseph, M. (1998). The effect of strong religious beliefs on coping with stress. *Stress Medicine 14*(4), 219–24.

Jost, J. T., and M. R. Banaji (1994). The role of stereotyping in system-justification and the production of false consciousness. *British Journal of Social Psychology 33*, 1–27.

Kalof, L. (2000). Ethnic differences in female sexual victimization. *Sexuality and Culture: An Interdisciplinary Quarterly 4*(4), 75–97.

Karumanchery, L. (2003). The colour of trauma: New perspectives on racism, politics, and resistance. *Dissertation Abstracts International Section A: Humanities and Social Sciences 64*(4-A), 1391.

Keane, T., D. Kaloupek, and F. Weathers (1996). Ethnocultural considerations in the assessment of PTSD. In A. Marsella, M. Friedman, E. Gerrity, and R. Scurfield, eds. *Ethnocultural Aspects of Posttraumatic Stress Disorder: Issues, Research, and Clinical Application*. Washington, DC: American Psychological Association.

Kendall, J., and D. Hatton (2002). Racism as a source of health disparity in families with children with attention deficit hyperactivity disorder. *Advances in Nursing Science 25*(2), 22–39.

Kennedy, D. (2000). The roots of child study: Philosophy, history, and religion. *Teachers College Record 102*(3), 514–38.

Kennedy, M. (2000). Christianity and child sexual abuse: The survivors' voice leading to change. *Child Abuse Review 9*, 121–24.

Kenny, M., and A. McEachern (2000). Racial, ethnic, and cultural factors of childhood sexual abuse: A selected review of the literature. *Clinical Psychology Review 20*(7), 905–22.

Kessler, R. C., K. D. Michelson, and D. R. Williams (1999). The prevalence, distribution, and mental health correlates of perceived discrimination in the United States. *Journal of Health and Social Behavior 40*, 208–30.

Kim, J., and M. Motsi (2002). "Women enjoy punishment": Attitudes and experiences of gender-based violence among PHC nurses in rural South Africa. *Social Science & Medicine 54*, 1243–54.

King, M., A. Coxell, and G. Mezey (2002). Sexual molestation of males: Associations with psychological disturbance. *British Journal of Psychiatry 181*, 153–57.

King, N., B. Tonge, P. Mullen, N. Myerson, D. Heyne, S. Rollings, R. Martin, and T. Ollendick (2000). Treating sexually abused children with posttraumatic stress disorder: A randomized clinical trial. *Journal of the American Academy of Child & Adolescent Psychiatry 39*(11), 1347–55.

Kleinke, C. L., and C. Meyer (1990). Evaluation of rape victims by men and women with high and low belief in a just world. *Psychology of Women Quarterly 14*, 343–53.

Klonoff, E. A., and H. Landrine (1999). Cross-validation of the schedule of racist events. *Journal of Black Psychology 25*, 231–55.

Klonoff, E. A., H. Landrine, and J. B. Ullman (1999). Racial discrimination and psychiatric symptoms among blacks. *Cultural Diversity and Ethnic Minority Psychology 5*, 329–39.

Koenig, M., S. Ahmed, M. Hossain, and A. Mozumder (2003). Women's status and domestic violence in rural Bangladesh: Individual and community level effects. *Demography 40*(2), 269–88.

Kopper, B. A. (1996). Gender, gender identity, rape myth acceptance, and time of initial resistance on the perception of acquaintance rape blame and avoidability. *Sex Roles 34*, 81–93.

Koss, M., L. Heise, and N. Russo (1994). The global health burden of rape. *Psychology of Women Quarterly 18*(4), 509–37.

Koss, M. (1993). Rape: Scope, impact, interventions, and public policy responses. *American Psychologist 48*, 1062–69.

Kvam, M. H. (2000). Is sexual abuse of children with disabilities disclosed? A retrospective analysis of child disability and the likelihood of sexual abuse among those attending Norwegian hospitals. *Child Abuse & Neglect 24*(8), 1073–84.

Landwehr, P. H., R. K. Bothwell, M. Jeanmard, L. R. Luque, R. Brown, and M. Breaux (2002). Racism in rape trials. *Journal of Social Psychology 142*, 667–69.

Laub, D., and D. Podell (1995). Art and Trauma. *International Journal of Psycho-Analysis 76*(5), 991–1005.

Ledray, L. (1994). *Recovering from Rape*. New York: A Henry Holt Book.

Lefly, H., C. Scott, M. Llabre, and D. Hicks (1993). Cultural beliefs about rape and victims response in three ethnic groups. *American Journal of Orthopsychiatry 63*(4), 623–32.

Leibowitz, S., M. Mendelsohn, and C. Michelson (1999). Child rape: Extending the therapeutic intervention to include the mother-child dyad. *South African Journal of Psychology 9*(3), 03–108.

Lev-Wiessel, R. (1998). Use of drawing technique to encourage verbalization in adult survivors of sexual abuse. *Arts in Psychotherapy 25*(4), 257–62.

Livanou, M., M. Basoglu, I. Marks, P. De Silva, H. Noshirvani, K. Lovell, and S. Thrasher (2002). Beliefs, sense of control, and treatment outcome in post-traumatic stress disorder. *Psychological Medicine 32*(1), 157–65.

Lock, J., and H. Steiner (1999). Gay, lesbian, and bisexual youth risks for emotional, physical, and social problems: Results from a community based-sample. *Journal of the American Academy of Child & Adolescent Psychiatry 38*(3), 297–304.

Loo, C. M., J. A. Fairbank, R. M. Scurfield, L. O. Ruch, D. W. King, L. J. Adams, and C. M. Chemtob (2001). Measuring exposure to racism: Development and validation of a race-related stressor scale (RRSS) for Asian American Vietnam veterans. *Psychological Assessment 13*, 503–20.

Loo, C., K. Singh, R. Scurfield, and B. Kilauano (1998). Race-related stress among Asian American veterans: A model to enhance diagnosis and treatment. *Cultural Diversity and Mental Health 4*, 75–90.

Lubin, H., M. Loris, J. Burt, and D. Johnson (1998). Efficacy of psychoeducational group therapy in reducing symptoms of posttraumatic stress disorder among multiply traumatized women. *American Journal of Psychiatry 155*(9), 1172–77.

Lutwak, N., B. E. Razzino, J. R. Ferrari (1998). Self-perceptions and moral affect: An exploratory analysis of subcultural diversity in guilt and shame emotions. *Journal of Social Behavior and Personality 13*, 333–49.

Lynch, M., and D. Cicchetti (1998). An ecological-transactional analysis of children and contexts: The longitudinal interplay among child maltreatment, community violence, and children's symptomatology. *Development & Psychopathology 10*(2), 235–57.

Madu, S. N., and K. Peltzer (2001). Prevalence and patterns of child sexual abuse and victim-perpetrator relationship among secondary school students in the Northern Province (South Africa). *Archives of Sexual Behavior 30*(3), 311–21.

Majors, R., and J. Billson (1992). *Cool Pose: The Dilemmas of Black Manhood in America.* New York: Lexington Books.

Marks, I., K. Lovell, H. Noshirvani, M. Livanou, and S. Thrasher (1998). Treatment of posttraumatic stress disorder by exposure and/or cognitive restructuring: A controlled study. *Archives of General Psychiatry 55*(4), 317–25.

Marsella, A., M. Friedman, and P. H. Spain (1996). Ethnocultural aspects of PTSD: An overview of issues and research directions. In A. Marsella, M. Friedman, E. Gerrity, and R. M. Scurfield. *Ethnocultural Aspects of Posttraumatic Stress Disorder: Issues, Research, and Clinical Applications.* Washington, DC: American Psychological Association.

Marsh, C. (1993). Sexual assault and domestic violence in the African American community. *Western Journal of Black Studies 17*(3), 149–55.

Martin, W. (1984). Religiosity and United States suicide rates. *Journal of Clinical Psychology 40*(5), 1166–69.

Massey, S., A. Cameron, S. Quellete, and M. Fine (1998). Qualitative approaches to the study of thriving: What can be learned? *Journal of Social Issues 54*(2), 237–44.

Maton, K., D. Teti, K. Corns, C. Vieira-Baker, and J. Lavine (1996). Cultural specificity of support sources, correlates and contexts. Three studies of African-American and Caucasian youth. *American Journal of Community Psychology 24*(4), 551–87.

Mattis, J. (2002). Religion and spirituality in the meaning making and coping experiences of African American women: A qualitative analysis. *Psychology of Women Quarterly 26*(4), 309–21.

McAdoo, H. (1995). Stress levels, family help patterns, and religiosity in middle and working class African American single mothers. *Journal of Black Psychology 21*(4), 424–49.

McCreary, M., L. Slavin, and E. Berry (1996). Predicting problem behavior and self-esteem among African-American adolescents. *Journal of Adolescent Research 11*(2), 216–34.

McFarlane, A., and G. Girolama (1996). The nature of traumatic stressors and the epidemiology of posttraumatic reactions. In B. van der Kolk, A. C. McFarlane, and L. Weisaeth, eds. *Traumatic Stress: The Effects of Overwhelming Experience on Mind, Body, and Society*, 3–23. New York: Guilford Press.

McFarlane, A., and R. Yehuda (1996). Resilience, vulnerability, and the course of posttraumatic reactions. In B. van der Kolk, A. C. McFarlane, and L. Weisaeth, eds. *Traumatic Stress: The Effects of Overwhelming Experience on Mind, Body, and Society*, 155–81. New York: Guilford Press.

McGinn, L., and C. William (2001). What allows cognitive behavioral therapy to be brief: Overview, efficacy, and crucial factors facilitating brief treatment. *Clinical Psychology: Science & Practice 8*(1), 23–37.

McKelvey, R., and J. Webb (1995). A pilot study of abuse among Vietnamese Amerasians. *Child Abuse & Neglect 19*(5), 545–53.

McNair, L., and H. Neville (1996). African-American women survivors of sexual assault: The intersection of race and class. *Women and Therapy 18*(3–4), 107–18.

McRae, M., P. Carey, and R. Anderson-Scott (1998). Black churches as therapeutic systems: A group process perspective. *Health Education & Behavior* Special Issue: Public health and health education in faith communities. 25(6), 778–89.

Meadows, E., and E. Foa (1998). Intrusion, arousal, and avoidance: Sexual trauma survivors. In V. Follette, J. Ruzek, eds. *Cognitive Behavioral Therapies for Trauma*, 100–23. New York: Guilford Press.

Merrill, G., and V. Wolfe (2000). Battered gay men: An exploration of abuse, help seeking, and why they stay. *Journal of Homosexuality 39*(2), 1–30.

Miles, G. M. (2000). "Children don't do sex with adults for pleasure": Sri Lankan children's views on sex and sexual exploitation. *Child Abuse & Neglect 24*(7), 995–1003.

Milliora, M. (2000). Beyond empathetic failures: Cultural racism as narcissistic trauma and disenfranchisement of grandiosity. *Clinical Social Work Journal 28*, 43–54.

Mize, L., B. Bentley, S. Helms, and J. Ledbetter (1995). Surviving voices: Incest survivors' narratives of their process of disclosure. *Journal of Family Psychotherapy 6*(4), 43–59.

Moghaddam, F., and C. Studer (1997). The sky is falling, but not on me: A cautionary tale of illusions of control, in four acts. *Cross-Cultural Research: The Journal of Comparative Social Science 31*, 155–67.

Moisan, P. A., K. Sanders-Phillips, P. M. Moisan (1997). Ethnic differences in circumstances of abuse and symptoms of depression and anger among sexually abused black and Latino boys. *Child Abuse & Neglect 21*(5), 473–88.

Monet, A., and R. Lazarus (1977). *Stress and coping: An Anthology*. Oxford, England: Columbia University Press.

Morgan, T., and A. Cummings (1999). Change experienced during group therapy by female survivors of childhood sexual abuse. *Journal of Consulting & Clinical Psychology 67*(1), 28–36.

Morris-Prather, C. E., J. P. Harrell, R. Collins, K. L. Jeffries-Leonard, M. Boss, and J. W. Lee (1996). Gender differences in mood and cardiovascular responses to socially stressful stimuli. *Journal of Ethnicity and Disease 6*, 109–22.

Muran, E., and R. DiGiuseppe (2000). Rape trauma. In F. Dattilio, and A. Freeman, eds. Cognitive-behavioral strategies in crisis intervention (2nd ed). New York, NY: Guilford Press, 150–65.

Nagata, D., and W. Cheng (2003). Intergenerational communication of race-related trauma by Japanese American former internees. *American Journal of Orthopsychiatry 73*, 266–78.

Naker, A. W., and S. P. Duncan (1985). Child sexual abuse: A study of prevalence in Great Britain. *Child Abuse & Neglect 9*, 457–67.

Neighbors, H., K. Elliot, and L. Gant (1990). Self-help and black America. In T. Powell, ed. *Working with Self-Help*, 189–217. Silver Spring, MD: National Association of Social Workers.

194

References

Neville, H., and A. G. Pugh (1997). General and culture-specific factors influencing African American women's reporting patterns and perceived social support following sexual assault: An exploratory investigation. *Violence against Women 3*, 361–81.

Nickerson, K. J., J. E. Helms, and F. Terrell (1994). Cultural mistrust, opinions about mental illness, and black students' attitudes toward seeking psychological help from white counselors. *Journal of Counseling Psychology 41*, 378–85.

Nisbet, P. (1996). Protective factors for suicidal black females. *Suicide & Life-Threatening Behavior 26*(4), 325–41.

Nyborg, V. (2003). The impact of perceived racism: Psychological symptoms among African American boys. *Journal of Clinical Child and Adolescent Psychology 32*, 258.

Ocampo, C. (2000). Psychophysiology and racism. *American Psychologist 55*, 1164–65.

Omalade, B. (1994). *The Rising Song of African American Women*. New York: Routledge.

Orzek, A. (1988). The lesbian victim of sexual assault: Special considerations for the mental health professional. *Women & Therapy* Special Issue: Lesbianism: Affirming nontraditional roles, 8(1–2), 107–17.

Paredes, M., M. Leifer, and T. Kilbane (2001). Maternal variables related to sexually abused children's functioning. *Child Abuse & Neglect 25*, 1159–76.

Parillo, K., R. Freeman, K. Collier, and P. Young (2001). Association between early sexual abuse and adult HIV-risky sexual behaviors among community-recruited women. *Child Abuse and Neglect 25*, 335–46.

Payne, H. (1994). Dance Movement Therapy. In D. Jones, ed. *Innovative Therapy: A Handbook*, 165–73. Buckingham, England: Open University Press.

Pellegrini, A. (1992). Shifting the terms of hetero/sexism: Gender, power, homophobia. In W. J. Blumenfeld, ed. *Homophobia: How We All Pay the Price*, 39–56. Boston: Beacon Press.

Pierce-Baker, C. (1998). *Surviving the Silence: Black Women's Stories of Rape*. New York: W. W. Norton.

Pillay, A., and C. Sargent (2000). Psycho-legal issues affecting rape survivors with mental retardation. *South African Journal of Psychology 30*(3), 9–13.

Poussaint, A. F., and A. Alexander (2000). *Lay My Burden Down: Unraveling Suicide and the Mental Health Crisis among African Americans*. Boston: Beacon Press.

Pynoos, R., and K. Nader (1988). Psychological first aid and treatment approach to children exposed to community violence: Research implications. *Journal of Yraumatic Stress 1*(4), 445–73.

Raj, A., J. G. Silverman (2003). Immigrant South Asian women at greater risk for injury from intimate partner violence. *American Journal of Public Health 93*(3), 435–37.

Rao, K., R. DiClemente, and L. Ponton (1992). Child sexual abuse of Asians compared with other populations. *Journal of the American Academy of Child and Adolescent Psychiatry 31*, 880–86.

Rickert, V. I., C. M. Wiemann, S. D. Harrykissoon, A. B. Berenson, and E. Kolb (2002). The relationship among demographics, reproductive characteristics, and intimate partner violence. *American Journal of Obstetrics and Gynecology 187*(4), 1002–7.

Ridley, C. R. (1995). *Overcoming Unintentional Racism in Counseling and Therapy*. Thousand Oaks, CA: Sage Publishers.

Rind, B., P. Tromovitch, and R. Bauserman (1998). A metal-analytic examination of assumed properties of child sexual abuse using college samples. *Psychological Bulletin 124*, 22–53.

Robinson, A. (2002). "There's a stranger in this house": African American lesbians and domestic violence. In C. W., ed. *Violence in the Lives of Black Women*, 125–32. New York: Haworth Press.

Robinson, G. E. (2003). Violence against women in North America. *Archive of Women's Mental Health 6*, 185–91.

Robinson, T., and J. Ward, Janie (1991). "A belief in self far greater than anyone's disbelief": Cultivating resistance among African American female adolescents. *Women & Therapy Special Issue: Women, girls & psychotherapy: Reframing resistance 11*(3–4), 87–103.

Roesler, T., and T. Wind (1994). Telling the secret: Adult women describe their disclosures of incest. *Journal of Interpersonal Violence 9*(3), 327–38.

Roosa, M., C. Reinholtz, and P. Angelini (1999). The relation of child sexual abuse and depression in young women: Comparisons across four ethnic groups. *Journal of Abnormal Child Psychology 27*(1), 65–76.

Root, M. (1996). *The Multiracial Experience*. Thousand Oaks, CA: Sage.

Rosenbloom, M. (1995). Implications of the Holocaust for social work. *Families in Society 76*, 567–76.

Roth, S., and R. Batson (1997). *Naming the Shadows: A New Approach To Individual and Group Psychotherapy for Adult Survivors of Childhood Incest*. New York: Free Press.

Rounds, D. (1996). Victimization of individuals with legal blindness: Nature and forms of victimization. *Behavioral Sciences & the Law 14*(1), 29–40.

Rozee, P. (2000). Sexual Victimization. In M. Biaggio and M. Hersen, eds. *Issues in the Psychology of Women*, 93–113. New York: Kluwer Academic–Plenum.

Rozee, P., and M. Koss (2001). Rape: A century of resistance. *Psychology of Women Quarterly 25*, 295–311.

Rubenzahl, S., and K. Corcoran (1998). The prevalence and characteristics of male perpetrators of acquaintance rape: New research methodology reveals new findings. *Violence Against Women 4*(6), 713–25.

Ruef, A. M., B. T. Litz, and W. E. Schlenger (2000). Hispanic ethnicity and risk for combat-related posttraumatic stress disorder. *Cultural Diversity and Ethnic Minority Psychology 6*, 235–51.

Rutter, M. (1993). Resilience: Some conceptual considerations. *Journal of Adolescent Health 14*, 626–31.

Ryan, P. (1998). Spirituality among adult survivors of childhood violence. *Journal of Transpersonal Psychology 30*(1), 39–51.

Saigh, P. (1991). The development of posttraumatic stress disorder following four different types of traumatization. *Behaviour Research & Therapy 29*(3), 213–16.

Sanchez-Hucles, J. (1998). Racism: emotional abusiveness and psychological trauma for ethnic minorities. *Journal of Emotional Abuse 1*, 69–87.

Saywitz, K., A. Mannarino, L. Berliner, and J. Cohen (2000). Treatment for sexually abused children and adolescents. *American Psychologist 55*(9), 1040–49.

Schlangenhauf, P. (2003). UNICEF report documents sexual exploitation of children. *The Lancet 362*, 1556.

Schneider, B. (1991). Put up and shut up: Workplace sexual assault. *Gender and Society* 5(4), 533–48.

Schneider, K. T., R. T. Hitlan, and P. Radhakrishnan (2000). An examination of the nature and correlates of ethnic harassment experiences in multiple contexts. *Journal of Applied Psychology 85*, 3–12.

Scott, C., H. Lefley, and D. Hicks (1993). Potential risk factors for rape in three ethnic groups. *Community Mental Health Journal 29*(2), 133–41.

Scurfield, R. (2001). Positive and negative aspects of exposure to racism and trauma: research, assessment, and treatment implications. *National Center for PTSD Clinical Quarterly 10*, 3–10.

Scurfield, R., and D. Mackey (2001). Racism, trauma, and positive aspects of exposure to race-related experiences: Assessment and treatment implications. *Journal of Ethnic and Cultural Diversity in Social Work 10*, 23–47.

Segal, U. A. (1995). Child abuse by the middle class? A study of professionals in India. *Child Abuse & Neglect 19*(2), 217–31.

Sellers, R. M., and J. M. Shelton (2003). The role of racial identity in perceived racial discrimination. *Journal of Personality and Social Psychology 84*, 1079–92.

Sellers, R. M., M. Smith, J. N. Shelton, S. J. Rowley, and T. M. Chavous (1998). Multidimensional model of racial identity: A reconceptualization of African American racial identity. *Personality and Social Psychology Review 2*, 18–39.

Sequira, H., P. Howlin, and S. Hollins (2003). Psychological disturbances associated with sexual abuse in people with learning disabilities. *British Journal of Psychiatry 183*, 451–56.

Shaw, J. A., J. E. Lewis, A. Loeb, J. Rosado, and R. A. Rodriguez (2001). A comparison of Hispanic and African-American sexually abused girls and their families. *Child Abuse & Neglect 25*, 1363–79.

Sheldon, G. (2001). Trauma and the conservation of African American racial identity. *Journal for the Psychoanalysis of Culture and Society 6*, 58–72.

Sheldon, J., and S. Parent (2002). Clergy's attitudes and attributions of blame toward female rape victims. *Violence against Women 8*(2), 233–56.

Sidebotham, P., J. Heron, and J. Golding, ALSPAC Study Team (2002). Child maltreatment in the "Children of the Nineties": Deprivation, class, and social networks in a UK sample. *Child Abuse & Neglect 26*, 1243–59.

Simi, N., and J. Mahalik (1997). Comparison of feminist versus psychoanalytic/dynamic and other therapists on self-disclosure. *Psychology of Women Quarterly 21*(3), 465–83.

Sims, M. (2002). Incest and child sexual abuse in the African American community: African American ministers' attitudes and beliefs. *Dissertation Abstracts International: Section B: The Sciences & Engineering 63*(5-B): 2605.

Smith, L., S. Friedman, and J. Nevid (1999). Clinical and sociocultural differences in African-American and European American patients with panic disorder and agoraphobia. *Journal of Nervous & Mental Disease 187*(9), 549–60.

Smyth, K., and P. Williams (1991). Patterns of coping in Black working women. *Behavioral Medicine 17*(1), 40–46.

Smythe, K., and H. Yarandi (1996). Factor analysis of the ways of coping questionnaire for African American women. *Nursing Research 45*(1), 25–29.

Sobsey, D., W. Randall, and R. K. Parrila (1997). Gender differences in abused children with and without disabilities. *Child Abuse & Neglect 21*(8), 707–20.

Solomon, S. (1999). Interventions for acute trauma response. *Current Opinion in Psychiatry 12*(2), 175–80.

Spasojevic, J., R. Heffer, and D. Snyder (2000). Effects of posttraumatic stress and acculturation on marital functioning in Bosnian Refugee Couples. *Journal of Traumatic Stress 13*(2), 205–18.

Spencer, G. A., and S. A. Bryant (2000). Dating violence: A comparison of rural, suburban, and urban teens. *Journal of Adolescent Health 27*, 302–5.

Spencer, L. (1997). *Heal Abuse and Trauma through Art: Increasing Self-Worth, Healing of Initial Wounds, and Creating a Sense of Connectivity*. Springfield, IL: Charles C. Thomas Publisher.

Steffen, P., A. Hinderliter, J. Blumenthal, A. Sherwood (2001). Religious coping, ethnicity, and ambulatory blood pressure. *Psychosomatic Medicine 63*(4), 523–30.

Stevenson, H., J. Reed, P. Bodison, A. Bishop (1997). Racism stress management: Racial social beliefs and the experience of depression and anger in African American youth. *Youth and Society 29*, 197–222.

Steward, R., H. Jo, D. Murray, W. Fitzgerald, D. Neil, F. Fear, and M. Hill (1998). Psychological adjustment and coping styles of urban African-American high school students. *Journal of Multicultural Counseling & Development 26*(2), 70–82.

Sudderth, L. (1998). "It'll come right back at me": The interactional context of discussing rape with others. *Violence against Women 4*, 572–94.

Sue, S. (1999). Science, ethnicity, and bias: Where have we gone wrong? *American Psychologist 54*, 1070–77.

Sue, D., and S. Sue (1995). Asian-Americans. In N. A. Vace, S. B. Devaney, and J. Wittmer, eds. *Experiencing and Counseling Multicultural and Diverse Populations*. 3rd ed., 63–89. Bristol, PA: Accelerated Development.

Sussman, S., C. Dent, A. Stacy, and D. Burton (1994). Psychosocial variables as prospective predictors of violent events among adolescents. *Health Values: The Journal of Health Behavior, Education & Promotion 18*(3), 29–40.

Swim, J., K. Aikin, W. Hall, and B. Hunter (1995). Sexism and racism: Old-fashioned and modern prejudices. *Journal of Personality and Social Psychology 68*, 199–214.

Tang, C. (2002). Childhood experience of sexual abuse among Hong Kong Chinese college students. *Child Abuse & Neglect 26*, 23–37.

Taylor, J., C. Gilligan, and A. Sullivan (1995). *Between Voice and Silence: Women and Girls, Race and Relationship*. Cambridge, MA: Harvard University Press.

Taylor, D. M., S. C. Wright, F. M. Moghaddam, and R. N. Lalonde (1990). The personal/group discrimination discrepancy: Perceiving my group but not myself to be a target of discrimination. *Personality and Social Science Bulletin 16*, 254–62.

Terrell, F., and S. L. Terrell (1981). An inventory to measure cultural mistrust among blacks. *Western Journal of Black Studies 5*, 180–84.

Thomas, C. (1987). Pride and purpose as antidotes to black homicidal violence. *Journal of the National Medical Association 79*(2), 155–60.

Thompson, C. (1992). On being heterosexual in a homophobic world. In W. J. Blumenfeld, ed. *Homophobia: How We All Pay the Price*. Boston, MA: Beacon Press.

Thompson, C. E., and H. A. Neville (1999). Racism, mental health, and mental health practice. *Counseling Psychologist 27*, 155–223.

Thompson, M. (2000). Life after rape: A chance to speak? *Sexual and Relationship Therapy 15*(4), 325–43.

Thompson, V., and M. Akbar (2003). The Understanding of Race and the Construction of African American Identity. *Western Journal of Black Studies 27*(2), 80–88.

Thompson Sanders, V. L. (2002). Racism: Perceptions of distress among African Americans. *Community Mental Health Journal 38*, 111–18.

Thompson Sanders, V. L. (1996). Perceived experienced of racism as stressful life events. *Community Mental Health Journal 32*, 223–33.

Tillet, S. (2003). Fragmented Silhouettes. In C. West ed. *Violence in the Lives of Black Women: Battered, Black, and Blue*. Binghamton, NY: Haworth Press.

Tillet, S. (2002). Fragmented silhouettes. *Women & Therapy 25*(3–4), 161–77.

Tjaden, P., and N. Thoennes (1998). Prevalence, incidence, and consequences of violence against women: Findings from the National Violence against Women Survey. *National Institute of Justice, Centers for Disease Control and Prevention, research brief*.

Tracy, S. (1999). Sexual abuse and forgiveness. *Journal of Psychology & Theology 27*(3), 219–29.

Turell, S., and C. Thomas (2001). Where was God?: Utilizing spirituality with Christian survivors of sexual abuse. *Women & Therapy 24*(3–4), 133–47.

Tyagi, S. (2001). Incest and women of color: A study of experiences and disclosure. *Journal of Child Sexual Abuse 10*(2), 17–39.

Ullman, S., and L. Brecklin (2002). Sexual assault history and health-related outcomes in a national sample of women. *Psychology of Women Quarterly 27*, 46–57.

U.S. Department of Health and Human Services (2001). *Mental Health: Culture, Race, Ethnicity: A Report of the Surgeon General*. Rockville, MD: Author.

Utsey, S. O., Y. A. Payne, E. S. Jackson, and A. M. Jones (2002). Race-related stress, quality of life indicators, and life satisfaction among elderly African Americans. *Cultural Diversity and Ethnic Minority Psychology 8*, 224–33.

Utsey, S. O., J. G. Ponteretto, A. L. Reynolds, and A. A. Cancelly (2000). Racial discrimination, coping, life satisfaction, and self-esteem among African Americans. *Journal of Counseling and Development 78*, 72–81.

Valanis, B., D. Bowen, T. Bassford, E. Whitlock, P. Charney, and R. Carter (2000). Sexual orientation and health: Comparisons in the Women's Health Initiative sample. *Archives of Family Medicine 9*(9), 843–53.

Valentine, S., L. Silver, and N. Twigg (1999). Locus of control, job satisfaction, and job complexity: The role of perceived racial discrimination. *Psychological Reports 84*, 1267–73.

van der Kolk, B. (2002). Posttraumatic therapy in the age of neuroscience. *Psychoanalytic Dialogues 12*, 381–92.

van der Kolk, B., and A. C. McFarlane (1996). The black hole of trauma. In B. A. van der Kolk, A. C. McFarlane, and L. Weisaeth, eds. *Traumatic Stress: The Effects of Overwhelming Experience on Mind, Body, and Society*, 3–23. New York: Guilford Press.

van der Kolk, B., D. Pelcovitz, S. Roth, F. Mandel, A. McFarlane, and J. Herman (1996). Dissociation, somatizations, and affect dysregulation: The complexity of adaptation to trauma. *American Journal of Psychiatry 153*(7S), 83–93.

van der Kolk, B., A. McFarlane, and L. Weisaeth (1996). *Traumatic Stress: The Effects of Overwhelming Experience on Mind, Body, and Society*. New York: Guilford Press.

van der Kolk, B. (1996). Dissociation and information processing in posttraumatic stress disorder. In B. van der Kolk, A. McFarlane, and L. Weisaeth, eds. *Traumatic Stress: The Effects of Overwhelming Experience on Mind, Body, and Society*. New York: Guilford Press.

van der Kolk, B. (1996). Trauma and memory. In B. van der Kolk, A. McFarlane, and L. Weisaeth, eds. *Traumatic Stress: The Effects of Overwhelming Experience on Mind, Body, and Society*. New York: Guilford Press.

van der Kolk, B. (1996). The body keeps the score: Approaches to the psychobiology of posttraumatic stress disorder. In B. van der Kolk, A. McFarlane, and L. Weisaeth, eds. *Traumatic Stress: The Effects of Overwhelming Experience on Mind, Body, and Society*. New York: Guilford Press.

van der Kolk, B., O. van der Hart, and C. Marmar (1996). Dissociation and information processing in posttraumatic stress disorder. In B. van der Kolk, A. McFarlane, and L. Weisaeth, eds. *Traumatic Stress: The Effects of Overwhelming Experience on Mind, Body, and Society*; New York, NY: Guilford Press, 303–27.

Vasquez, M. (1998). Latinos and violence: Mental health implications and strategies for clinicians. *Cultural Diversity & Ethnic Minority Psychology* 4(4), 319–34.

Villena-Mata, D. (2002). The "Don't Rules" in societal trauma and its healing. *Nonviolent Change Journal 16*, 3–10.

Vogel, L., and L. Marshall (2001). PTSD symptoms and partner abuse: Low income women at risk. *Journal of Traumatic Stress 14*(3), 569–84.

Wade-Gayles, G. (1993). *Pushed Back To Strength: A Black Woman's Journey Home*. New York: Avon Books.

Walker, L. (2000). *Abused Women and Survivor Therapy: A Practical Guide for the Psychotherapist*. Washington, DC: American Psychological Association.

Walker, L. (1994). *Abused Women and Survivor Psychotherapy: A Practical Guide for the Psychotherapist*. Washington, DC: American Psychological Association.

Walsh, F. (1998). Beliefs, spirituality, and transcendence: Keys to family resilience. In M. McGoldrick, ed. *Re-Visioning Family Therapy: Race, Culture, and Gender in Clinical Practice*, 62–77. New York: Guilford Press.

Walters, K. L., and J. M. Simoni (2002). Native women's health: An "indigenist" stress-coping model. *American Journal of Public Health 92*, 520–24.

Ward, T. (2000). Sexual offenders' cognitive distortions as implicit theories. *Aggression and Violent Behavior 5*, 491–507.

Warshaw, R. (1988). *I Never Called It Rape: The Ms. Report on Recognizing, Fighting, and Surviving Date and Acquaintance Rape*. New York: Harper & Row.

Warwick, L. (2001). Self-in-relation theory and women's religious identity in therapy. *Women & Therapy 24*(3–4), 121–31.

Warwick, L. (1996). Relationality, lesbian identity, and rape recovery: Meaning made by three lesbian survivors of male rape. Dissertation, Abstracts International, Section B, the Sciences and Engineering 57(1-B), 0716.

Washington, P. A. (2001). Disclosure patterns of black female sexual assault survivors. *Violence against Women 7*, 1254–83.

Weaver, T., H. Resnick, S. Glynn, and D. Foy (1999). Behavior therapy. In M. Hersen and A. Bellack, eds. *Handbook of Comparative Interventions for Adult Disorders*, 433–61. New York: John Wiley & Sons.

Webb, N. (1999). *Play Therapy with Children in Crisis: Individual, Group, and Family Treatment*. New York: Guilford Press.

Weems, R. (1995). *Battered Love: Marriage, Sex, and Violence in the Hebrew Prophets*. Minneapolis: Fortress Press.

Weems, R. (1993). *I Asked for Intimacy: Stories of Blessing, Betrayals, and Birthings*. San Diego: LuraMedia.

West, C. M. (2000). Developing an "oppositional gaze" toward the image of black women. In J. C. Chrisler, C. Golden, and P. D. Rozee, eds. *Lectures on the Psychology of Women*, 220–44. New York: McGraw-Hill.

White, A. (1999). Talking feminist, talking black: Micromobilization processes in a collective protest against rape. *Gender and Society 13*(1), 77–100.

White, A., M. Strube, and S. Fisher (1998). A Black feminist model of rape myth acceptance: Implications for research and antirape advocacy in black communities. *Psychology of Women Quarterly 22*(2), 157–75.

White, K., S. Bruce, A. Farrell, and W. Kliewer (1998). Impact of exposure to community violence on anxiety: A longitudinal study of family social support as a protective factor for urban children. *Journal of Child & Family Studies 7*(2), 187–203.

Williams, D. R., H. W. Neighbors, and J. S. Jackson (2003). Racial/ethnic discrimination and health: Findings from community studies. *American Journal of Public Health 93*, 200–208.

Williams, D. R., and R. Williams-Morris (2000). Racism and mental health: The African American experience. *Ethnicity and Health 5*, 243–68.

Williams, W. (1992). Benefits of nonhomophobic societies: An anthropological perspective. In W. J. Blumenfeld, ed. *Homophobia: How We All Pay the Price*. Boston: Beacon Press.

Wolfer, T. A. (2000). Coping with chronic community violence. The variety and implications of women's efforts. *Violence and Victims 15*, 283–302.

Wood, G., and S. Roche (2001). Representing selves, reconstructing lives: Feminist group work with women survivors of male violence. *Social Work with Groups 23*(4), 5–23.

Woodard, L. (2001). Racial oppression as a form of insidious trauma among African Americans. Unpublished doctoral dissertation. Boston: University of Massachusetts.

Wright, N., and S. Owen (2001). Feminist conceptualizations of women's madness: A review of the literature. *Journal of Advanced Nursing 36*(1), 143–50.

Wyatt, G. E. (1997). *Stolen Women: Reclaiming Our Sexuality, Taking Back Our Lives*. New York: John Wiley & Sons.

Wyatt, G. E., M. D. Newcomb, and M. H. Riederle (1993). *Sexual Abuse and Consensual Sex*. Newbury Park, CA: Sage Publications.

Wyatt, G. E. (1992). The sociocultural context of African American and white American women's rape. *Journal of Social Issues 48*, 77–91.

Wyatt, G. (1990). Sexual abuse of ethnic minority children: Identifying dimensions of victimization. *Professional Psychology: Research & Practice, 21*(5), 338–43.

Wyatt, G., M. Newcomb (1990). Internal and external mediators of women's sexual abuse in childhood. *Journal of Consulting & Clinical Psychology 58*(6), 758–67.

Wyatt, G. E. (1985). The sexual abuse of Afro-American and white American women in childhood. *Child Abuse & Neglect 8*, 507–19.

Yimin, C., L. Shouqing, Q. Arzhu, Z. Yuke, W. Jianhua, Z. Jinxin, Q. Yanli, W. Xiaodun, J. An, P. Li, and W. Shaomin (2002). Sexual coercion among adolescent women seeking abortion in China. *Journal of Adolescent Health 31*, 482–86.

Youssef, R., M. Attia, and M. Kamel (1998). Children experiencing violence: Parental use of corporal punishement. *Child Abuse & Neglect 22*(10), 959–73.

Index

About the Author

THEMA BRYANT-DAVIS is an internationally recognized counselor, educator, and advocate, and an expert on the cultural context of trauma recovery. Her doctorate in Clinical Psychology is from Duke University and she completed her post-doctorate training at the Harvard Medical Center Victims of Violence Program. Formerly the American Psychological Association representative to the United Nations and Senior Staff Coordinator of the Princeton University SHARE Program against sexual violence and harassment, she is now Director of Oasis Institute International in Los Angeles. Oasis staff members provide training on the issues of trauma and culture to judges, nurse examiners, doctors, counselors, police officers, government officials, advocates, volunteers, students, and survivors.